DEFINING MOMENTS
WORKERS UNITE!
THE AMERICAN
LABOR MOVEMENT

DEFINING MOMENTS
WORKERS UNITE!
THE AMERICAN
LABOR MOVEMENT

Kevin Hillstrom

Omnigraphics

P.O. Box 31-1640
Detroit, MI 48231

Omnigraphics, Inc.

Kevin Hillstrom, *Series Editor*
Cherie D. Abbey, *Managing Editor*

Peter E. Ruffner, *Publisher*
Matthew P. Barbour, *Senior Vice President*

Elizabeth Collins, *Research and Permissions Coordinator*
Kevin M. Hayes, *Operations Manager*

Allison A. Beckett and Mary Butler, *Research Staff*
Cherry Stockdale, *Permissions Assistant*
Shirley Amore, Martha Johns, and Kirk Kauffmann, *Administrative Staff*

Copyright © 2011 Omnigraphics, Inc.
ISBN 978-0-7808-1130-0

Library of Congress Cataloging-in-Publication Data

Hillstrom, Kevin, 1963-
  Workers unite! : the American labor movement / by Kevin Hillstrom.
    p. cm. -- (Defining moments)
  Includes bibliographical references and index.
    ISBN 978-0-7808-1130-0 (hbk. : alk. paper) 1. Labor movement--United States--History--Juvenile literature. 2. Industrial relations--United States--History--Juvenile literature. I. Title.
  HD8066.H55 2010
  331.880973--dc22

2010026548

This book is printed on acid-free paper meeting the ANSI Z39.48 Standard. The infinity symbol that appears above indicates that the paper in this book meets that standard.

Printed in the United States of America

TABLE OF CONTENTS

NARRATIVE OVERVIEW

BIOGRAPHIES

PRIMARY SOURCES

PREFACE

Throughout the course of America's existence, its people, culture, and institutions have been periodically challenged—and in many cases transformed—by profound historical events. Some of these momentous events, such as women's suffrage, the civil rights movement, and U.S. involvement in World War II, invigorated the nation and strengthened American confidence and capabilities. Others, such as the McCarthy era, the Vietnam War, and Watergate, have prompted troubled assessments and heated debates about the country's core beliefs and character.

Some of these defining moments in American history were years or even decades in the making. The Harlem Renaissance and the New Deal, for example, unfurled over the span of several years, while the American labor movement and the Cold War evolved over the course of decades. Other defining moments, such as the Cuban missile crisis and the Japanese attack on Pearl Harbor, transpired over a matter of days or weeks.

But although significant differences exist among these events in terms of their duration and their place in the timeline of American history, all share the same basic characteristic: they transformed the United States' political, cultural, and social landscape for future generations of Americans.

Taking heed of this fundamental reality, American citizens, schools, and other institutions are increasingly emphasizing the importance of understanding our nation's history. Omnigraphics' *Defining Moments* series was created for the express purpose of meeting this growing appetite for authoritative, useful historical resources. This series will be of enduring value to anyone interested in learning more about America's past—and in understanding how those historical events continue to reverberate in the twenty-first century.

Each individual volume of *Defining Moments* provides a valuable resource for readers interested in learning about the most profound events in our nation's history. Each volume is organized into three distinct sections— Narrative Overview, Biographies, and Primary Sources.

- The **Narrative Overview** provides readers with a detailed, factual account of the origins and progression of the "defining moment" being examined. It also explores the event's lasting impact on America's political and cultural landscape.

- The **Biographies** section provides valuable biographical background on leading figures associated with the event in question. Each biography concludes with a list of sources for further information on the profiled individual.

- The **Primary Sources** section collects a wide variety of pertinent primary source materials from the era under discussion, including official documents, papers and resolutions, letters, oral histories, memoirs, editorials, and other important works.

Individually, each of these sections is a rich resource for users. Together, they comprise an authoritative, balanced, and absorbing examination of some of the most significant events in U.S. history.

Other notable features contained within each volume in the series include a glossary of important individuals, places, and terms; a detailed chronology featuring page references to relevant sections of the narrative; an annotated bibliography of sources for further study; an extensive general bibliography that reflects the wide range of historical sources consulted by the author; and a subject index.

New Feature – Research Topics for Student Reports

Each volume in the *Defining Moments* series now includes a list of research topics, detailing some of the important topics that recur throughout the volume and providing a valuable starting point for research. Students working on essays and reports will find this feature especially useful as they try to narrow down their research interests.

These research topics are covered throughout the different sections of the book: the narrative overview, the biographies, the primary sources, the chronology, and the important people, places, and terms section. This wide coverage allows readers to view the topic through a variety of different approaches.

Students using *Defining Moments: Workers Unite! The American Labor Movement* will find information on a wide range of topics suitable for conducting historical research and writing reports.

Acknowledgements

This series was developed in consultation with a distinguished Advisory Board comprised of public librarians, school librarians, and educators. They evaluated the series as it developed, and their comments and suggestions were invaluable throughout the production process. Any errors in this and other volumes in the series are ours alone. Following is a list of board members who contributed to the *Defining Moments* series:

Gail Beaver, M.A., M.A.L.S.
Adjunct Lecturer, University of Michigan
Ann Arbor, MI

Melissa C. Bergin, L.M.S., NBCT
Library Media Specialist
Niskayuna High School
Niskayuna, NY

Rose Davenport, M.S.L.S., Ed. Specialist
Library Media Specialist
Pershing High School Library
Detroit, MI

Karen Imarisio, A.M.L.S.
Assistant Head of Adult Services
Bloomfield Twp. Public Library
Bloomfield Hills, MI

Nancy Larsen, M.L.S., M.S. Ed.
Library Media Specialist
Clarkston High School
Clarkston, MI

Marilyn Mast, M.I.L.S.
Kingswood Campus Librarian
Cranbrook Kingswood Upper School
Bloomfield Hills, MI

Rosemary Orlando, M.L.I.S.
Library Director
St. Clair Shores Public Library
St. Clair Shores, MI

Comments and Suggestions

We welcome your comments on *Defining Moments: Workers Unite! The American Labor Movement* and suggestions for other events in U.S. history that warrant treatment in the *Defining Moments* series. Correspondence should be addressed to:

Editor, *Defining Moments*
Omnigraphics, Inc.
P.O. Box 31-1640
Detroit, MI 48231

E-mail: editorial@omnigraphics.com

HOW TO USE THIS BOOK

*D*efining Moments: Workers Unite! The American Labor Movement provides users with a detailed and authoritative overview of the rise of American labor unions and their subsequent impact on the economy and culture of the United States. The preparation and arrangement of this volume—and all other books in the *Defining Moments* series—reflect an emphasis on providing a thorough and objective account of events that shaped our nation, presented in an easy-to-use reference work.

Defining Moments: Workers Unite! The American labor Movement is divided into three primary sections. The first of these sections, the **Narrative Overview**, provides an in-depth survey of the history of the American labor movement from its earliest origins to the present day. The volume includes comprehensive coverage of the colonial foundations of the American workplace, the impact of nineteenth-century industrialization and free market capitalism on workers and the wider American society, and major events and individuals that drove the growth of labor unions during the Progressive, New Deal, and post-World War II eras. It also chronicles the declining influence of the labor movement over the past half-century and examines various proposals for revitalizing American unions in the twenty-first century.

The second section, **Biographies**, provides valuable biographical background on America's most famous and influential labor leaders. Profiled individuals range from early pioneers in labor organizing and activism, including Samuel Gompers, Eugene Debs, and Mother Jones, to later labor giants like Walter Reuther and George Meany. Each biography concludes with a list of sources for further information on the profiled individual.

The third section, **Primary Sources**, collects essential and illuminating documents related to the evolution of labor unions in the United States. Selections include an 1890 essay by Eugene V. Debs urging "workingmen" to organize for economic and social justice; Clarence Darrow's famous defense of labor unions in the 1907 murder trial of "Big Bill" Haywood; excerpts from a federal investigative report on the 1914 Ludlow Massacre; Frances Perkins's recollection of the political maneuvering behind the passage of the National Labor Relations Act; and a 2009 debate over the future of American labor. Other documents included in this section feature perspectives on labor issues from such diverse sources as United Mine Workers President John L. Lewis and President Ronald Reagan.

Other valuable features in *Defining Moments: Workers Unite! The American Labor Movement* include the following:

- Attribution and referencing of primary sources and other quoted material to help guide users to other valuable historical research resources.

- Glossary of Important People, Places, and Terms.

- Detailed Chronology of events with a *see reference* feature. Under this arrangement, events listed in the chronology include a reference to page numbers within the Narrative Overview wherein users can find additional information on the event in question.

- Photographs of the leading figures and major events associated with the development and growth of the American labor movement.

- Sources for Further Study, an annotated list of noteworthy works about the event.

- Extensive bibliography of works consulted in the creation of this book, including books, periodicals, and Internet sites.

- A Subject Index.

RESEARCH TOPICS FOR
WORKERS UNITE! THE
AMERICAN LABOR MOVEMENT

Starting a research paper can be a challenge, as students struggle to decide what area to study. Now, each book in the *Defining Moments* series includes a list of research topics, detailing some of the important topics that recur throughout the volume and providing a valuable starting point for research. Students working on essays and reports will find this feature especially useful as they try to narrow down their research interests.

These research topics are covered throughout the different sections of the book: the narrative overview, the biographies, the primary sources, the chronology, and the important people, places, and terms section. This wide coverage allows readers to view the topic through a variety of different approaches.

Students using *Defining Moments: Workers Unite! The American Labor Movement* will find information on a wide range of topics suitable for historical research and writing reports.

- Work arrangements from apprenticeships to slavery in the British colonies and early America.

- The impact of wider social and economic trends like immigration, industrialization, and urbanization on American work.

- Union organizing and union-busting activities in mining, railroads, and other leading nineteenth-century industries.

- The influence of radical political thought on the growth and direction of early American labor organizations.

- Similarities and differences in the ways that Samuel Gompers, Eugene Debs, "Big Bill" Haywood, John L. Lewis, and other labor leaders viewed the struggle to strengthen worker rights.

- Franklin D. Roosevelt's New Deal labor policies and their impact on labor unions and working-class families.

- Landmark clashes in U.S. labor history, ranging from the Homestead and Pullman Strikes of the late nineteenth century to the Flint Sit-Down Strike of 1936-37.

- Factors that have contributed to the labor movement's decline in power, influence, and popularity from the mid-twentieth century to the opening years of the twenty-first century.

NARRATIVE OVERVIEW

PROLOGUE

⚛️

To many long-time labor activists and organizers in the United States, the mid-1930s must have seemed like the completion of a journey that they thought would never end. Since the mid-nineteenth century, trade unions and social reformers had pushed and fought for higher wages, better working conditions, and union recognition against powerful and politically connected corporations. More often than not, the corporations had prevailed in these tense and sometimes bloody clashes. Over the years, the record of union setbacks and tragedies grew to include such events as the Homestead Strike of 1892, the Pullman Strike of 1894, and the Ludlow Massacre of 1914. But the American labor movement persevered, and in the 1930s it was finally rewarded for its long years of struggle.

Ironically, this breakthrough came during the Great Depression, a period of terrible economic trouble and mass unemployment. The Depression threw millions of people out of work and plunged numerous families into economic jeopardy or outright poverty. But it also ushered in the "New Deal" policies of President Franklin D. Roosevelt. After his arrival in the White House in early 1933, Roosevelt worked not only to get American businesses back on their feet, but also to provide long-suffering American workers with greater rights and financial security. To accomplish this latter goal, Roosevelt and his fellow New Dealers passed legislation that dramatically strengthened the nation's labor unions.

Laws such as the 1935 National Labor Relations Act gave the American labor movement sweeping new legal rights in its clashes with management, and unions were quick to take advantage of them. By the close of 1936 union activity was surging in a number of important industries. A particularly dramatic example of the rapidly changing workplace landscape could be seen in Flint, Michigan. On December 30, 1936, a group of autoworkers employed by industry giant General Motors (GM) brought the company's operations to a standstill by launching in a "sit-down" strike at one of GM's key manufacturing facilities. They announced that they would not end their strike until GM recognized the United Auto Workers (UAW) labor union as the legitimate bargaining agent for GM workers.

When General Motors first learned of the events taking place in Flint, company spokesmen vowed that GM would never recognize the UAW. One day later, on December 31, 1936, GM received a blunt warning from labor leader John L. Lewis, president of the Committee for Industrial Organizations (CIO), a labor federation to which the UAW belonged. Speaking with unmistakable confidence, Lewis informed the executives of General Motors—and all other industry leaders across America—that whether they liked it or not, a new day of labor-management relations was at hand:

> The year 1936 has witnessed the beginning of this great movement in the mass production industries. The year 1937 will witness an unparalleled growth in the numerical strength of labor in the heretofore unorganized industries, and the definite achievement of modern collective bargaining on a wide front where it heretofore had not existed. Not only the workers, but our nation and its entire population will be the beneficiaries of this great movement. Labor demands collective bargaining and greater participation by the individual worker, whether by hand or brain, in the bountiful resources of the nation and the fruits of the genius of its inventors and technicians.

> Employers talk about possible labor trouble interfering with continued expansion and progress of industry. They ignore the fact that unless people have money with which to buy, the wheels of industry slow down, and profits and likewise capital disappear. It would be more fitting and accurate to talk about "employer trouble"—that is something from which wage earners are suffering. I refer you to the refusal of some of the largest and most powerful corporations in this country to follow modern labor practice or to obey the law of the land. They deny the entirely reasonable and just demands of their employees for legitimate collective bargaining, decent incomes, shorter hours, and for protection against a destructive speed-up system.

It is the refusal of employers to grant such reasonable conditions and to deal with their employees through collective bargaining that leads to wide-spread labor unrest. The strikes which have broken out in the last few weeks, especially in the automotive industry, are due to such "employer trouble." Modern collective bargaining, involving negotiations between organized workers and organized employers on an industry basis, would regularize and stabilize industry relations and reduce the economic losses occasioned by management stupidity. The sit-down strike [in Flint] is the fruit of mismanagement and bad policy toward labor. Employers who tyrannize over the employees, with the aid of labor spies, company guards, and the threat of discharge, need not be surprised if their production lines are suddenly halted....

The steel corporations are likewise trying to avoid collective bargaining with their employees. They have tried, by fostering and subsidizing company unions, to get around the law. Instead, they have transgressed the law. The steel companies, themselves, are organized, and they appreciate and exploit the value of organization in the conduct of their business enterprises. The United States Steel Corporation is trying to enforce upon its two hundred and twenty thousand employees the outmoded labor policy adopted by its Board of Directors in 1901, a policy which denies the right of self-organization to any employee of that Corporation or its subsidiaries....

Huge corporations, such as United States Steel and General Motors, have a moral and public responsibility. They have neither the moral nor the legal right to rule as autocrats over the hundreds of thousands of employees. They have no right to transgress the law which gives to the worker the right of self-organization and collective bargaining. They have no right in a political democracy to withhold the rights of a free people.

The workers in the steel industry are organizing; the workers in the automotive industry are organizing; the workers in other industries are organizing; any sane concept of industrial relations would indicate that the labor problems of these industries should be settled across the council table....

Labor desires a peaceful solution of the problems of its relationships in the mass production industries. The organizations associated with the Committee for Industrial Organizations are not promoting industrial strike—they are hoping for industrial peace on a basis that recognizes the rights of the workers as well as the employers. Peace, however, cannot be achieved by employers' denial of the right to organize; by denial of conferences for bargaining purposes; by the purchase and use of arms, ammunition, and tear gas; by a continued policy of arrogance and repression.

The time has passed in America when the workers can be either clubbed, gassed, or shot down with impunity. I solemnly warn the leaders of industry that labor will not tolerate such policies or tactics. Labor will also expect the protection of the agencies of the Federal Government in the pursuit of its lawful objectives.[1]

As it turned out, many of Lewis's bold predictions came true. The Flint Sit-Down Strike ended in a historic victory for labor, and by the early 1940s the UAW was representing the workforce of the entire American auto industry. Labor registered major victories in other industries as well, and the days when workers could be "clubbed, gassed, or shot down with impunity" did indeed fade into the history books.

But in other respects the American labor movement's journey remained a troubled one. In the decades since Lewis's historic speech, in fact, American labor unions have been swallowed in turmoil. And as the labor movement moves deeper into the twenty-first century, its future looks considerably more uncertain than it did on the day Lewis gave this speech.

---

[1] Lewis, John L. "I Solemnly Warn the Leaders of Industry," Speech delivered on the Red Network, National Broadcasting Company, Washington, DC, December 31, 1936.

Chapter One

AMERICAN WORKERS IN AN INDUSTRIALIZING WORLD

‹‹‹‹‹‹‹‹‹‹‹‹›››››

Labor is the great producer of wealth. It moves all other
causes.

—Daniel Webster

When Europeans colonized the North American continent, they
brought with them familiar systems and concepts of labor. In the
New World, however, working life changed in ways that reflected
both the opportunities and challenges contained in America. Some people
suffered enormously from the colonies' heavy demand for cheap labor—most
notably the legions of Africans who were forced to serve as slaves in Southern
crop fields. Others endured years of servitude in exchange for eventual freedom in America. And still other workers prospered from the outset, their fortunes boosted by the fact that skilled craftsmanship was in short supply in the
lightly peopled colonies. Skilled workers enjoyed this leverage throughout
the colonial era and even after the American Revolution. In the nineteenth
century, however, the setting for American workers changed with disorient-
ing speed. Rocked by stormy new economic and social forces like industrialization and mass immigration, laborers began to explore ways of joining
together to improve their lives.

An Era of Abundant Land and Labor Shortages

When the first English colonists arrived in the New World in the early
1600s and began carving farms and settlements out of the American wilder-
ness, their efforts were made much more difficult by their small numbers.
Building homes and barns, clearing forests for fields, and tending livestock

were all time-consuming and exhausting tasks in this pre-industrial era, and the supply of labor in these early communities was extremely limited. These labor shortages subsided somewhat as the colonies took on a progressively more permanent and prosperous aura. This sense of stability made them more attractive to European workmen looking for a better life, and the colonies themselves began to produce new generations of native-born Americans. Nonetheless, labor shortages of varying levels of severity remained a fact of life in the colonies throughout the mid-1700s.

The main reason for the continued scarcity of labor in the colonies was that land in America was both abundant and cheap to acquire (the original inhabitants of these territories, the Indians, were dismissed by most Europeans as temporary occupants rather than owners of the land). The availability of large tracts of inexpensive and fertile land convinced many of the early colonists to launch their own farming operations rather than seek employment with someone else. As a result, the colonies that developed up and down the Atlantic seaboard in the seventeenth century, from New England to Georgia and the Carolinas, featured large numbers of farm owners, mill operators, and other businesses—but relatively few ordinary workers to help owners run these enterprises.

> *"There is a continual Demand for more Artisans of all the necessary and useful kinds. Tolerably good Workmen in any of those mechanic Arts are sure to find Employ, and to be well paid for their Work."*
> *– Benjamin Franklin, 1782*

Chronic labor shortages resulted in high wages for workers in many parts of the country. This delighted laborers, of course, but made it more difficult for colonial farms and businesses to turn a profit. This problem eventually became so bad that colonial authorities intervened with regulations that placed a ceiling on wages. Some colonies also instituted severe penalties—including whipping—for members of the community who engaged in "idleness." Work regulations varied from colony to colony, though, so they were not very effective. Workmen simply migrated to the areas that offered the friendliest regulatory environment, thus deepening the labor problems of those colonies that had imposed the wage scales and idleness penalties in the first place.

Steadily rising levels of immigration to the New World could not completely fill this labor "hole," either, because the frontier to the West was so vast. When one valley became filled to capacity with white settlers, the overflow simply spilled deeper into the interior, where additional land lay for the taking. This dynamic played out time and time again, keeping labor supplies in many of the colonies extremely tight. The most notable exception to this state of affairs existed in the South, which used slavery as its antidote to labor shortages.

Family Labor and Indenture in Colonial America

The labor force that existed in colonial America was composed of several different types of workers. On family-owned farms—by far the most common type of business enterprise in America during both the colonial era and after independence—family members were an essential source of labor. Sons were of particular value because of their strength and stamina in the fields, but wives and daughters also contributed mightily. In addition to their cooking, cleaning, sewing, and other household responsibilities, women and children helped with planting, harvesting, and caring for livestock. The economic advantages of free family labor were so great, in fact, that even married sons and daughters often stayed on the family farm. "Only by concentrating the efforts of two or even three generations within a single operation," explained one scholar, "could families accumulate sufficient capital to provide for an English standard of living, with the normal complement of pewter plates, woolen cloth, printed Bibles, and flintlock muskets."[1]

Early American farmers, planters, mill owners, freight movers, and other business interests also depended to a great degree on various forms of "bound labor." The most common form of bound labor, which accounted for about half of all immigration to the colonies from 1700 to 1775, was indentured servitude. Indentured servants were poor English, Irish, Welsh, Scottish, and German men and women who signed contracts of service to New World masters in exchange for passage to America. Their ranks were further supplemented by poor orphans and minors. These children, viewed by English authorities as likely future paupers, were herded onto boats and forced into indentured servitude in the colonies. The term "kidnapping," in fact, originated with this harsh practice. All told, about one out of three people who immigrated to America during the colonial era came as indentured servants.

Terms of indenture typically lasted from four to seven years, and they were strictly enforced. Indentured servants received room and board from their masters, but they received no wages. They also had extremely limited legal rights throughout their period of servitude. For instance, many families that came to the colonies as indentured servants were separated from one

Colonial farmers in America relied heavily on family members as a labor source, as seen in this wood engraving.

another for years. Husbands and wives and siblings did not have the power to make themselves a "package deal," so they were sometimes auctioned off to masters who lived dozens or even hundreds of miles from one another.

Once they settled in the New World, the daily quality of life of indentured servants depended a great deal on the temperament and character of their masters. Many indentured servants were treated with respect and kindness by their masters. Some masters even bestowed land on valued servants when their terms of service expired. A number of colonies, eager to encourage settlement and economic development within their borders, rewarded completed terms of service as well. In Georgia in the 1730s, for example, indentured servants who completed their obligations received between twenty and fifty acres of farmland, cattle, a set of farming tools, and a cash allowance.[2] Other indentured servants were treated cruelly, however. Stories of beatings and other mistreatment at the hands of masters were not uncommon, and many indentured servants who fulfilled their contracts entered American society as free citizens with little else besides the shirts on their backs.

For most of the seventeenth century and into the early eighteenth century, indentured servitude stood as the only option for poor Europeans to reach the colonies. In the later 1700s, though, a related type of bound labor known as redemption emerged. Under this practice, which was especially utilized by German immigrants to the New World, cash-strapped workers who wanted to emigrate signed contracts in which they agreed to "redeem" their fares when they reached America. Under this arrangement, the ship's captain put the emigrant, his family, and his possessions aboard ship and delivered them to America. Once they arrived, redemptioners usually received a grace period of two weeks or so to obtain the money owed the shipper, either through work or the aid of friends and family already in the colonies. If the redeemer could not fully pay off the debt, however, he would be sold into indentured servitude by the ship's captain. The length of this servitude varied enormously, depending on the size of his debt.[3]

The final subset of white bound laborers who came from Europe to America consisted of convicted criminals. England's Parliament decided at the beginning of the 1700s that it could take care of two problems at one time by depositing some of the convicts in its overcrowded prisons in the labor-starved colonies. This practice became much more frequent after 1718, when Parliament passed a Transportation Act that gave courts the option of banishing convicted "rogues, vagabonds, and sturdy beggars" to the colonies. From that time until the Revolutionary War, about 52,000 convicted criminals were shipped to America—about one quarter of all British immigrants during those years. These undesirables included prisoners who had been found guilty of crimes ranging from prostitution, burglary, and horse theft to more serious crimes like murder, rape, and highway robbery. The convicts typically served much longer periods of servitude than ordinary indentured servants, but once they had completed their term they too received their freedom.

Many colonial owners of farms, mills, shipyards, and other businesses welcomed this steady infusion of laborers and heartily approved of the policy. Other colonists were outraged not only by the policy, but by the way in which the British Crown ignored their complaints. As one critic sarcastically summarized in a 1751 edition of the *Pennsylvania Gazette,* "Our Mother knows what is best for us. What is a little Housebreaking, Shoplifting, or Highway-robbing; what is a son now and then corrupted and hanged, a Daughter debauched, or Pox'd, a wife stabbed, a Husband's throat cut, or a child's brains beat out with an Axe, compared with this 'Improvement and Well peopling of the Colonies?'"[4]

Slavery and King Cotton in the American South

Indentured servitude was less common in the Southern provinces. Unlike the North, the colonial South had developed economic and social systems that depended primarily on African slaves for labor. In Maryland, Virginia, Georgia, and the Carolinas, individual planters had been able to acquire huge expanses of land for agricultural development. But these fields required large numbers of unskilled laborers, and over time the entire region became progressively more dependent on African slaves to provide that labor. During the first half of the eighteenth century, the number of Africans dragged across the Atlantic to the British colonies jumped from 5,000 a year to 45,000 a year. In addition, individual colonies passed laws to ensure that the children of these slaves would themselves be doomed to lives of slavery.

After the colonies waged their successful revolutionary war of independence from Great Britain (1775 to 1783) and formed the United States, some Americans argued that slavery should be abolished. They described it not only as a great evil, but as a stain on the founding principles of equality and justice described in America's Declaration of Independence. But most of the nation's early political leaders studiously avoided discussing the subject, even as America's first census, carried out in 1790, revealed that almost 700,000 of the 3.89

Wealthy Southern planters began using slaves to tend their tobacco and cotton fields early in the colonial era.

million people living in the United States were slaves. Fearful that their fragile new nation would be torn apart if they tried to end slavery, they privately expressed the hope that the practice would slowly fade away on its own.

Instead, the South's dependence on slavery became even greater in the next century. Early in the 1800s, mechanical inventions like the cotton gin and the power loom transformed cotton, which grew very well in Southern

13

fields, into an enormously profitable commodity. The emergence of "King Cotton," which could only be harvested by using large numbers of field laborers, made white Southerners more dependent on slavery for their economic prosperity and way of life than ever before.

By the mid-1800s, about one out of three people living in the South were slaves. Some of these slaves received fairly good food and shelter and moderate workloads—in part because many slaveowners equated slaves with carriage horses or other valuable plantation "property" that required smart care and maintenance. Other slaves were treated mercilessly by masters who had the power to whip them, humiliate them, or sell their spouses or children to distant plantations whenever they pleased.

Free Workmen and Apprentices in Early America

About half of white immigrants to colonial America possessed the financial resources to book passage for themselves and their families with no strings attached. When these "freemen" completed the arduous voyage across the Atlantic and stepped on American soil, they had two options: 1) establish farms, shops, and businesses for themselves, or 2) find jobs in which they received a wage for their services. Many of the freemen were skilled craftsmen, also known as artisans, in such professions as shoemaking, sailmaking, shipbuilding, glass making, tanning, printing, and weaving—all trades that promised a good living in the colonies.

These artisans typically passed their skills and knowledge on to other colonists through apprenticeship arrangements. Apprenticeships were usually entered into either by male youths who had the consent of their parents/guardian, or by adults who had completed their terms of indenture (smaller numbers of girls also received apprenticeship instruction in weaving and other "womanly" trades). Apprentices did not receive a wage, but they received room and board and training in a skilled trade from their artisan masters in return for their labor. Apprenticeships, which usually ran until the age of twenty-one for boys and sixteen or eighteen for girls, thus served as a kind of vocational school for colonial youth. Apprentices who completed their terms of service either opened their own businesses or became "journeymen" (wage-earning employees). Some of the most famous citizens of early America, including such luminaries as Benjamin Franklin, Mark Twain, and Horace Greeley, got their start in the world of work as apprentices.

Many colonial craftsmen relied on apprentices and indentured servants to assist them in their business ventures. In return, these workers learned valuable trades such as carpentry.

Prior to American independence, most skilled craftsmen who emigrated from Europe chose to establish their own shops and businesses in the New World. By the late 1700s and early 1800s, many of these enterprises were booming thanks to the growth of American towns and an overall rise in population. To keep up with escalating demand for their products, though, skilled sailmakers, carpenters, shoemakers, stonecutters, and other entrepreneuers became increasingly reliant on employees. Many of these workers could pick and choose from various employment options, as Benjamin Franklin observed in 1782. "There is a continual Demand for more Artisans of all the necessary and useful kinds," he declared. "Tolerably good Workmen in any of those mechanic Arts are sure to find Employ, and to be well paid for their Work."[5] These were the workers who would form America's first trade societies, the earliest union-type organizations in the United States.

Early Craft Guilds and Societies

Guilds and other formal organizations of merchants and craftsmen had been a feature of European life for centuries. Guild members worked together as a single entity to build the best possible economic benefits for themselves in the wider society. These types of societies did not appear in America until the late eighteenth century, however. Up to that point, the demand for the goods and services of artisans had been so high that there simply was not any economic need for them to form an alliance with other craftsmen. The only organizations that remotely resembled the European guilds were 1) occasional temporary alliances of house carpenters and other master craftsmen who negotiated price and wage agreements with city officials, and 2) "mutual-aid" societies, which became popular in American population centers in the mid-1700s. This type of group usually included both the masters and journeymen of a given trade in a particular town. The societies were formed not for the purposes of economic advancement, but to provide various sickness and death benefits for their memberships. By the 1790s, almost every important trade in New York, Boston, and Philadelphia—America's largest cities—had established mutual-aid societies.

The first efforts to establish organizations of workers dedicated to their collective *economic* betterment did not stir to life until the 1770s and 1780s. It was at that time that the supply of workers in America finally began to catch up with labor demand. As a result, many artisans found that they no longer had the leverage to demand top wages from employers. Business owners could simply replace them with journeymen willing to accept lower wages and longer working hours.

In addition, the increased availability of cheap workers coincided with a great expansion in postwar commerce within America's leading population centers. "Under constant pressure to reduce costs in meeting the highly competitive conditions of this new world of business, employers sought to hold down wages, lengthen the working day of their employees, and tap new sources of cheap labor," summarized one account of this period. "They tried to break down the restrictions of the traditional apprenticeship system; they

America's labor picture began to change in the late eighteenth century with the emergence of craft guilds like the General Society of Mechanics and Tradesmen, honored here in an artist's engraving.

began to employ both women and children wherever possible; they introduced the sweatshop and the practice of letting out contracts to prison labor."[6]

Workers in the skilled trades responded to this power shift by organizing themselves into temporary societies authorized to "bargain collectively" with employers to determine wages, hours, and working conditions. They recognized that a united group of workers stood a much better chance of negotiating good wages than an individual craftsman.

Early forerunners of the modern labor union popped up all across America from the 1780s through the early nineteenth century. They enjoyed a measure of immediate acceptance from workers and the American public at large because they were seen as a natural outgrowth of the principles that had led the colonies to declare their independence from England in 1776. Indeed, leaders of this movement consciously drummed up support for their stance by arguing that workers were protesting against the same sort of ruling-class oppression that had sparked the Revolutionary War.

During the 1780s and 1790s some of these societies called strikes—work stoppages—to press employers for better wages and working conditions. Organizations of printers and shoemakers in New York and Philadelphia were among the earliest to use strikes as a weapon against unyielding employers. Of these early societies, an organization of Philadelphia shoemakers called the Federal Society of Journeymen Cordwainers (FSJC) is frequently cited by historians as the nation's first genuine trade union. Founded in 1794, this organization of journeymen cordwainers (a term for artisans who made shoes out of cordovan, a type of leather) endured for twelve years.

During its first years of existence, the FSJC called strikes and picketed masters' shops in a successful campaign to win higher wages and convince Philadelphia shoe manufacturers to hire only FSJC members. The group eventually fell apart, however, in a manner that cast a long and grim shadow over workers' rights to organize. In 1805 an FSJC strike for better wages triggered a harsh response from Philadelphia shoemakers. They convinced city officials to arrest eight leaders of the society and charge them with violating conspiracy prohibitions contained in English common law. When the leaders were found guilty of these charges, they received only small fines. But the court's judgment in the case, known as *Commonwealth v. Pullis*, essentially branded labor unions as unlawful organizations. This highly publicized ruling did not end all union organizing in the United States, but it greatly hindered union efforts to gain acceptance from workers or the general public.

Economic Shifts Change Worker Fortunes

During the first two decades of the nineteenth century, skilled workers in many different trades followed the lead of New York and Philadelphia printers and shoemakers and formed their own workers' societies. These journeymen organizations continued to frame their calls for higher wages and better working conditions as defensive measures against an increasingly ruthless, employer-dominated system of capitalism. But their campaigns for worker "solidarity" proved to be no match for a multi-year economic depression that began in 1819. When sales of goods and services slowed across the United States, employers began letting high-wage workers go or replacing them with less expensive help. As unemployment rose, even skilled craftsmen became so desperate for work that they accepted low-paying positions with long hours or dangerous workplace conditions. The local trade unions that had arisen in the early nineteenth century tried to fight back against these trends. But the poor economic conditions convinced many members to go their own way, and most of these early worker societies simply were not strong enough to survive the loss of membership.

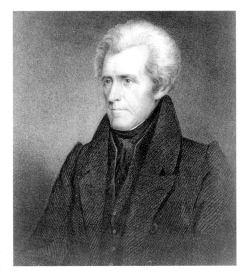

During the 1830s, President Andrew Jackson engineered many political and social changes that benefited America's working class.

The fortunes of workers lifted again in the mid-1820s, when general economic conditions improved. New societies of workers emerged in many of the skilled trades, and some of the unions that formed during this time even managed to squeeze higher wages and shorter working hours out of employers. Ship carpenters in Philadelphia, cabinet makers in Baltimore, stonecutters in New York, and tailors in Buffalo all secured gains in wages or hours after organizing themselves.[7]

Other rumblings from the world of labor were heard during this time as well. In Philadelphia, a labor group called the Mechanics' Union of Trade Associations was established in 1827. This organization was the first union in American history to bring together workers from multiple trades. Around this same period, factory workers in the textile mills of New England and the ironworks of Pennsylvania made their first tentative attempts to organize into unions (see "A Textile Mill Worker Mourns the Hardships of the Factory System," p. 153). Their demands for higher wages and better treatment from the companies that employed them went mostly unanswered. But the willingness of "unskilled" factory workers to follow the lead of tradesmen and explore the benefits of unionization was an important development.

Finally, American workers gained greater political power in the 1830s than they had ever enjoyed before. They were lifted to this newfound status by a popular social movement known to historians as Jacksonian Democracy. This movement was named after President Andrew Jackson, who led a successful campaign to extend voting rights to all white male adult citizens, not just landowners (women and free blacks were still denied the vote). Following Jackson's lead, American culture also became much more celebratory of the "common man," while at the same time dismissing educated and affluent "elites" as selfish, arrogant, and untrustworthy.

Worker Gains Under Jacksonian Democracy

Jacksonian Democracy gave labor organizers a big boost, and by the mid-1830s so-called workingmen's parties were even fielding their own candidates for political office. Other politicians, meanwhile, discovered that they could only obtain the votes of the "common man" if they promised to defend the interests of trade societies and other workers. Oftentimes this meant working on wider societal issues that were important to workingmen, like instituting public education for their children.

American trade groups achieved several momentous victories during this time, but none was bigger than the fight for a ten-hour workday. Prior to the 1830s, most artisans and mechanics had toiled from sun-up to sunset. By the close of that decade, however, craftsmen in Baltimore, Boston, Philadelphia, and other towns were enjoying ten-hour workdays. A few years later, the federal government even passed regulations that made the ten-hour day standard for all government work projects.

Despite these gains, however, workers remained intensely vulnerable to economic downturns. In 1837, for example, another depression rolled across America. Employers took the usual steps to weather the crisis until business picked up again. They replaced highly-paid workers with cheap labor or demanded longer working hours for the same pay. As had happened in 1819, the rising competition for jobs made it difficult for worker societies to stay unified.

Other changes in American society took a toll on workers as well. One major development was a mid-century surge in immigration, which greatly boosted the supply of cheap labor available to employers. Another key was that these immigrants arrived at a time when America's Industrial Revolution was roaring to life. These new arrivals provided cheap labor for the nation's

20

new factories and mills and swelled the size of its cities. The output of these factories quickly lifted the United States to new heights of economic power, but the introduction of industrial manufacturing also transformed workers into replaceable "cogs" in a vast machine. Given all of these factors, it is little wonder that the American labor movement spent the second half of the nineteenth century struggling for its very survival.

Notes

1. Innes, Stephen. "Fulfilling John Smith's Vision: Work and Labor in Early America." In *Work and Labor in Early America.* Edited by Stephen Innes. Chapel Hill: University of North Carolina Press, 1988, p. 22.
2. Morgan, Kenneth. *Slavery and Servitude in Colonial North America: A Short History.* New York: NYU Press, 2001, p. 47.
3. Smith, Abbott Emerson. *Colonists in Bondage: White Servitude and Convict Labor in America, 1607-1776.* Baltimore: Genealogical Publishing, 2009, p. 20.
4. Quoted in Dulles, Foster Rhea, and Melvyn Dubofsky. *Labor in America: A History.* 5th ed. Wheeling, IL: Harlan Davidson, 1993, p. 6.
5. Quoted in Boorstin, Daniel J. *The Americans: The Colonial Experience.* New York: Random House, 1958, p. 194.
6. Dulles, p. 26.
7. Dulles, p. 31.

Chapter Two
SWEAT AND BLOOD

Whether you work by the piece or work by the day,
Decreasing the hours increases the pay.

—Nineteenth-century labor slogan penned by Mary Steward,
the wife of a Boston machinist and union organizer

Relations between American workers and their employers worsened greatly in the decades following the Civil War. Workers recognized that the nation's growing industrial might was giving factory owners, bankers, and executives the means to build lives of fantastic luxury for themselves. Millions of working men, women, and children, however, remained trapped in dangerous, exhausting jobs that paid poorly. Desperate to improve their circumstances, laborers organized themselves into unions that demanded better wages and working conditions for their memberships. But their calls for a more equitable distribution of America's growing wealth were rejected by the powerful corporations that came to prominence in the late nineteenth century. Spasms of violence between the two sides erupted with increasing frequency, ushering in an era of economic and political turmoil that rocked America to its core.

Civil War Brings Industrial Changes

When the United States entered the second half of the nineteenth century, progress in its economic and industrial development was blunted by rising hostilities between the North and South over slavery. The South's reliance on the enslavement of blacks for its labor needs had been a source of tension

23

with the North since America's earliest days of existence. But America's internal struggle over slavery reached fresh heights during the 1840s and 1850s. At that time, debates over whether slavery should be permitted in the country's newly settled western territories sparked the growth of a powerful abolitionist movement in the North.

In 1861 the longstanding sectional divide over slavery finally exploded into the American Civil War. This four-year conflict between the nation's northern and southern states ultimately claimed the lives of about 620,000 Union and Confederate soldiers. But it also ended slavery in the United States, freeing about four million African Americans from lives of bondage.

The war also had a tremendous impact on America's industrial development. As the conflict progressed, the North—which already possessed huge advantages in population, industrial capacity, and capital—invested in new factories and equipment to make uniforms, guns, ammunition, wagons, and other military supplies. When the war ended, these factories stood ready to make a huge assortment of products for peacetime consumers. The postwar South, on the other hand, was left reeling from a conflict that not only destroyed a familiar way of life, but also smashed much of its limited industrial infrastructure, including railroads and factories. As a result, many Southern states became even more deeply wedded to agriculture for their survival.

Northern lawmakers tried to help the South recover from its deep war wounds during the Reconstruction era of 1865-1877, but these efforts failed to erase the deep racial bigotry that existed throughout the region. Once Reconstruction ended, whites refused to give black workers equal opportunities to prosper in the postwar South. Instead, they passed a variety of blatantly discriminatory laws against blacks. White southerners also instituted campaigns of terror and intimidation against black families that sometimes ended in beatings or lynchings. These grim developments convinced growing numbers of black men, women, and children to move to the industrial cities of the North beginning in the 1890s.

A New World of Mass Production

The men and women who constituted the leading edge of the great black migration to the North found a labor world that was far unlike the one they left behind. In the years following the Civil War, northern cities and towns

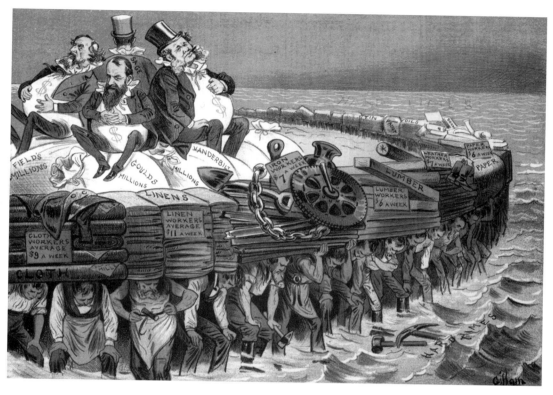

This 1883 cartoon shows "robber barons" Cyrus Field, Jay Gould, Cornelius Vanderbilt, and Russell Sage reclining on a platform of riches that is supported by working men of various professions.

were completely transformed by the arrival of millions of new immigrants as well as stunning changes in industrialization. Technological innovations like the Bessemer steelmaking process, the steam-powered engine, and the telegraph had an explosive impact on the economy, as did the increased size and efficiency of manufacturing and transportation operations. Chicago, for example, experienced a meteoric rise in the space of a mere fifty years—from a humble fort of less than 200 souls in the 1830s to a chaotic but vibrant metropolis of 800,000 people by the late 1880s.

These changes to American business and society lifted the United States to a whole new level of international influence and prestige. Observers in Europe and America alike described this emergence as evidence that the world's next great empire was in the process of being built. But the rapidly changing economic and industrial landscape also had its dark side. The rise of large corporations employing hundreds or thousands of workers made labor-management relations much more impersonal than they had been in the colonial era of small shops and apprenticeships. Factories also instituted systems of mass production in which employees were assigned to carry out the same limited, repetitive, and tedious tasks for their entire shift. "Mass production left no place for the individual craftsman—the tailor who made the whole suit, the shoemaker who made the whole shoe, the mechanic who made the whole machine," summarized one historian. "In his place you had many workers dependent upon one another to make *one* product, each swiftly trained to do his narrow part of the job."[1]

The powerful entrepreneurs who built and directed these massive corporate trusts became increasingly focused on the idea that long-term financial success and industry control hinged on keeping operating costs low. Since wages paid out to workers were one of their biggest costs, many business owners focused on keeping wages low, while at the same time pressuring workers to work at a fast—and at times even exhausting—pace. Yet these same companies tossed workers off their payrolls whenever they pleased, and they made little effort to provide a pleasant or safe working environment. "If workers survived the threat of unemployment, they still faced the twin specters of injury and early death," wrote one historian. "Every working-class occupation had its difficulties and dangers, from the explosions, fires, cave-ins, debilitating 'miner's lung,' and other notorious perils of hard-rock mining in the West to the 'Monday morning sickness,' asthma, byssinosis, tuberculosis, and maimings in the textile mills of the East."[2]

America's courts and legislatures offered no sanctuary for powerless workers, either. Corporate giants used their wealth to secure much greater access to politicians and judges than ordinary workers could ever hope for. As a result, most of the laws passed during this era were slanted decisively in favor of management. Workers felt helpless in the face of these trends, and they came to regard America's leading industrialists—men like railroad tycoons Cornelius Vanderbilt and Jay Gould, telegraph tycoon Cyrus Field, steel magnate Andrew Carnegie, oilman John D. Rockefeller, and financiers Russell Sage and J.P. Morgan—as greedy and unscrupulous "robber barons" who looked at workers in the same way they looked at timber, cotton, and coal: as raw material to be used for their own enrichment.

26

The Molly Maguires

Molly Maguires were Irish-American miners from Pennsylvania's dangerous anthracite coal fields who organized into a secret—and extremely violent—union in the 1860s and 1870s. The union, formally called the Workingmen's Benevolent Association, arose in response to the terrible working and living conditions that existed in the coal mining industry at that time. When their calls for wage increases and other improvements were ignored by the coal companies, the Molly Maguires turned to violent strike actions and outright murder of local policemen who were allied with the mine owners.

The Molly Maguires' tightening grip over the Pennsylvania region was broken in 1877, when an undercover agent working on behalf of the mine owners exposed the union's leadership. Nineteen members were arrested for murder, and all were convicted in trials that were rife with irregularities and questionable evidence. All nineteen men were eventually hanged—including ten in a single day, June 21, 1877.

The Emergence of National Unions

During the late 1860s and 1870s, workers in several industries formally banded together in an effort to check the power of the corporations and improve their own lots in life. They became convinced that only labor unions—which could organize strikes, work stoppages, and boycotts in response to unfair labor practices—had the potential to give employees any hope of prevailing in clashes with management. These early organizations had wildly different characteristics. Some of these groups were mutual aid societies of modest scope, designed primarily to provide injury and death benefits to members and their families. Others were strictly local unions organized to negotiate higher wages and a shorter workday. Indeed, securing an eight-hour workday was a major focal point of organized labor activity in the decades following the Civil War.

Many of these union organizations pursued their goals through peaceful negotiations and strike actions, even when owners engaged in activities—like unilateral wage cuts—that deeply angered them. The most successful of these

27

groups were unions of skilled tradesmen who could not easily be replaced, like the Pennsylvania-based Amalgamated Association of Iron, Steel, and Tin Workers. Other unions embraced violence and intimidation as a way of striking back against mine owners, laborers reluctant to join their groups, and the replacement workers or "scabs" that businesses hired to take the place of strikers. The Molly Maguires of the Appalachian coal country were the most notorious purveyors of this sort of mayhem (see "The Molly Maguires," p. 27).

Some of these local unions registered notable victories for their memberships, especially in industries like silver mining, which experienced a huge boom in the postwar years. But the most important development in union organizing after the Civil War was the emergence of *national* unions—labor organization that united workers across different regions of the country.

The first major effort in this area took place in 1866, when the National Labor Union (NLU) was founded in Baltimore, Maryland. Led by an iron molder named William H. Silvis, the NLU rose in a few years to include about 200,000 workers from 300 local unions. Seizing the eight-hour day as its central goal, the union's leadership asserted that a new age of labor-management relations was dawning. "I love this union cause!" Silvis declared in one speech to NLU rank and file. "Singlehanded we can accomplish nothing, but united there is no power of wrong that we cannot openly defy."[3]

Silvis's optimism was dashed within a few years. The NLU was mortally wounded in 1872, when it launched a failed bid to form a new political party devoted to the labor cause. Within a few years of this setback the union itself was no more. But its early years of success inspired other union organizers, and in the 1870s and 1880s two major national unions—the Knights of Labor and the American Federation of Labor—burst onto the scene.

Changing Fortunes in an Era of Upheaval

The Knights of Labor, initially founded in Philadelphia in 1869 by a group of tailors headed by Uriah Smith Stephens, grew slowly in its early years. But it expanded rapidly in the late 1870s and early 1880s for three reasons: 1) it drew in members of the National Labor Union after the NLU's final collapse in 1873; 2) it was accepting of both skilled and unskilled workers, and welcomed women and blacks in an era when few other unions were willing to do so; and 3) it benefited from strong leadership from labor giants like Terence Powderly and Mary Harris "Mother" Jones.

The Knights of Labor generally avoided strike actions and other confrontational tactics in its first years of existence. This stance was mostly due to an economic depression that swept across the United States in September 1873 and lingered for most of the remaining decade. The depression led many businesses to shed workers and slash wages, which angered the Knights and other unions. But organized labor knew that if it resorted to strikes in response, legions of desperate unemployed workers would gladly take those jobs, even at extremely low wages. This concern was especially strong among unskilled workers, but job security fears were also present among skilled craftsmen. Shoemakers, printers, glassmakers, stonemasons, and mechanics were harder to replace than miners, longshoremen, and other "unskilled" workers. Sales slumps during economic downturns, though, put the jobs of even skilled workers at risk because there simply was not that much work to be found. As a result, when companies imposed wage cuts or demanded longer hours on the job during economic downturns, even skilled workers felt they had no choice but to swallow hard and obey.

Terence Powderly led the Knights of Labor during its years of greatest success.

On several occasions, sharp wage cuts and rising unemployment brought explosions of violence from furious workers. The most notorious of these incidents came in July 1877, when wage cuts by powerful railroad companies triggered a series of violent riots in cities across the country, from Baltimore to San Francisco. These outbreaks temporarily paralyzed the nation's rail system, which was the foundation of most of its economic activity. Federal troops were subsequently sent into several cities to put down the revolt. Violence between workers and soldiers flared up in some cities, but in most places the arrival of troops brought an end to strike activity. The strikers grimly returned to work because "they knew when they were beaten; they knew that they had no chance with the government upholding the railroads. By the end of July, the trains were generally running again and the strikes were over."[4]

The hard economic times led many struggling Americans to explore new political belief systems that held out the hope of a better life. These political philosophies included anarchism (a belief that society should have no government), communism (a belief that all private ownership should be abolished and all wealth shared equally within the community), and socialism (a belief that society should be organized for the benefit of all members, with state ownership of industry). All of these philosophies found some measure of acceptance within the struggling labor movement, although other union leaders and rank-and-file members rejected them.

The depression conditions of the late 1870s also shattered many of the fragile national unions that had been formed after the war. One labor-oriented newspaper, the *Labor Standard,* reported in 1877 that the number of national unions in America had fallen from thirty to nine in the space of four years, and that the total number of unionized workers had declined from 300,000 to no more than 50,000.[5]

When the United States finally emerged from its economic difficulties at the end of the 1870s, though, these same workers were extremely receptive to union organizers. Battered by years of declining wages, nonexistent job security, and workdays that were once again creeping up into dawn-to-dusk territory, they liked the sound of an organization that promised them a measure of power and self-determination. As one Massachusetts mechanic said in 1879, "For the last five years the times have been growing worse every year, until we have been brought down so far that we have not much farther to go. What do the mechanics of Massachusetts say to each other? I will tell you: 'We must make a change. Any thing is better than this. We cannot be worse off, no matter what the change is.'"[6]

The unions that managed to survive the nightmarish 1870s were able to capitalize on this despair and recruit hundreds of thousands of new members in the following decade. The Knights of Labor was at the forefront of this explosion in union growth (see "The Knights of Labor Explain Their Cause and Issue Demands," p. 158). The organization boosted its membership rolls from 19,000 in 1881 to 700,000 by late 1886. One key to this astounding growth was the Knights' success in two dramatic strike actions. Dropping its long-time opposition to such confrontational tactics, it carried out a successful strike against the powerful Union Pacific Railroad in 1884, then followed up one year later with an effective strike against the Wabash Railroad, which was owned by the hated union-buster Jay Gould.

This illustration of the Haymarket tragedy, titled "The Anarchist Riot in Chicago—A Dynamite Bomb Exploding Among the Police," appeared in the issue of *Harper's Weekly* dated May 15, 1886.

The Haymarket Tragedy

The gains in wages and other benefits that members received from these labor actions convinced many other workers to hitch their stars to the Knights of Labor, but in 1886 the organization suffered two crushing blows. The first was a tragic series of events in Chicago in the opening days of May. On May 1, tens of thousands of American workers gathered together in the heart of the city to take part in a "national strike day" organized by labor leaders to demand an eight-hour workday across all industries. The Knights of Labor supported this action, but other unions were primarily responsible for organizing the Chicago demonstration (similar demonstrations were carried out in other cities across America as well).

The next two days unfolded peacefully, but on the evening of May 3 Chicago police shot and killed two strikers demonstrating outside a factory. Outraged labor leaders decided to hold a rally in Chicago's Haymarket Square the next day to denounce police brutality. About 3,000 workers gathered at Haymarket. They conducted themselves peacefully, but when police decided to break up the rally later that night, an unknown assailant threw a bomb into the police ranks, killing one officer. The frightened and furious police then opened fire into the crowd of mostly unarmed men and women. A full-blown riot erupted, and by the time it was over seven policemen and eight civilians were dead.

The Haymarket riot triggered a tremendous backlash against organized labor in general and the Knights of Labor in particular, since it ranked as the nation's largest union. After Haymarket, the American public became much more sympathetic to mine owners, railroad companies, and other corporate interests who argued that unions were populated with thugs, radicals, and losers who did not respect the nation's laws or traditions.

Pro-business newspapers continued to drive this message home during the June 1887 trial of eight rally organizers who were arrested for inciting murder at Haymarket. The prosecutors were unable to provide any evidence linking the men to the bomb attack—in fact, several of the accused were not even present in the square when the bomb throwing occurred—but the jury returned guilty verdicts against all eight men after only three hours of deliberations. One man was sentenced to fifteen years in prison, while the other seven were sentenced to death. Four were eventually executed by hanging and one committed suicide in prison. The best known of the executed men was August Spies, a labor leader and anarchist who boldly predicted that the Haymarket convictions would not quiet the working man's demands for fair and humane treatment. "If you think that by hanging us you can stamp out the labor movement … then hang us! Here you will tread upon a spark, but everywhere flames blaze up." The other three Haymarket convicts were released from prison in 1893. They were pardoned by Illinois Governor John Peter Altgeld, who asserted that the convictions had been a glaring miscarriage of justice.

Founding of the American Federation of Labor

The second major event that damaged the Knights of Labor was the 1886 founding of the American Federation of Labor (AFL). Initially composed of 13 distinct craft unions of skilled workers, the AFL experienced tremendous growth under the leadership of Samuel Gompers, a London-born cigar maker. Many skilled workers in the Knights of Labor switched to the AFL after the Haymarket riot, and Gompers proved adept at bringing thousands of new unionists into the fold as well. "[Union members] are forced by the conditions which surround them to organize for self-protection," he declared. "Where trade unions are most firmly organized, there are the rights of the people most respected."[7] Within six years of its formation, the AFL had almost one million members.

The AFL's roster of unions in the early 1890s included the United Mine Workers (UMW), one of the nation's leading organizations of "unskilled" industrial workers. But the UMW, which claimed a membership of about 100,000 workers in 1890, was unlike virtually every other union under the AFL banner. Gompers believed that workers with specialized skills, such as carpenters, glassmakers, masons, mechanics, and printers, were much better equipped than unskilled

In 1886 the American Federation of Labor (AFL) was established under the leadership of London-born cigar maker Samuel Gompers.

laborers to demand higher wages, fewer hours, and better workplace conditions from their employers. This conviction led him to focus nearly all his energies on gathering tradesmen to the AFL—and to stay away from the work forces in mass-production industries.

Mindful that enemies of the Knights of Labor were able to use Haymarket to paint that union as a collection of wild-eyed radicals, Gompers also worked very hard to keep the AFL respectable in the eyes of the American public and the executives and public officials with which it negotiated. Certainly, he was capable of using fiery language to recruit workers, condemn "wealthy parasites," and criticize corruption in America's capitalist system (see "Samuel Gompers Answers the Question 'What Does Labor Want?'" p. 164). But Gompers steered the organization away from anarchists, Communists, and other controversial "radicals," and he remained uninterested in joining forces with unskilled workers. In addition, Gompers and the AFL excluded women, African Americans, and other minorities from membership. Finally, Gompers and the rest of the federation's leadership adopted a strong anti-immigration position because they thought that new immigrants represented a threat to the job security of AFL members, thus weakening their bargaining position with management.

Divisions within the Labor Movement

The unwelcoming stance of the AFL and some other unions towards immigrants was not based entirely on economics. The leaders of these groups were mostly of German, Irish, and English ancestry. Many of them looked down on the Italians, Slavs, and other southern and eastern European peoples that dominated immigration to America from the post-Civil War years through the early twentieth century. This sense of racial superiority also contributed to their hostility toward African Americans, Chinese, and other minorities, especially in industries where competition for even exhausting, low-paying jobs was fierce.

"I love this union cause!" said William H. Silvis of the National Labor Union. "Singlehanded we can accomplish nothing, but united there is no power of wrong that we cannot openly defy."

But it was also true that the vast wave of immigrants that entered America from the 1870s through the mid-1920s *did* constitute a huge pool of desperate workers who were willing to take low pay for even the most exhausting and dangerous jobs. This reality led unions like the Knights of Labor to lend their active support to federal legislation that placed restrictions on immigration to America, like the 1885 Alien Contract Law. Similarly, African-American laborers who streamed into northern cities from the South competed for factory jobs long held by whites, and their financial desperation sometimes did result in lower wages for the entire work force. This reality led Gompers to describe blacks as a "continuous convenient whip placed in the hands of the employers to cow the white men and to compel them to accept abject conditions of labor."[8] Occasionally, these racial animosities even exploded into violence, as was the case when white coal miners in Rock Springs, Wyoming, murdered 28 Chinese miners in an 1885 riot.

These tensions made it even more difficult for America's workers to overcome the differences in culture, language, and appearance that existed between ethnic groups. And as long as these walls of division remained high, workers of different ethnicities found it difficult to find common ground and present a united front for better wages and working conditions. Employers recognized this basic truth, and so they adopted policies that purposely pitted ethnic groups against one another. For example, corporations frequently used blocs of African Americans, Chinese, or eastern European immigrants as strikebreakers when unions filled with white members of west European descent organized work stoppages to seek better wages or working conditions.

This particular strategy paid enormous dividends for corporations because strikebreakers—or "scabs," as union members called them—were hated by organized labor with white-hot intensity. The Socialist writer Jack London, author of *Call of the Wild* and other famous stories of the Yukon, summarized union sentiment when he wrote that "After God had finished the rattlesnake, the toad, and the vampire, he had some awful substance left with which he made a scab. A scab is a two-legged animal with a corkscrew soul, a water brain, a combination backbone of jelly and glue. Where others have hearts he carries a tumor of rotten principles."[9] Holders of such views made no allowance for the fact that the strikebreakers were often just as desperate to feed themselves and their families as the strikers were.

Some elements within the American labor movement did try to bridge these ethnic divisions and unite all workers under the same working-class banner. The National Labor Union was an early pioneer in this regard, and other organizers sensibly argued that including African Americans and immigrants could greatly boost the negotiating power of labor. But these efforts remained the exception rather than the rule until the early 1900s. Instead, minorities and eastern European immigrants continued to wander America's cities as outcasts from labor groups that could have benefited mightily from their inclusion. As one black observer bitterly commented in 1899, "They hang the negro in the South, but they are not so bad in the North; they just simply starve him to death by labor unions."[10]

American Society on the Edge

By the early 1890s the people of the United States could look back with pride on three successive decades of immense population growth, startling territorial expansion, ingenious technological advances, and escalating industrial power. These elements had brought many Americans, from office workers and shopkeepers to skilled AFL tradesmen, to new heights of comfort and security. Moreover, this so-called "gilded age" of American history lifted the nation's elite upper class—the families who owned and directed America's great banks, railroads, mines, and factories—into lives of incredible wealth and luxury. But America was also a powder keg of rage and frustration, for millions of working-class Americans had been left behind in this era of economic expansion. By 1890, in fact, the richest 1 percent of the country's population had more wealth than the total of the other 99 percent.[11] As one historian observed, "never before or since in American history have the rich been so rich and the poor so poor."[12]

Whether they toiled in the silver and copper mines of the West, the coal and oil fields of Pennsylvania, or the mills and factories of the big cities, millions of unskilled workers remained mired in poverty. The anger and despair felt by these workers was further intensified by the fact that the only shelter they could usually afford for their families took the form of filthy, crowded tenement buildings or threadbare shacks. Nor could they afford decent food or clothing for themselves or their children. Yet when they issued cries for better pay or safer workplaces, they were treated to humiliating verbal attacks from wealthy countrymen like Baptist minister Russell H. Conwell, who famously sermonized that "Ninety-eight out of one hundred of the rich men of America are honest. That is why they are trusted with money….While we should sympathize with God's poor—that is, those who cannot help themselves—let us remember there is not a poor person in the United States who was not made poor by his own shortcomings, or by the shortcomings of some one else. It is all wrong to be poor, anyhow."[13]

> *"There is not a poor person in the United States who was not made poor by his own shortcomings, or by the shortcomings of some one else," declared Baptist minister Russell H. Conwell. "It is all wrong to be poor, anyhow."*

The long years of working-class struggle—with few signs of meaningful progress—finally convinced many industrial labor unions that if they ever hoped to claim a greater share of the wealth they were helping to create, they needed to take bolder steps against the companies that employed them. These steps ranged from major strike actions to acts of sabotage and other violence against corporations. Management responded with harsh and sometimes vicious strikebreaking strategies. Often working in league with allies in the state and federal governments, they worked to imprison labor leaders and smash unions with greater energy than ever before. By the time it was all over, the 1890s had hosted some of the most famous labor-management clashes in American history.

The Homestead Strike

In 1892 alone, approximately 1,300 labor strikes flared across the American business landscape.[14] Some of these resulted in union victories in the form of higher wages or shorter working days, but the most famous of these strikes—the Homestead Steel Strike—was a crushing defeat. This labor battle

The 1892 strike action at Carnegie Steel in Homestead, Pennsylvania, was broken when the governor of Pennyslvania ordered state troops to take the factory back from strikers.

in Pennsylvania pitted the Amalgamated Association of Iron and Steel Workers, a union of skilled workers in the steel industry, against Carnegie Steel, the most powerful steel company in the United States.

The president of Carnegie Steel was Henry Clay Frick, who viewed unions as little more than criminal organizations designed to extort money from business owners. When the union issued demands for better pay and other management concessions in July 1892, Frick responded by shutting the plant down. He believed that the plant closure would destroy the Amalgamated union and force the workers back to their jobs, but instead the union orchestrated a seizure of the factory. Furious at this development, Frick hired a 300-man army from the Pinkerton Detective Agency. This company provided many of America's top corporations with "security services," including strikebreaking and harassment of union organizers. The arrival of the Pinkertons, though, set off a deadly exchange of rifle fire and dynamite attacks. The strikers successfully turned back the Pinkertons, but they had only a short time to celebrate before state troops came and took control of the plant under orders of Pennsylvania Governor Robert E. Pattison.

With the factory back under his control, Frick used trains to bring in strikebreakers. Many of these men, lured by vague promises of work, did not even know they were being used as strikebreakers until they arrived at Homestead. This last blow shattered the union beyond repair. Broken by Frick's ruthless tactics, the strikers gradually returned to work. Strike leaders were arrested and charged with a variety of crimes, including murder. Although they were eventually acquitted, Carnegie Steel blacklisted them and then spent the next several years stamping out the few remnants of union activity that remained in the region.

The Pullman Strike

Dozens of other strikes, boycotts, and work stoppages garnered newspaper headlines across the United States in the final years of the nineteenth century. The only one that rivaled Homestead in notoriety and long-term influence, though, was the Pullman Strike of 1894.

The Pullman Palace Car Company was a Chicago-based manufacturer of luxury railroad cars for wealthy travelers. Financial success had enabled it to follow the lead of other big manufacturers and form a company-owned "town" for its employees to live in. The establishment of these towns, which featured company-owned grocery stores, shops, services, and rental homes, enabled corporations to recoup virtually all the wages they paid out to their workers.

The Pullman company town was nicer than many other company towns of the era, but the workers still recognized that they were living their entire lives in the grip of their employer. As residents of the town often said, "We are born in a Pullman house, fed from the Pullman shop, taught in the Pullman school, catechized in the Pullman church, and when we die we shall be buried in the Pullman cemetery and go to the Pullman hell."

Nonetheless, Pullman workers grudgingly accepted this state of affairs until May 1894. At that time, the company responded to sluggish economic conditions by abruptly firing some workers and imposing steep cuts in wages

This drawing from a contemporary American newspaper shows hundreds of freight cars set afire in a Chicago rail yard by rioting workers during the 1894 Pullman Strike.

and hours to the remaining employees. This blow was further worsened by the company's refusal to reduce the rent on the company-owned homes in which the workers and their families lived.

The outraged workers subsequently turned to the American Railway Union (ARU), which not only organized a strike against the Pullman factory but also instigated a nationwide boycott in which ARU members refused to run trains containing Pullman cars. This strike was spearheaded by ARU president Eugene V. Debs, who was already well on his way to becoming one of the most famous figures in American life (see "Eugene Debs Asks 'What Can We Do for Working People?'" p. 160). In some parts of the country the boycotts spiraled into riots in which angry workers vandalized or destroyed freight cars and other railroad property.

Company owner George Pullman called on Illinois Governor John Peter Altgeld to use state troops to break the strike. Altgeld not only refused Pullman's request, but publicly sided with the strikers. This was a stunning development not only for Pullman, but also for other corporations across the country that had always been able to rely on government military support when they fell into disputes with labor.

When the ARU ignored a federal court order to end the strike, President Grover Cleveland sent 12,000 U.S. troops to Chicago to confront the strikers. Thirteen strikers were killed in clashes with the troops, who successfully put down the strike and arrested Debs. The labor leader was eventually sentenced to six months in jail for defying a federal court order. Debs underwent a political conversion to socialism during his imprisonment, and after his release he became the most prominent Socialist figure in America.

The Pullman Strike itself, meanwhile, further darkened the mood of tension and anxiety hanging over the United States. Even after it ended, Americans from all walks of life continued to debate what it meant for the country's future. "The entire nation felt the shock of the Pullman strike," observed one study of the conflict. "Conservatives were dismayed by the governor's sympathy for laboring men who had defied the courts. And for those who felt that the country was in the grip of plutocracy [government by the wealthy], the Pullman strike was almost a last straw. To them, the railroad owners merely had to snap their fingers to have judges and soldiers come rushing to force workingmen back to underpaid and unorganized labor."[15]

Notes

[1] Meltzer, Milton. *Bread-And Roses: The Struggle of American Labor, 1865-1915.* New York: Knopf, 1967, p. 4.

[2] McGerr, Michael. *A Fierce Discontent: The Rise and Fall of the Progressive Movement in America.* New York: Oxford University Press, 2005, pp. 16-17.

[3] Quoted in Meltzer, p. 77.

[4] Dulles, Foster Rhea, and Melvyn Dubofsky. *Labor in America: A History.* 5th ed. Wheeling, IL: Harlan Davidson, 1993, p. 115.

[5] Dulles, p. 106.

[6] Quoted in Meltzer, p. 12.

[7] Gompers, Samuel. Testimony of Samuel Gompers, August 1883. *Report of the Committee of the Senate upon the Relations between Labor and Capital.* Vol. 1. Washington, DC: GPO, 1885, p. 365.

[8] Quoted in McGerr, p. 129.

[9] London, Jack. "What Is a Scab?" In *Ferment in Labor,* edited by Jerome Wolf. Glencoe Press, 1968, p. 78.

[10] Foner, Philip S. *Organized Labor and the Black Worker, 1619-1973.* New York, International Publishers, 1976, p. 79.

[11] Meltzer, p. 53.

[12] Diamond, Sigmund. *Nation Transformed: The Creation of an Industrial Society.* New York: Braziller, 1963, p. vii.

[13] Conwell, Russell H. *Acres of Diamonds. His Life and Achievements.* Robert Shackleton. New York: Harper's, 1915, p. 21.

[14] Weisberger, Bernard A., and the Editors of Time-LIFE. *Reaching for Empire. Volume 8: 1890-1901 of the LIFE History of the United States.* New York: Time-Life Books, 1964, p. 85.

[15] Weisberger, p. 90.

Chapter Three

RADICALS, PROGRESSIVES, AND THE WORKING MAN

⟨⟨⟨⟨⟨⟨⟩⟩⟩⟩⟩⟩

Where trade unions are most firmly organized, there are the
rights of the people most respected.

—Samuel Gompers

During America's Progressive Era—a two-decade period stretching
roughly from the end of the nineteenth century through the United
States' entrance into World War I in 1917—organized workers
secured some improvements in wages and working conditions. Most of these
gains stemmed from organized labor activity, while others arose from progressive social reformers who wanted to reduce the power of corporations and
end child labor and other controversial employment practices. Still, the path
to greater prosperity for American workers remained a bumpy one, filled with
nearly as many defeats as victories.

The American Worker at the Turn of the Century

As the United States entered the 1900s, it remained heavily dependent on
manual workers for its industrial and agricultural wealth. More than half of
the nation's men and women—and a good number of its children—toiled with
their hands to bring in wages. The occupations in which they worked varied
enormously. Some worked as builders of bridges, subways, and railroad termi-
nals in America's great cities. Some spent their days cleaning households,
stocking shop shelves, harvesting crops from fields and orchards, and tending
cattle and sheep. Still others worked in paper mills, slaughterhouses,
foundries, and other types of factories.

By the early years of the twentieth century, immigrant workers were pouring into American cities in greater numbers than ever before. Their labor helped lift the United States to new heights of industrial productivity.

But wherever they worked and whatever their occupation, the majority of these laborers worked very long hours and earned very little money. One exception to this rule was the craft tradesman, who was usually enrolled in one of the American Federation of Labor's member trade unions. Blessed with a highly valued set of skills, these AFL men were able to carve out somewhat more comfortable places for themselves in industrial America. But even they had little margin for economic error, for any extended bout of illness, injury, or unemployment was likely to send them into poverty. All told, unskilled and skilled wage workers in American industry earned less than half as much as "white collar" or clerical employees. And some of the most dangerous and exhausting industries to work in, such as mining, paid very low wages. Families that depended on income from these jobs frequently struggled to obtain even the necessities of life, like decent shelter, clothing, and food.

Immigrants constituted an ever-growing percentage of these unskilled or semiskilled laborers. By 1900 more than a third of the U.S. population—about 26 million people—were either immigrants themselves or native-born Americans with at least one foreign-born parent. This immigrant surge showed no signs of abating, either. In 1905 alone, more than a million people emigrated from foreign shores to America to start new lives for themselves. Some of these immigrants joined native-born Americans in labor unions, but many of these organizations enjoyed only a few short years of existence before expiring. In 1901 only 1.125 million Americans were unionized—less than 10 percent of the nation's work force. And the country's largest labor union—the American Federation of Labor (AFL)—was not welcoming of new arrivals from eastern Europe, China, Mexico, and other foreign nations.

The continued limited growth of organized labor, even in the face of grinding poverty and hazardous working conditions, stemmed from several factors. For example, tensions between different ethnic groups and between skilled and unskilled workers often kept workers from presenting a united front in negotiations with management. In addition, courts and lawmakers at the state and federal levels remained much more sympathetic to big business than to struggling workers. But most of all, union growth was stifled by profit-hungry corporations that were utterly determined to keep workers from effectively organizing. They did this not only with a variety of union busting and strikebreaking strategies, but also with regular volleys of propaganda that painted all unionists as anti-American radicals.

Bitter Defeat and Stunning Victory

Some of the most famous battles between labor and management early in the Progressive Era took place in the mining camps of Colorado and northern

Idaho. These particular conflicts were rooted in wider changes taking place across the American West. During the last few decades of the nineteenth century, corporate giants like Anaconda, Kennecott, and Colorado Fuel and Iron had acquired control over vast western fields of copper, coal, and other minerals vital to America's industrial expansion. These companies filled their payrolls with unskilled immigrant workers, most of whom had little choice but to raise their families in "company towns"—clusters of rental homes, schools, shops, and churches all established, owned, and managed by the mine operators.

"It is well known that we have markedly differed and still differ from the policy of the officers of the Western Federation of Miners," declared AFL President Samuel Gompers. "Their conception and ours of the work and tactics of labor are as far apart as the poles."

In the 1890s union organizers successfully tapped into widespread mine worker anger and discontent and formed the Western Federation of Miners (WFM). Over the next several years, the WFM clashed repeatedly—and violently—with mine owners in Colorado and Idaho's Coeur d'Alene territory. These conflicts bore many of the hallmarks of all-out war. On several occasions, governors in league with mine owners sent militia troops to round up and imprison hundreds of striking workers. During one of these crackdowns the entire male population of a union town was arrested. WFM members retaliated with escalating violence against companies and strikebreakers, including an 1899 dynamite attack that obliterated operations at a Colorado Fuel and Iron mine in the Coeur d'Alenes.

The war between the increasingly radical WFM and western mine operators culminated in 1903-04 in Cripple Creek, Colorado. This conflict was sparked by several factors. One issue was worker anger over the refusal of the state's anti-union Republicans, including Governor James H. Peabody, to implement a voter-approved referendum imposing an eight-hour workday in mining and other hazardous industries. Tension also arose over mine owners' refusal to recognize the unionization rights of mine and smelter employees. The WFM leadership subsequently called a strike that dragged on for months. During this time, both sides used violence and intimidation to try and advance their cause. The crisis reached new heights in June 1904, when a union sympathizer set off a dynamite explosion that destroyed a train station and killed thirteen strikebreakers. In response, Colorado militia troops, the Cripple Creek Mine Owners Association, and an anti-union vigilante group known as the Citizens Alliance worked together to round up more than 200 union leaders and strikers and force them out of Colorado at gunpoint. This expulsion broke the back of the strike action. The WFM never recovered, and most of the Cripple Creek miners and smelters could only watch helplessly as their jobs were handed over to unorganized immigrant workers.[1]

Following the example of their hard rock mining colleagues, western coal mining companies were able to take similar steps to neutralize union "agitators" in their own industry in 1904. Employing a mix of state troops and company-sponsored vigilante groups, western coal operators master-minded a series of mass arrests and expulsions that smashed union-led strikes across Colorado.

Roosevelt Sides with the United Mine Workers

In the final analysis, though, these victories of the big western mining operators were not nearly as momentous as a labor triumph over manage-ment that occurred at virtually the same time in Pennsylvania. This struggle pitted 150,000 members of the United Mine Workers of America (UMWA), which was led by John Mitchell, in a strike action against anthracite coal field owners in Pennsylvania, home of the nation's richest anthracite fields.

The mine workers launched their May 1902 strike not only to secure better wages and working conditions, but also to force management to recog-nize the UMWA as the workers' legitimate representative in negotiations (see "The Importance of Collective Bargaining," p. 52). Union leaders and rank-and-file members alike knew that these ambitious goals would be bitterly contested by Pennsylvania's coal companies, most of which were actually owned by powerful railroad interests. "This will be the fiercest struggle in which we have yet engaged," declared Mitchell. "It will be a fight to the end, and our organization will either achieve a great triumph or it will be com-pletely annihilated."[2]

The strike dragged on inconclusively through the summer of 1902, to the growing frustration of U.S. President Theodore Roosevelt. The "coal kings" refused to even meet with Mitchell or other union leaders, and so min-ing of anthracite coal—the chief fuel for heating homes in America—slowed to a trickle in Pennsylvania. Roosevelt and other political leaders began to express fears about a wintertime "coal famine." In early October Roosevelt decided to step in by organizing a White House meeting between coal execu-tives and the UMWA.

In 1902 President Theodore Roosevelt (center) adopted a sympathetic stance toward striking coal mine workers. Roosevelt's attitude signaled a dramatic shift in the federal government's usual position on labor-management issues.

Once the meeting got underway, though, the mine operators made a serious tactical mistake. Not only did they treat the union representatives with contempt, they also acted as if Roosevelt had no choice but to support their corporate interests in the dispute. They dismissed Roosevelt's appeals for both sides to make patriotic sacrifices for the "greater good" of the American people. Instead, they demanded that Roosevelt use federal troops to force the strikers back to work. By the time the meeting ended, the president had become very angry about the "insolence" shown by mining executives like George F. Baer, president of the Philadelphia and Reading Railroad and chief spokesman for the mine owners. "If it wasn't for the high office I hold, I would have taken [Baer] by the seat of the breeches and the nape of the neck and chucked him out of that window," Roosevelt later wrote.[3]

Shortly after this White House meeting, Roosevelt informed the mine owners that he was thinking about using federal troops to operate the mines until the owners agreed to settle the strike through binding arbitration—a process in which labor-management disputes are resolved by an impartial government "arbitrator." This veiled threat finally pierced the fog of confident self-righteousness in which the mine owners had cloaked themselves. Stunned by the realization that Roosevelt could not be counted on to support them—and by growing public criticism of their stance—the coal executives grudgingly agreed to submit to arbitration from a government commission. This concession convinced the strikers to return to the coal mines on October 23, thus averting a disastrous winter of coal shortages. Five months later, the arbitration commission completed its work. It did not give the UMWA the formal recognition it desired. But it did grant a 10 percent pay raise, a shorter workday, and several other work improvements demanded by the union.

Today, the Anthracite Coal Strike is regarded as a momentous historical event for several reasons. First, it helped establish Roosevelt, who had been in office for less than a year when the strike began, as a bold progressive reformer unafraid to take on powerful corporate interests. In addition, the Roosevelt administration's actions during the strike "marked the turn of the U.S. Government from strikebreaker to peacemaker in industrial disputes," in the words of one labor historian.[4] But perhaps most importantly, the partial victory claimed by the UMWA gave an enormous boost of confidence to organized labor throughout America. Most than twenty years after it occurred, labor leader Samuel Gompers described the 1902 strike as the "most important single incident in the labor movement of the United States.... From then on the miners became not merely human machines to produce coal but men and citizens."[5]

Rise of the Wobblies

The full historical impact of the 1902 Anthracite Coal Strike did not reveal itself for years, however. Labor activists and union members were happy with the victory, but they knew that other triumphs had been short-lived. This sense of ongoing struggle, combined with setbacks like the 1904 Colorado mining strikes, led to the founding in June 1905 of a radical labor organization known as the Industrial Workers of the World (IWW).

The IWW was established during a secret meeting in Chicago attended by WFM refugees and a number of America's most prominent Socialists, anarchists, and radical union activists. Famous labor organizers including Mary Harris "Mother" Jones, William "Big Bill" Haywood, Eugene V. Debs, Daniel

Socialist Eugene Debs was a pivotal figure in the founding and early development of the International Workers of the World (IWW).

De Leon, and William E. Trautmann participated in the gathering, which was designed to create a "general industrial union embracing all industries."

The IWW founders offered a blunt perspective on American society. The organization's founding statement, in fact, flatly declared that "the working class and the employing class have nothing in common. There can be no peace so long as hunger and want are found among millions of working people and the few, who make up the employing class, have all the good things in life." According to the IWW, the solution to America's problems of social injustice was to bring *all* workers together in opposition to the ruling class of employers. And, they added, if the ruling class continued using violence and intimidation to keep workers down, the IWW was perfectly willing to respond with violence of its own.

This position placed the Industrial Workers of the World in direct opposition to the AFL. Under the direction of Samuel Gompers, the AFL and its membership of skilled tradesmen had navigated decades of turbulence that had dashed numerous other union groups to bits. But IWW members, known to both friend and foe as "Wobblies," viewed the AFL trade union as an elitist organization that did not care about industrial and agricultural workers who did not possess commercially valuable trade skills. They charged that the AFL's membership policies, which kept women, minorities, recent immigrants, and unskilled workers out of the organization, constituted an unforgivable betrayal of basic principles of worker solidarity. As the IWW complained, "the trade unions foster a state of affairs which allows one set of workers to be pitted against another set of workers in the same industry, thereby helping defeat one another in wage wars."[6]

Gompers and the rest of the AFL leadership brushed aside these complaints. They insisted that if they opened membership to wider groups of workers, the union's existing membership of tradesmen would get drawn into damaging labor disputes that did not directly concern them. This belief was so deeply felt within the AFL that when member unions like the United Metal Workers Industrial Union and the United Brewery Workers tried to form more general industrial unions in 1905 and 1907, respectively, Gompers and the rest of the leadership expelled them from the AFL.[7]

AFL leaders also framed their negative views of women, African Americans, and eastern European immigrants as a sensible stance. They observed that these groups had the potential to take jobs held by AFL members, or to flood labor markets with cheap workers who would undercut wages earned by AFL members. Still, the organization's long-standing hostility to African Americans and eastern European immigrants was based on bigotry as well as fears about competition for jobs. Similarly, the AFL's continued opposition to women in the workplace reflected fears about their possible negative impact on wages and job competition. But it also displayed deep-seated anxieties about the social impact if women strayed from their traditional roles. "The demand for female labor [is] an insidious assault upon the home," explained one conservative labor leader. "It is the knife of the assassin, aimed at the family circle."[8]

The founders of the IWW promised to build an organization that would serve as a sort of anti-AFL. They vowed to accept all workers—male and female, skilled and unskilled, native-born and immigrant, white and black— and meld them into a single great weapon that would crush "the corporations" and transform American society once and for all. Not surprisingly, this vow alarmed the executives who led the nation's great industries and the politicians who were responsible for maintaining social order. But it also sparked doubt and fear in the hearts of millions of Americans who favored addressing the nation's problems through reforms—not revolution.

Labor Gains in an Era of Progressive Reform

The need for a radical organization like the IWW was hotly debated by American workers and progressive reformers. Many people felt that the opening years of the twentieth century were already bringing important changes to American business and society. During this time, for example, President Roosevelt and like-minded progressive reformers implemented a wide range of

The Importance of Collective Bargaining

Labor organizers in the nineteenth and early twentieth centuries viewed management recognition of unions as essential to improving the fortunes of workers. They felt this way because once recognition was granted, workers could then engage in "collective bargaining"—a type of negotiation in which authorized union representatives bargain with management over wages, hours, and work rules applicable to all union members. In 1914 famed UMWA leader John Mitchell explained the importance of collective bargaining in testimony before Congress:

> There can be no permanent prosperity to the workingmen, there can be no permanent industrial peace, until the principle is firmly and fully established that in industrial life the settlements of wages, hours of labor, and all the important conditions of work, are made between the employers and the workingmen collectively and not between employers and working men individually. The individual workman theoretically bargains with his employer as to the wages to be paid by his employer; but practically there is no bargaining. The individual workman must accept the wages and conditions of employment that are offered to him by his employer. It is a matter of no concern at all to an employer if one workingman refuses employment. He thinks nothing about it, because there is another workingman ready to take the job. This "system of individual bargaining" gives too great an advantage to management, but collective bargaining evens the playing field.

Source:

Quoted in *Major Problems in the Gilded Age and Progressive Era.* Edited by Leon Fink. Washington, DC: Heath, 1993, p.40.

policies at the federal and state levels to address problems of excessive corporate power, urban poverty, social justice, and environmental destruction.

Many of these policies improved the lives of the American worker. For example, legislators passed numerous laws regulating the working conditions of women, boosting safety standards in dangerous workplaces, and limiting the employment of children. In addition, many states—35 by 1915—established modest systems of workmen's compensation for injured workers. State legislatures also passed housing reforms to clean up the worst tenement slums in their cities. This atmosphere of reform even led some private corporations to voluntarily introduce job-safety and retirement programs for workers.

These progressive gains lifted the fortunes of many working families, and they were embraced by a wide assortment of liberal labor activists and social reformers. Yet the largest union of all, the American Federation of Labor, voiced mixed feelings about these governmental attempts to combat poverty, disease, crime, and other problems in industrial America. AFL leaders acknowledged these problems, but they worried that the reforms might reduce their members' loyalty to the federation. The Progressive Era also highlighted Gompers's longstanding belief in limited government. He wanted the government to guarantee basic worker rights, like the right to bargain collectively, but he did not believe that additional governmental "interference" in society's affairs was warranted. "We do not want to place more power in the hands of the government to investigate and regulate the lives, the conduct and the freedom of America's workers," he said in 1915. "Where there is unwillingness to accept responsibility for one's life and for making the most of it, there is a loss of strong, red-blooded, rugged independence and will power."[9]

Most newspapers and legislators did not share this concern. Instead, they treated the wave of progressive reforms as evidence that the United States was poised on the cusp of a grand new era of widespread prosperity. In addition, the reform spirit running through America gave advocates of pro-labor socialism an opening to move into positions of actual political influence. The Socialist labor leader Eugene Debs made the first of five consecutive runs for the presidency in 1900, and while none of these efforts came close to lifting him to the White House, millions of working-class Americans came to see him as a wise and inspiring figure. At the local level, meanwhile, Socialist administrations were actually voted into office in cities like Milwaukee, Wisconsin, and Flint, Michigan, during the early 1900s. Unions themselves experienced rapid growth as well. Led by the AFL, the nation's total union membership jumped from fewer than 900,000 workers in 1900 to more than 2 million by 1904.

In reviewing these changes to American society, mainstream labor organizations like the AFL argued that Wobblies actually hindered the cause of workers by taking radical positions that reduced public support for labor.

AFL President Samuel Gompers (right) consciously worked to keep his labor organization from being identified with the more radical Wobblies.

They pointed, for example, to highly publicized events like the 1907 murder trial of "Big Bill" Haywood. A longtime radical unionist, WFM president, and co-founder of the IWW, Haywood was charged with arranging the 1905 assassination of former Idaho governor Frank Steunenberg, who had played a major role earlier in the decade in smashing the Western Federation of Miners. Haywood was eventually acquitted, thanks in no small part to the efforts of famed defense attorney Clarence Darrow (see "Clarence Darrow Defends Unions in the 'Trial of the Century,'" p. 170). But the trade unionists of the AFL openly worried that labor-related violence and mayhem made the American public wary of *all* union efforts. "It is well known that we have markedly differed and still differ from the policy of the officers of the Western Federation of Miners," declared Gompers in an attempt to keep the AFL from being tainted by the Steunenberg killing. "Their conception and ours of the work and tactics of labor are as far apart as the poles."[10]

Wobblies and other confrontation-minded unionists responded by stating that the AFL's membership did not understand or care about the horrible conditions that still prevailed in many industries. They also pointed out that whatever the other gains achieved during the Progressive Era, worker wages still paled when compared to the fabulous riches being raked in on a daily basis by America's "ruling class." They argued that these inequities proved that even more radical actions were needed to get workers what they deserved.

Big Business Strikes Back

Debate within the labor movement over whether workers should continue working within America's existing political and economic systems to

improve their lives (the AFL position)—or simply battle to completely
remake those systems (the position of
IWW and its Socialist and anarchist
allies)—dragged on inconclusively. In
the meantime, big business interests
launched a sustained counterattack
against organized labor.

Corporations worked to block any
further labor gains through several different strategies. One strategy used by anti-
union employers was to mount anti-
labor public relations and lobbying campaigns through corporate organizations
like the Citizens' Industrial Association
(founded in 1903) and the National
Association of Manufacturers (founded
in 1895). These associations fought for
industry priorities like the "open shop,"
a workplace that could employ both
union and non-union employees. Another industry goal was to advance the use
of "yellow dog" employment contracts,
which obligated signers to stay out of
unions as a condition of employment.

United Mine Workers President John Mitchell
and other labor leaders repeatedly described
U.S. courts as anti-labor puppets of big
business.

These anti-union drives, which
were particularly strong in the mass production industries, also relied heavily
on the U.S. court system. Many American courts of the early twentieth century were strongly pro-industry and anti-union in their orientation. This stance
was due partly to the fact that judges themselves came primarily from privileged upper-class backgrounds rather than working-class beginnings. But the
courts were also by their very nature defenders of societal stability. As a
result, they were often skeptical of organized labor campaigns to change the
ways in which American business and society had long operated.

As a result, worker gains during the Progressive Era were limited by
unfavorable court rulings. In some instances, advances made by organized
labor were even rolled back by judges who sided with industry in important

Children Caught in the Crossfire

Public relations blunders by management have been cited by historians as one of the main reasons that the 1912 Lawrence Strike in Massachusetts ended in victory for the striking textile workers. When the strike began in

Children of Lawrence strikers in New York City.

court cases. In 1904, for example, judges in Illinois and Wisconsin ruled that employers had every right to maintain open shops. Four years later, the U.S. Supreme Court overturned a federal ban on yellow dog contracts in the railroad business. Worst of all from the perspective of labor unions, dozens of judges issued injunctions—court orders—against actions that organized workers used to win battles with management.

January, the textile owners engaged in several strikebreaking tactics that actually increased public support for the workers, such as harassment of the young female picketers. But the owners' most disastrous move was to direct state police to stop strikers from sending their children away to sympathetic families in other cities, where they would be fed and cared for until the strike ended.

On February 24, 1912, dozens of families gathered at the Lawrence train station to send a group of children to waiting caregivers in Philadelphia. Before the children could board the train, however, police launched a vicious assault on the families. "When the time came [for the children] to depart," recalled one victim, "the police ... closed in on us with their clubs, beating right and left with no thought of the children who then were in desperate danger of being trampled to death. The mothers and the children were thus hurled in a mass and bodily dragged to a military truck and even then clubbed, irrespective of the cries of the panic-stricken mothers and children. We can scarcely find words with which to describe this display of brutality."

The police arrested a total of thirty-five women and children that day. The immediate public outcry over the incident soon prompted the authorities to release them, but by then it was too late. News of the attack on unarmed women and children turned public opinion decisively against the mill owners. Condemned by newspapers across the country as unfeeling monsters, the textile owners watched with mounting alarm as Congress also launched an investigation of the industry's strikebreaking activities. Bombarded by this negative publicity, the owners reluctantly decided to meet the strikers' demands, and by the end of March the triumphant textile workers were working again.

Injunctions were rarely issued against specific strike actions. But they were often used to keep unions from organizing large-scale boycotts or "general" strikes—work stoppages involving multiple industries in a single community or region. And sometimes they were even used to keep workers from picketing, meeting, or even shouting "scab" at strikebreakers.[11] "No weapon has been used with such disastrous effect against trade unions as the injunction in labor disputes," charged UMW President John Mitchell. "It is difficult to speak in measured tone or moderate language of the savagery and venom with which unions have been assailed by the injunction."[12]

The union cause also continued to suffer from self-inflicted wounds. In addition to its well-publicized internal squabbles, the movement's reputation with the wider general public suffered whenever labor disputes flared up in violence. To be sure, some of these explosions of bloodshed were triggered by industry thugs or strikebreaking militia troops. But the more aggressive unionists, some of whom remained closely allied with anarchists and other revolutionaries, were not blameless. Union members sometimes beat up strikebreakers or harassed men who did not want to join their organizations. And labor radicals occasionally engaged in outright acts of terrorism, such as the 1911 bombing of the offices of the *Los Angeles Times* by AFL member James B. McNamara, which claimed 21 lives.

From Lawrence to Ludlow

Yet despite all of these massive problems and obstacles, workers in the early twentieth century continued to make strides in organizing unions and improving their economic fortunes. These gains never would have been possible without the grit and determination displayed by millions of workers. But the movement was also energized by historical events that dramatically increased public support for labor rights and curbs on corporate power.

One of these events was the 1911 Triangle Shirtwaist Fire, in which 146 employees (mostly young women) died when a fire raged through a New York City sweatshop factory. This tragedy, which was caused by management's practice of locking stairwells and exits to keep workers from leaving the shop floor on breaks, sparked public outrage not only in New York but across the nation. It also prompted a wave of new workplace safety regulations, generated momentum for government investigations of industrial conditions, and helped a major new union, the International Ladies' Garment Workers Union, get established.

Another milestone in the labor movement was a successful strike waged by mostly female textile workers in Lawrence, Massachusetts. The ten-week "Bread and Roses" strike, which was organized and led in large measure by Elizabeth Gurley Flynn, Bill Haywood, and other IWW leaders, ended in a decisive victory for labor (see "Children Caught in the Crossfire of a Labor

A distraught man stands in the remains of the Ludlow tent colony that was destroyed by fire during the 1914 Ludlow Massacre.

Dispute," p. 56). Wages for textile workers were boosted all across New England under the terms of settlement. In addition, the Lawrence strike gave women new levels of acceptance in the wider labor movement.

In 1914 the United States was rocked by another dark event in its troubled labor history, this time in Ludlow, Colorado. And like the Triangle Shirtwaist Fire of three years earlier, the impact of this horrible event was felt for many years afterward. The violence that erupted in Ludlow on April 20, 1914, had been brewing for a long time. Coal miners in the employ of major operators in the region endured long hours of exhausting work for little pay, and most of their meager earnings went right back to the operators via their company stores. In September 1913 the United Mine Workers of America (UMWA) organized a strike of Colorado coal miners that focused on Colorado

Fuel and Iron (CFI). This company was the largest and most powerful coal company in the West, and it had a reputation for being ruthlessly anti-union. It was owned by the fabulously wealthy industrialist John D. Rockefeller, who by some estimations ranks as the richest individual in American history.[13]

The principal demands of the miners were for UMWA recognition, a 10 percent increase in wages, an eight-hour workday, and the right to choose their own housing, stores, and physicians. The CFI executives rejected all these demands and evicted the families of the striking miners from their rental housing. The families relocated in a series of tent cities put together by the union. The largest of these tent colonies, containing about 1,200 people, was set up outside of the town of Ludlow. As the strike dragged on, these tents provided little shelter against the fierce Colorado winter. The misery of the miners' families was further deepened by continued harassment from guards and thugs hired by CFI. But the Ludlow colony persevered until April 20, 1914, when Colorado National Guardsmen launched an unprovoked and fearsome attack on the colony. Using machine guns and kerosene, the guardsmen destroyed the tent city. In the process, they killed six miners, two women, and eleven children. Most of the children suffocated to death when they tried to take refuge from the attack in a pit beneath one of the tents that was set afire.

News of the Ludlow Massacre sparked outrage throughout Colorado's coal country. Striking miners at other locations attacked mine after mine, setting fire to buildings and shooting guards. Much of Colorado became a virtual war zone between gun-wielding strikers and company guards and state troopers. These clashes were finally put to rest when President Woodrow Wilson sent in a large contingent of federal troops to disarm the strikers and replace the state militia and corporate guards. The strike itself dragged on for several more months, but on December 10, 1914, the UMWA ran out of funds to support the striking miners. The union thus called off the strike, even though it had been unable to secure any of its demands. Some of the strikers were able to go back to their old jobs, but many were replaced.

The labor defeat in the so-called Colorado Coal Wars of 1913-1914 was difficult for unionists to take. To many workers, the shedding of innocent blood at Ludlow proved once again that wealthy owners like Rockefeller valued dollars more than human life and dignity. Over the long term, though, government investigations of the events in Colorado sparked new demands for meaningful reforms in mining and other industries (see "Investigating the

Ludlow Massacre," p. 173). In addition, the Ludlow Massacre became a powerful rallying cry for new generations of labor activists.

Notes

[1] Jameson, Elizabeth. *All That Glitters: Class, Conflict, and Community in Cripple Creek.* Urbana: University of Illinois Press, 1998.

[2] Quoted in Cornell, Robert J. *The Anthracite Coal Strike of 1902.* New York: Catholic University Press of America, 1957, p. 91.

[3] Quoted in Reynolds, Robert L., "The Coal Kings Come to Judgment," *American Heritage* [online], April 1960, volume 11, issue 3. Available online at http://www.americanheritage.com.

[4] Grossman, Jonathan. "The Coal Strike of 1902—Turning Point in U.S. Policy," n.a. Available online at http://www.dol.gov/oasam/programs/history/coalstrike.htm.

[5] Gompers, Samuel. *Seventy Years of Life and Labor.* Vol. 2. New York: Dutton, 1925, pp. 117, 126.

[6] Kornbluh, Joyce L. *Rebel Voices: An IWW Anthology.* Ann Arbor: University of Michigan Press, 1964, p. 8.

[7] McGerr, Michael. *A Fierce Discontent: The Rise and Fall of the Progressive Movement in America.* New York: Oxford University Press, 2005, p. 132.

[8] Quoted in Kessler-Harris, Alice. "The Labor Movement's Failure to Organize Women Workers." *Feminist Studies,* Fall 1975, p. 92.

[9] Quoted in Dulles, Foster Rhea, and Melvyn Dubofsky. *Labor in America: A History.* 5th ed. Wheeling, IL: Harlan Davidson, 1993, p. 192.

[10] Quoted in Lukas, J. Anthony. *Big Trouble: A Murder in a Small Western Town Sets Off a Struggle for the Soul of America.* New York: Simon and Schuster, 1997, p. 381.

[11] McGerr, p. 144.

[12] Mitchell, John. *Organized Labor: Its Problems, Purposes and Ideals and the Present and Future of American Wage Earners.* Philadelphia, 1903, p. 324.

[13] "The Richest Americans Ever." *New York Times,* July 15, 2007. Available online at http://www.nytimes.com/ref/business/20070715_GILDED_GRAPHIC.html#.

Chapter Four

THE NEW DEAL
LIFTS UNIONS

⟨⟨⟨ ✿ ⟩⟩⟩

It is one of the characteristics of a free and democratic nation
that it have free and independent labor unions.

—Franklin Delano Roosevelt

From World War I through the 1920s, the American labor movement
struggled mightily. It was buffeted not only by a resurgence in the
strength of big business, which remained hostile to unions, but also by
a wave of political conservatism that cast a cloud of suspicion over the beliefs
and actions of labor organizers. The problems of organized labor deepened
with the onset of the Great Depression in 1929. This terrible multi-year economic collapse triggered severe levels of unemployment and wage cuts across
virtually all industry sectors. In the mid-1930s, however, the so-called "New
Deal" policies of President Franklin D. Roosevelt provided important assistance to workers and made it much easier for unions to establish themselves
and grow. The New Deal, in fact, laid the groundwork for several decades of
tremendous union growth in America.

Organized Labor during World War I

When the great powers of Europe took up arms against each other in
1914 in the conflict that came to be known as World War I, the United States
tried to stay neutral. America insisted that it did not want to take the side of
either the Allied nations, which were led by Great Britain, or the Central
Powers, dominated by Germany. In 1917, though, a series of German subma-
rine attacks on American ships convinced the United States to join forces
with Great Britain and declare war against Germany.

During World War I "Big Bill" Haywood and dozens of other Wobbly leaders were convicted of violating the 1917 Espionage Act. Haywood fled to Russia after his conviction, and he remained there for the rest of his life.

American labor divided down the middle over this decision to enter the war. The American Federation of Labor (AFL) vowed to support the war effort. Its membership even promised that it would not undertake any strikes or other activities that might disrupt U.S. industrial activities in wartime. This stance brought praise from American business executives, newspaper editorials, and lawmakers, and it has also been credited with boosting AFL membership during the war years. But labor groups with strong Socialist, pacifist, or Communist elements loudly condemned the decision to enter the war. Organizations like the Socialist Industrial Workers of the World (IWW) charged that the war was needlessly throwing away the lives of soldiers—many of whom were poor workers—to benefit industrialists who profited from the bloodshed.

When American soldiers began going overseas to fight, the Wobblies and a number of other left-wing unions who opposed U.S. participation in the war became the targets of violence and repression. They were attacked as unpatriotic and traitorous in newspaper editorials and Congressional speeches, and some war critics within the labor movement even came under physical attack. One leading IWW critic of the war, Frank Little, was even dragged out of a Montana jail cell and lynched by vigilantes for his antiwar views.

This backlash against left-wing political beliefs became even more severe in October 1917, when a bloody political revolution swept across Russia and displaced the dictatorial monarchy that had long existed there. The so-called Russian Revolution placed Bolsheviks atop the Russian government. Under the leadership of Vladimir Lenin, the Bolsheviks installed a fiercely Communist regime that regarded America's political and economic systems with outspoken contempt.

With public opinion on its side, the administration of President Woodrow Wilson moved to crush the IWW radicals. In June 1917 the United States passed the Espionage Act into law, making it illegal for anyone to interfere with the war effort or military recruitment. Later amendments to the Espionage Act, most notably the 1918 Sedition Act, even made it illegal for American citizens to harshly criticize the U.S. government during wartime.

In September 1917 the Federal Bureau of Investigation (FBI) raided nearly fifty IWW meeting halls across the country. Agents arrested 165 IWW leaders for conspiring to interfere with America's military draft, encouraging desertion from the army, and other acts of "sabotage" against the war effort. More than 100 activists were eventually put on trial, including William "Big Bill" Haywood. All were found guilty and sentenced to heavy fines and federal prison terms of ten to twenty years. When Haywood managed to gain a temporary release from custody on bail, he fled to Russia, where he lived until his death.

By the end of 1918, the Espionage Act was being openly used to target anarchists, Socialists, pacifists, and Communists within the labor movement. Notable radicals like Emma Goldman and Alexander Berkman were deported under the act, and Socialist legend Eugene Debs received a ten-year prison sentence for speaking out against the war. Imprisoned on April 13, 1919, he actually ran for president from his jail cell a year later. On Christmas Day 1921 his sentence was commuted by President Warren G. Harding and he was released from prison.

The Great Strike of 1919

World War I ended with an Allied victory in November 1918. Once the war ended, unions that had promised not to make any fuss about wages and working conditions during the conflict issued demands for improved benefits from employers—many of which had reaped huge profits from wartime orders. Many labor leaders focused particular attention on the eight-hour workday, which remained a fantasy in many major industries. Indeed, workers in steel mills, oil fields, canneries, and transportation industries commonly worked twelve-hour days—and many of them worked seven days a week as well. "The very workers most in need of a strong union to demand shorter hours are often too exhausted at night to attend meetings," complained Grace Hutchins, a Communist labor activist.[1]

A labor leader addresses a crowd of striking steel workers in Gary, Indiana, during the Great Strike of 1919.

When these calls for higher wages and shorter workweeks were rejected, some of the nation's largest industries—including shipping, coal, steel, and textiles—were roiled by massive strike actions. The impact of these strikes was greatly increased by the participation of the American Federation of Labor, which accounted for more than three out of four union members in America by 1920. Most of the strikes ended in complete defeat for the AFL and its fellow unions, however. One reason for their defeat was the presence in industrial cities of large numbers of African Americans who had fled the South in search of a better life. This additional source of cheap labor greatly reduced union leverage to squeeze better wages and working conditions out of employers.

An even greater factor in the union losses of 1919, though, was the so-called Red Scare. During this period of American history, fears about treacherous "reds"—Communists who wanted to bring down the nation from within—were widespread. Big business owners and their allies in government and the news media capitalized on these concerns by portraying *all* striking workers as dangerous radicals who threatened the American way of life. They also insinuated that since many strikers were recent immigrants, they were not "real" Americans.

These accusations deeply angered the great majority of striking workers. They argued that they were loyal Americans who were taking principled stands against corporate greed and social injustice on behalf of their families and their fellow laborers. But the efforts to persuade fellow Americans of the justness of their cause fell short, and without popular support their strikes and boycotts were doomed. It took many years for the labor movement to recover from the disappointments of 1919.

Corporate Paternalism in the Roaring Twenties

The labor movement's downturn in strength and vitality lasted for more than a decade. During the course of the 1920s the number of American workers in unions fell by over 1.6 million members.[2] In the meantime, pro-management and anti-union politicians took the reins of American government. To men like President Calvin Coolidge, who famously said that "the chief business of America *is* business," the needs and desires of American corporations were of the highest priority. This environment made it next to impossible for unions to make gains, either in size or influence. Instead, they spent much of their time and energy simply defending the small wage increases and other gains they had made in earlier decades.

Nonetheless, the condition of some American workers did improve somewhat during the "Roaring Twenties," a nickname given to the decade by affluent Americans who enjoyed the era's colorful and exuberant music, art, and culture. During this period, some large corporations showed an increased willingness to voluntarily approve small wage hikes, reduce workweeks, extend health and recreational benefits, or provide other benefits to employees. Many of these initiatives, sometimes called welfare capitalism or corporate paternalism, placed employers in the role of parental authority figures—and the workers in the role of children dependent on the kindness and wisdom of their elders. For example, several leading companies offered language and citizenship classes to immigrant workers, while others imposed strict guidelines of worker behavior that extended to their home lives. The Ford Motor Company, the largest automobile maker in the world, even created a Sociological Department that sent field agents to workers' homes to monitor them for cleanliness and order.

The growth in welfare capitalism was not generally driven by the warm and sympathetic feelings of business owners toward their workers. Rather, it was fueled by a desire to attract the most talented workers and by evolving ideas about business productivity and efficiency. Most notably, some employers became convinced that rates of worker absenteeism and disability could be greatly reduced if employees did not have to work such long hours. Major steelmakers, for example, voluntarily cut the hours of many of their exhausted workers—a move that also had the benefit of creating a demand for new workers who could fill those extra hours.

"We began it as an experiment, but we shall probably keep the five day week permanently," said Henry Ford in 1922. "The men are better off with two days a week of complete rest."

The best known example of a voluntary diminishment of work hours, though, came from the Ford Motor Company. In the late 1910s company founder and president Henry Ford began looking into using a five-day workweek in his factories and offices. "We began it as an experiment, but we shall probably keep the five day week permanently," Ford explained in 1922. "We thought that in the present labor situation we should be performing a service if we employed a larger force of men over five days rather than a smaller force over six days—provided, of course, we could do so without increasing our costs and therefore the cost to the public.... The men are better off with two days a week of complete rest, and we think that we shall be able to make the five day week permanent."[3] In 1926 this policy became official throughout the company.

Despite such high-profile initiatives, though, most employers remained reluctant to reduce hours. They did not see any reason to change the profitable status quo, in which workers labored ten or twelve hours a day, six or seven days a week. Some of these large corporations sought to deflect criticism of their stance by pointing out the various programs of welfare capitalism they provided to their workers. But since these benefits were not regulated or mandated by the government, the companies were of course free to end the benefits whenever they chose. So when the hard times of the Great Depression rolled over America and the world in 1929, corporations were quick to pull the plug on many of these programs.

The Great Depression brought crushing levels of unemployment to cities throughout the United States. This image shows unemployed workers in Detroit lined up at a charity bread line.

Labor Conditions in the Great Depression

The Great Depression was the most devastating economic collapse in the history of the United States. It began with the stock market crash of October 1929, which exposed dreadful weaknesses in the nation's banking and financial systems. From that point forward, the American people—and people in many other nations as well—endured years of incredible economic hardship. The worst years were the early 1930s, but the Depression did not fully pass away until the early 1940s, when America's involvement in World War II spurred huge increases in governmental military spending that revitalized industry and created millions of new jobs.

The economic downturn happened with terrifying speed as well. When the Great Depression first began, fewer than one million Americans were out of work. By January 1930, however, the number of unemployed had passed four million. By the end of that year, more than ten million Americans were without jobs. In March 1932 the jobless count stood at twelve million, and by January 1933 more than fourteen million Americans could not find jobs. In March 1933—the month that Democrat Franklin D. Roosevelt succeeded pro-business Republican Herbert Hoover as president of the United States—the number of unemployed workers across the United States had surpassed fifteen million.[4] The situation was even more dire for African Americans, who even in good times were typically "last to be hired, first to be fired" by white employers.

As unemployment soared, so too did levels of hunger and homelessness. The desperate situation eroded longstanding convictions among America's working class that hard work could bring a brighter future for themselves and their families. "Workers who once believed in the American myth of success, who dreamed of inching up the occupational ladder, acquiring property of their own, and watching their children do even better occupationally and materially, had their hopes blasted by the Great Depression," wrote historian David Dubofsky.[5]

After Roosevelt took office, he promised to put the government to work to fight the nation's many problems. He did this through numerous programs and legislative acts designed to reduce unemployment, revitalize banks, and relieve the overall misery that had enveloped so many American families. As part of this so-called "New Deal," the Roosevelt administration also signaled its support for labor unions (see "America's First Female Secretary of Labor," p. 72). This attitude greatly alarmed big business owners, who launched a variety of efforts to keep the unionization at bay. Some companies harassed or fired union organizers. Others bluntly warned that they would replace workers who dared to organize.

Another popular tactic was to form "company unions"—organizations of workers that were actually founded and bankrolled by the companies themselves. Employers claimed that these company unions would give workers the means to negotiate with owners over wages, hours, and other workplace issues, just like regular labor unions. Labor activists condemned company unions as a blatant attempt to lure workers away from "real" unions, but corporations worked very hard to sell the company union concept to their workers. One Pennsylvania steelworker recalled that the company he worked for "called us together and said, 'We're going to get big-hearted now.' ... And the company was very lavish with the money. Oh, they were lavish. They put on some of the most beautiful picnics you ever saw. They spent up to ten thousand dollars. They brought nationally known, prominent bands and comedians here. They gave the kids all the pop and soda and hotdogs they wanted. They brought in all kinds of rides and concessions. They went all out! In other words, they spent unlimited money to keep the union out."[6]

Unionization and the National Industrial Recovery Act

The early centerpiece of Roosevelt's New Deal job creation efforts was the National Industrial Recovery Act (NIRA). Signed into law by Roosevelt on June 16, 1933, the NIRA created the Public Works Administration (PWA), an agency designed to put millions of unemployed Americans to work building highways, hospitals, schools, dams, and other infrastructure. The legislation also established the National Recovery Administration (NRA). The NRA established wage and competition guidelines for corporate America. In addition, it contained a provision—Section 7a—that guaranteed labor unions the right to organize and collectively bargain with employers.

Labor leaders seized on this opportunity to rebuild their long-suffering unions. Under the leadership of John L. Lewis, the United Mine Workers (UMW) managed to gain official recognition from a number of big coal companies, and before long UMW mines accounted for 90 percent of the country's soft coal production. Sidney Hillman of the Amalgamated Clothing Workers Association (ACWA) used the Section 7a provision to double his union's membership by the close of 1933. The International Ladies' Garment Workers' Union (ILGWU), which was helmed by David Dubinsky, experienced an even greater jump in membership, from 40,000 workers to 200,000 workers.[7]

But many companies still refused to negotiate in good faith with labor representatives, in part because the NRA did not contain meaningful penalties for such behavior. Instead, numerous companies organized company unions. In the steel industry alone, for example, the number of company unions jumped from seven in 1932 to ninety in 1934.[8]

Mounting worker frustration with this situation resulted in a series of labor strikes in the summer of 1933. Roosevelt and his fellow New Dealers responded to this development, which threatened hopes of an economic recovery, by establishing a National Labor Relations Board (NLRB). The NLRB

America's First Female Secretary of Labor

Secretary of Labor Frances Perkins.

One of the most important New Dealers in the administration of President Franklin D. Roosevelt was Labor Secretary Fannie Coralie "Frances" Perkins, the first woman to be appointed to a cabinet position in the United States. Perkins was born in Boston, Massachusetts, on April 10, 1880. She spent her early career as a progressive social reformer in Chicago and New York. In 1918 she was appointed to the New York State Industrial Commission, where she worked on workplace safety issues. In 1929 Roosevelt, who was serving at that time as governor of New York, promoted Perkins to leadership of the Commission. When the Great Depression struck in late 1929, Roosevelt gave her a leading role in managing various relief programs across the state.

quickly moved to establish a set of regulations that would outlaw some of the anti-union actions of industry and strengthen collective bargaining rights. In the meantime, though, worker anger continued to escalate. In 1934 the nation was rocked by another wave of labor strikes, some of which spiraled into violence. The worst of these events occurred in Minneapolis, where repeated bloody clashes between striking members of the International Brotherhood of Teamsters and police (who were also supported by "deputies" paid by city trucking companies) forced Minnesota Governor Floyd Olson to place both Minneapolis and the neighboring city of St. Paul under martial law.

The Wagner Act

In 1935 the chaotic world of labor-management relations underwent another dramatic change. Frustrated by the continued difficulty of enforcing

When Roosevelt became president in 1933, he tapped Perkins to serve as his secretary of labor. A strong advocate for working Americans as well as the millions of Americans who had lost their jobs in the economic downturn, Perkins helped craft a variety of laws and programs to help these segments of the population, including the 1933 National Industrial Recovery Act, the 1935 Social Security Act, and the 1938 Fair Labor Standards Act. In addition, Perkins's tenure as secretary of labor was marked by steadfast opposition to using federal or state troops to break up union-organized strikes.

Perkins enjoyed the trust and respect of Roosevelt throughout her years at the helm of the Labor Department, despite repeated conservative charges that she was a Communist sympathizer. She led the department for twelve years and did not step down until May 1945, one month after Roosevelt's death. One year later President Harry S. Truman appointed her to the Civil Service Commission, on which she served for the next seven years. In the 1950s she left government to take a faculty position at Cornell University. She died on May 14, 1965.

Sources:

Downey, Kirstin. *The Woman Behind the New Deal: The Life of Frances Perkins, FDR's Secretary of Labor and His Moral Conscience.* New York: Doubleday, 2009.

Pasachoff, Naomi. *Frances Perkins: Champion of the New Deal.* New York: Oxford University Press, 1999.

decisions made by the NLRB, lawmakers in Washington who supported union rights began discussing new ways to ensure labor's ability to organize and bargain collectively with employers. Then, in May 1935, the U.S. Supreme Court handed down a unanimous ruling that the National Industrial Recovery Act, which had created the NRA, was unconstitutional. The Supreme Court decision paved the way for members of many service industries, like hotels and restaurants, to push for a return to twelve-hour workdays and seven-day weeks, which had faded away under NRA rules. This proved to be an unwise move, however, for progressive lawmakers became even more determined to pass labor-friendly legislation.

The leader of this Washington effort to strengthen labor rights was Democratic Senator Robert Wagner of New York. Wagner had been one of the lawmakers most responsible for putting labor standards into the 1933 NRA,

President Franklin D. Roosevelt (seated) signed numerous bills that were designed to reduce unemployment and bolster workers' rights. This photograph shows a signing ceremony for a 1933 unemployment bill crafted by Representative Theodore A. Peyser of New York (left) and Senator Robert Wagner of New York (right), and witnessed by Secretary of Labor Frances Perkins (center).

so when he saw the need for additional legislation he stepped up once again. "Running through all of Wagner's thinking was not just concern for social justice," explained historian Anthony Badger, "but also a conviction that the American economy could not operate at its fullest capacity unless mass purchasing power was guaranteed by government spending, welfare benefits, and the protection of workers' rights."[9]

Working with other concerned legislators and officials, Wagner crafted a new labor rights law, then pushed tirelessly for its passage (see "Laying the

Groundwork for the National Labor Relations Act," p. 180). He initially received little help in this effort from the Roosevelt administration. When it became clear that the legislation had enough votes for passage in both the Senate and the House of Representatives, however, Roosevelt became more enthusiastic about its potential impact. Roosevelt signed Wagner's National Labor Relations Act—popularly known as the Wagner Act—into law on July 5, 1935.

The Wagner Act was a tremendous victory for organized labor and worker rights. It expanded the powers of the National Labor Relations Board to oversee employee votes to unionize. This provision alone prevented companies from torpedoing such elections or ignoring their results. In addition, the act outlawed company unions and identified numerous unfair labor practices—including espionage, blacklisting, and discriminatory treatment of union members—that would no longer be permitted under U.S. law.

In the months following the signing of the Wagner Act, significant other pro-labor measures were signed into law as well. The Public Contracts Act of 1936, also known as the Walsh-Healey Act, required all companies doing work for the government worth $10,000 or more to establish a maximum eight-hour workday and forty-hour workweek for their employees. The 1938 Fair Labor Standards Act (FLSA) prohibited "oppressive child labor," established minimum wage standards in many industries, and guaranteed "time and a half" pay for overtime for many types of jobs. Roosevelt summarized the FLSA as a law that would ensure that working Americans received "a fair day's pay for a fair day's work."

Rise of the CIO

This rapidly changing labor landscape provided America's largely non-unionized "industrial" workers—employees within the nation's mass-production industries—with a golden opportunity to organize. Up to this point in U.S. history, most of the strength of the American labor movement had been concentrated in craft unions—organizations of machinists, pipefitters, carpenters, and other workers with specialized skills. These unions were the foundation of the AFL, which had long dominated organized labor.

During the early 1930s AFL leaders like William Green had explored the idea of expanding into "industrial unionism," in which both skilled and unskilled workers within a company or industry would join together in a single union. After all, the majority of American workers *were* unskilled or semi-

John Lewis helped organize millions of industrial workers under the banner of the Congress of Industrial Organizations.

skilled employees in mass-production industries like steelmaking and automobile manufacturing and service industries such as freight transport. John Lewis of the United Mine Workers, one of the few AFL unions with a largely unskilled workforce, also argued for a new emphasis on organizing workers in these industries. But other officials in the AFL worried that expansion into these areas would reduce the negotiating leverage of their existing members in the skilled trades, and so the AFL never really moved forward on the issue.

This stance angered and frustrated many industrial workers, who felt powerless and forgotten. "In the AFL in those days nobody seemed interested in us," recalled a worker who helped make refrigerators for General Electric. "They were only interested in skilled people: tool and die makers, carpenters, tinsmen, and the like. No one seemed interested in the semiskilled or the unskilled.... I mean, what about the common guy in the shop that runs a machine, or a sheet-metal man that runs shears, or a punch-press operator that sets up a press, or a man that repairs tools and dies and that kind of stuff?"[10]

Continued AFL inaction also infuriated Lewis, who believed that all workers would benefit if the labor movement could establish a strong presence in America's steel mills and automobile factories. In 1935 Lewis finally decided that if the AFL would not act, he would spearhead a drive for industrial unionism on his own. That November he established the Committee for Industrial Organizations (CIO), which became a major force in American business and industry within months of its founding. The CIO was technically part of the AFL at its outset, but strained relations resulted in the CIO's formal break from the older organization in 1938. It was at that time that the CIO changed its name to the Congress of Industrial Organizations.

Taking full advantage of the protections contained in the Wagner Act and other New Deal legislation, the CIO organized workers in a vast array of industries with stunning speed. And since the ranks of mass-production workers it recruited were heavily populated with African Americans, Mexican Americans, white women, and immigrants from southern and eastern Europe, the federation of unions under the CIO umbrella became much more representative of the American population as a whole than the white male-dominated AFL had ever been.

The Flint Sit-Down Strike

The CIO's amazing growth was due in large part to several highly publicized clashes with employers that ended in victory for CIO unions. These included a successful 1936 strike by the United Rubber Workers against the Goodyear Tire and Rubber Company in Akron, Ohio, over poor working conditions, as well as collective bargaining agreements with corporate giants like U.S. Steel, RCA, and General Electric in the late 1930s.

The single greatest triumph, however, was undoubtedly the 1936-37 Flint Sit-Down Strike, which pitted the fledgling United Automobile Workers (UAW) against General Motors (GM), one of the most powerful corporations in the country. The UAW's chief goal was to force GM to recognize the UAW as the representative of its work force for collective bargaining purposes. To accomplish this, UAW organizers launched a "sit-down" strike on December 29, 1936, at one of GM's most important plants in Flint, Michigan. Unlike previous strikes that combined work stoppages and picketing, the strikers in Flint simply occupied a key facility that contained the dies for the automaker's 1937 car models. By seizing control of the plant and keeping management from retrieving the dies, the UAW effectively paralyzed the entire corporation's manufacturing operations.

Outraged GM executives promptly demanded that Michigan Governor Frank Murphy call in National Guard troops to evict the strikers. But Murphy, who was sympathetic to labor demands, refused to do so out of concern that such a move might trigger an outpouring of bloodshed. When Flint police launched a botched—and bloody—attempt to seize the plant, though,

A striking auto worker enjoys a brief reunion with his dog during the 1936-37 Flint Sit-Down Strike.

Murphy ordered troops to Flint to keep the peace and prevent another explosion of violence. The tense showdown continued for several more weeks, as GM tried unsuccessfully to get the courts to intervene. In the meantime, the UAW ferried food and other supplies to the sit-down strikers (who took control of another key facility in the plant in early February) and organized marches and other demonstrations of support.

The clash ended quietly on February 11, 1937, when Murphy negotiated a settlement between the two parties (see "Remembering the Flint Sit-Down Strike," p. 184). Under the agreement, GM formally recognized the UAW as the exclusive bargaining representative for General Motors employees who joined the union over the following six months. Lewis and the UAW rejoiced, for they knew that the terms would convince many non-UAW workers of the union's stability and strength. As they anticipated, membership in the UAW soared in the weeks following the settlement. More than 100,000 workers from General Motors alone joined the union, and the UAW's total membership jumped from fewer than 100,000 in February 1937 to more than 400,000 by the end of that summer.

Other UAW victories soon followed. The auto executives at Chrysler accepted the UAW as the official bargaining representative of their workers later in 1937, and in 1941 the UAW managed to unionize the fiercely anti-union Ford Motor Company after years of bitter conflict. To be sure, the CIO and its constituent unions were not always victorious during this time. In 1937, for example, a sit-down strike aimed at a group of smaller steel companies in the Midwest known collectively as "Little Steel" was soundly defeated. Nonetheless, the overall trend was toward unionization. From 1933 to 1941 the percentage of union workers in nonagricultural industries jumped from 11.5 percent to 28.5 percent, and by the end of World War II more than one-third of the American work force was unionized.[11] And for the first time in the twentieth century, the AFL relinquished its place as the largest federation of labor in the country. By the close of the 1930s the CIO's unionization of vast swaths of the auto, steel, rubber, and electric product industries—all of which were pillars of the U.S. economy—had enabled it to vault over the AFL and claim its place as the most influential union in the land.

Notes

[1] Hutchins, Grace. *Labor and Silk*. New York: International Publishers, 1929, p. 120.

[2] Roediger, David R., and Philip S. Foner. *Our Own Time: A History of American Labor and the Working Day.* New York: Greenwood Press, 1989, p. 210.

[3] Interview with Samuel Crowther. "Ford's Four Production Principles." *Factory: The Magazine of Management,* July 1922, p. 15.

[4] Roediger, p. 243.

[5] Dubofsky, Melvyn. "Not So Radical Years." In Boris, Eileen, and Nelson Lichtenstein, eds. *Major Problems in the History of American Workers: Documents and Essays.* Lexington, MA: Heath, 1991, p. 376.

[6] Quoted in Bodnar, John. *Workers' World: Kinship, Community, and Protest in an Industrial Society, 1900-1940.* Baltimore: Johns Hopkins University Press, 1982, p. 131.

[7] Badger, Anthony J. *The New Deal: The Depression Years, 1933-1940.* Chicago: Ivan R. Dee, 1989, p. 121.

[8] Badger, p. 119.

[9] Badger, p. 127.

[10] Quoted in Bodnar, p. 154.

[11] Barnard, John. *American Vanguard: The United Auto Workers during the Reuther Years, 1935-1970.* Detroit: Wayne State University Press, 2004.

Chapter Five

BANNER DAYS FOR AMERICAN UNIONS

⟨⟨⟨⟨⟨⟨⟩⟩⟩⟩⟩⟩

By raising the living standards of millions, labor miraculously created a market for industry and lifted the whole nation to undreamed of levels of production. Those who attack labor forget these simple truths, but history remembers them.

—Martin Luther King Jr.

During World War II the American economy came roaring back to life, and the economic fortunes of U.S. workers remained on the upswing long after the war drew to a close. These sustained gains were made possible in large part by American labor unions, which reached new heights of influence in many of the nation's largest industry sectors. From the mid-1940s through the early 1960s, in fact, the United Automobile Workers (UAW) and other industrial unions negotiated wage and benefit increases that lifted many of their members into the ranks of America's middle class. As the 1960s unfolded, though, the ship of labor began taking on water from a variety of sources, including damaging revelations of union corruption and increased employer investments in automated machinery. By the close of the decade, these storm clouds threatened to bring the labor movement's postwar run of growth and prosperity to an end.

American Industry Becomes an "Arsenal of Democracy"

On December 7, 1941, the nation of Japan launched a devastating surprise attack on the U.S. naval base at Pearl Harbor in Hawaii. The assault convinced the United States to abandon its policy of neutrality in World War II, which had erupted two years earlier, and join England and other Allied nations in their fight against Nazi Germany, Japan, and Italy (the so-called Axis Powers).

America's entrance into World War II proved to be a tremendous boon for numerous industries that been struggling for years to regain their economic footing. As governmental orders for rifles, uniforms, medicine, tanks, jeeps, planes, food, ships, grenades, boots, blankets, tents, gasoline, and other military supplies poured into factory offices, companies all across the United States were finally able to shake off the Great Depression. America's transformation into a wartime "arsenal of democracy," as President Franklin D. Roosevelt described it, restored financial health and profitability to numerous industries.

The revitalization of American factories, mills, foundries, and rail yards also lifted the fortunes of the nation's workers. Cities and towns that had been grappling with high levels of unemployment since the opening months of the Depression suddenly found themselves awash in job openings, especially after millions of American men joined the armed forces. Women, African Americans, and other minorities benefited especially from the high demand for workers. Labor unions benefited as well, adding more than four million workers to their ranks from 1941 to 1945.[1]

Postwar Turmoil

By 1945, when the United States, Great Britain, and the rest of the Allies claimed victory in World War II, about 15 million Americans were members of one union or another. Most of these unions had held off on strike activity during the war because they did not want to hamper the U.S. war effort. The most notable exception to this trend was the United Mine Workers (UMW), which called a strike in 1943 for better wages and other benefits. This work stoppage, which was orchestrated by UMW President John L. Lewis, eventually succeeded in squeezing significant concessions from the mine owners, including wage hikes, pension benefits, and safety improvements. But the decision to strike during a time of national crisis infuriated President Franklin D. Roosevelt, Congress, and the American public, all of whom viewed the UMW's actions as unpatriotic and selfish.

Once the war was over, however, other unions warned that they were willing to engage in strikes and other actions to force concessions from employers. Union spokesmen expressed particular determination to boost

OUR FRIEND

NATIONAL CITIZENS POLITICAL ACTION COMMITTEE

Our Friend, lithograph/poster by Ben Shahn, 1944. Art © Estate of Ben Shahn/Licensed by VAGA, New York, NY.

This 1944 political poster, which features a profile of President Franklin D. Roosevelt amid hats bearing union insignias, symbolized the alliance that developed between American unions and Roosevelt's Democratic Party.

wages, which had remained flat during the war years even though the cost of groceries, clothing, gasoline, and many other daily essentials had increased sharply. Many employers resisted these calls for wage hikes and new benefits. They argued that these new expenses could be dangerous for them, given the expense of switching back to peacetime production practices and the economic uncertainty surrounding the end of the war. But the labor movement was in no mood to put off its demands. In the year following the end of World War II the United States was rocked by an incredible number of strike actions—more than 4,630 work stoppages involving a total of five million workers.[2]

Some of these strikes paid off for individual unions. A four-month strike waged by the United Auto Workers against General Motors (GM), the largest automobile manufacturer in the world, ended only after GM agreed to generous new wage and benefit packages. Similarly, striking steelworkers secured hefty wage increases from steel companies, who received permission from the federal government to pay for the higher wages through higher steel prices. The tactics employed by unions in securing these victories, though, angered many Americans who feared that economic disruptions like strikes might plunge the country into another Depression. And some strikes—like a nationwide railway strike in 1946 that brought passenger and freight transportation to a standstill for several weeks—were extremely unpopular with the American public.

The railway strike also drove a deep wedge between the labor movement and the Democratic Party. During the New Deal era, American workers' gratitude for the pro-labor policies of Roosevelt and his fellow Democrats had made them very loyal to Democrats at election time. And once organized labor became convinced that Democrats were looking out for its interests, labor activists who continued to issue radical demands for revolutionary social change rapidly lost influence. As historian Melvin Dubofsky wrote, "Roosevelt's Democratic Party had become, in effect, the political expression of America's working class."[3]

But the railway strike of 1946 threatened to blow up this alliance. When the striking railway workers turned down a compromise settlement proposed by Democratic President Harry S. Truman, the president became so angry and concerned about the economic impact of a long strike that he prepared a plan to have the U.S. Army operate the railroads. "This is no longer a dispute between labor and management," he declared in a May 25, 1946, speech to Congress. "It has now become a strike against the Government of the United States itself.... What we are dealing with here is not labor as a whole. We are dealing with a handful of men who are striking against their own government and against every one of their fellow citizens, and against themselves. We are dealing with a handful of men who have it within their power to cripple the entire economy of the nation."[4]

In the midst of his speech to Congress requesting authorization for government operation of the railroads—and to draft striking rail workers into the armed forces—Truman received word that the strike had just been settled according to the terms he had previously laid out. News of the settlement relieved Americans everywhere, but it did not patch up the hard feelings between the labor movement and the Truman administration. Instead, labor leaders viewed Truman's actions as clear evidence that he could not be trusted to help them in future showdowns with the nation's big corporate powers.

The Taft-Hartley Act of 1947

As it turned out, however, American unions had a much bigger problem than President Truman on their hands. Collectively, the big mid-1940s wave of labor strikes intensified anti-union feelings in many parts of the country. Sensing an opportunity to deliver a blow against the labor movement, business interests, conservative congressmen, and anti-union newspapers all began arguing that American labor unions had become *too* powerful and arrogant as a result of the Wagner Act and other New Deal labor legislation. These critics insisted that a new law was necessary that would curb the power of the unions and strike a better balance of power in labor-management negotiations.

In April 1947 the House of Representatives approved a labor bill sponsored by Republican Fred A. Hartley Jr. of New Jersey that placed major new restrictions on union activities and rights. A short time later, the Senate approved a similar measure championed by Republican Senator Robert Taft of Ohio. The bill, formally known as the Labor-Management Relations Act but much better known as Taft-Hartley, then went to Truman's desk for his signature. Instead, Truman vetoed the bill on June 20, 1947. The president described the bill's many anti-union provisions as deeply unfair. Union leaders rejoiced at Truman's stand, but the Republican-controlled Congress overrode the president's veto. On June 23, 1947, the Taft-Hartley Act became the law of the land.

The Taft-Hartley legislation changed the landscape of labor-management relations in numerous ways. It outlawed the "closed shop" (unionized places of work that required all new employees to be members of that union) and made it much more difficult for labor groups to institute the "union shop" (labor agreements that required all workers to join the workplace union). The act also forbade unions from engaging in secondary boycotts and jurisdictional strikes, severely restricted the ability of unions to make political contributions, and expanded the rights of management to express their views about unionization to their employees. In addition, the legislation gave the president of the United States the authority to suspend (through injunctions) any strike which he thought posed a threat to the nation's basic health and security. Most importantly, Section 14(b) of the Taft-Hartley Act cleared the way for individual states to ban union shops altogether. Conservative legislatures in southern

In the 1940s and 1950s labor unions negotiated wage and benefit contracts that enabled members to move their families into comfortable middle-class neighborhoods such as this one in Washington state.

and western states quickly seized on this provision and established themselves as "right-to-work" states—places in which labor-management agreements could no longer make union membership a condition of employment.

The passage of Taft-Hartley was a stunning blow to the labor movement, which now recognized that the worker-friendly Washington that had existed during the New Deal era was no more. But it also went a long way toward repairing relations between unions and the Democratic Party. Since Republicans had been the chief force behind passage of the hated bill—and Truman had made a valiant attempt to stop Taft-Hartley from becoming law—labor leaders returned to the Democratic fold, where they remained for the next half-century.

Union Members Enter the American Middle Class

Labor leaders accurately interpreted the passage of Taft-Hartley as evidence that unions had a big image problem in Congress and with the wider American public. With this in mind, many unions adopted a less confrontational approach in their dealings with management. In addition, labor unions responded swiftly to the political and social impact of the Cold War, a term used to describe the post-World War II tensions that arose between the United States and its allies and the Soviet Union and other Communist countries. In the late 1940s, for example, the UAW kicked all known Communists off its membership rolls. In 1950 the Congress of Industrial Organizations (CIO) adopted a similar policy, expelling eleven unions that were determined to be under Communist influence.

Efforts to improve labor's image did not make strikes a complete thing of the past, however. Work stoppages were still employed by unions, and occasionally a big strike—such as a controversial 53-day strike by the United Steel Workers (USW) in the spring of 1952—garnered national attention. In many industries, though, unions and employers settled into a fairly routine pattern of collective bargaining and contract-signing. These contracts, which ran from three to five years in most cases, gave a sense of stability and security to workers and management alike.

The terms of many of these contracts also lifted the standard of living of many union families into the middle class. This was especially true of powerful unions like the UAW, which operated in a prosperous industry and had an immensely talented leader in Walter Reuther. Under Reuther's direction, the UAW negotiated a series of contracts in the 1950s and early 1960s that gave members significant wage hikes and supplementary pay during layoff periods (a benefit commonly known as the "annual wage"). UAW contracts from this period also featured a wide assortment of other benefits that would have seemed unbelievable to workers of the 1920s and 1930s, including retirement pensions, medical and life insurance, dental coverage, paid vacations and holidays, generous allotments of sick days, and increased workplace rights.

These gains enabled hourly wage earners in the automobile industry to purchase the same types of homes, automobiles, fishing boats, clothing, and appliances that salaried white-collar employees enjoyed. "As conditions and wages improved in the plants, workers were able to have a more settled home life and raise families," summarized UAW organizer Gonora (Johnson) Dollinger:

> The children did better in school, and they got to the point where they could go to college. After a few years of saving, the parents had the money to send them to colleges and universities. That's the period, in the 40s and 50s, when the college system began to proliferate across the country because of workers being able to send their kids. There was so much pride in the family: "My son is studying to become a doctor or a lawyer." Or "My daughter is studying to become a librarian." They had hopes that were outside the factory. And so the whole family was changed. I think that was the biggest change of all.[5]

Few other industrial workers could match the economic advances made by UAW members. But rates of home ownership and other indicators of economic health rose among workers in virtually all industries. Even non-union workers benefited from the economic good times of the 1950s—demand for workers remained so high across the board that companies had to provide competitive compensation or risk losing valuable employees. Still, the unionized sectors of the economy were the ones that registered the biggest gains in terms of wage increases and fringe benefits. And since there were more than 18 million union members in the mid-1950s—more than a third of all nonagricultural workers in the United States—this meant a dramatic expansion in the size of America's middle class. As one Department of Labor analysis concluded in 1959, "[the hourly] wage earner's way of life is well-nigh indistinguishable from that of his salaried co-citizens. Their homes, their cars, their babysitters, the style of clothes their wives and children wear, the food they eat ... their days off—all of these are alike and are becoming more nearly identical."[6]

AFL-CIO

The American labor movement of the 1950s also experienced a historic merger of its two major organizational camps, the nine-million-member American Federation of Labor (AFL) and the six-million-member Congress of Industrial Organizations (CIO). Since its founding in 1886, the AFL's membership had been primarily composed of craft unions, while the upstart CIO, established in 1937, had garnered its strength from industrial workers who felt ignored or underrepresented by the older federation. The competitive relationship between the two groups had intensified during the 1940s, as AFL leaders established their own industrial unions to counter the growth of the CIO. But this increased openness of the AFL to industrial unionism also narrowed the differences between the organizations.

Other events contributed to merger discussions as well. During the 1940s and early 1950s, the two great labor federations found themselves working together on important causes, from lobbying for pro-worker laws to election campaigns for pro-labor politicians. The emergence of a new generation of labor leaders also played a key role. In 1952 William Green, who had led the AFL for thirty years, died and was replaced by George Meany, a long-time labor executive who had gotten his start as a New York plumber. That same year, CIO President Philip Murray passed away and was replaced by the hard-charging Reuther.

Both Meany and Reuther believed that if the AFL and CIO united, the American labor movement as a whole would be greatly strengthened. As a result, both men worked diligently to craft a merger agreement. On February

Labor leaders George Meany (left) and Walter Reuther celebrate following the 1955 merger of the American Federation of Labor (AFL) and the Congress of Industrial Organizations (CIO).

Cesar Chavez and the California Grape Boycott

Cesar Chavez at a 1971 United Farm Workers rally.

The famed Latino labor leader Cesar Chavez was born in Yuma, Arizona, on March 31, 1927. When the Great Depression wiped out his family's small farm and country store, Cesar and his parents and four siblings relocated to California. They became migrant farm laborers, traveling all across the West to pick crops with the various harvesting seasons. This nomadic existence was very hard on Chavez, who attended 38 different schools before turning to fieldwork full-time in his mid-teens.

In 1948 Chavez married Helen Favela, with whom he eventually had seven children. In the 1950s he became deeply interested in civil rights activism, workers' rights, and community organizing. In 1962 Chavez formed the National Farmworkers Association (NFWA), an organization dedicated to providing community services and legal assistance to poor farmworkers across the West. Three years later, Chavez's career as a labor organizer began in earnest when he and the NFWA joined forces with the Agricultural Workers Organizing Committee (AWOC). The mostly Filipino AWOC had just called a strike against grape growers in Delano, California, who had announced sharp cuts to the already meager wages

9, 1955, they announced that they had succeeded in their quest. Meany and Reuther framed the agreement not only as a victory for American workers, but as a blessing for national security. "We feel confident," they declared in a joint statement, "that the merger of the two union groups which we represent will be a boon to our nation and its people in this tense period. We are happy that, in our way, we have been able to bring about unity of the labor move-they paid field workers. This strike became much more effective once it had the support of the mostly Mexican NFWA.

As the strike deepened in 1966, Chavez oversaw the merger of NFWA and AWOC into the United Farm Workers of America (UFW). As the months passed by, Chavez focused much of his efforts on educating the public on the miserable conditions that migrant farm workers faced. Aided by other labor groups, idealistic students, and religious organizations, Chavez and the UFW were able to launch a nationwide grape boycott. At its height, an estimated 13 million Americans took part in the boycott. In 1968, meanwhile, Chavez conducted a 25-day fast that became a major news story on television broadcasts and in newspapers across the country. His campaign not only exacted a financial toll on the Delano grape growers, it also turned public opinion decisively against them.

In 1969 the growers essentially admitted defeat by signing a labor contract with Chavez and the UFW. Three years later the UFW joined the American Federation of Labor (AFL), and in 1975 California passed the Agricultural Labor Relations Act (ALRA), the first American law recognizing the rights of farm workers to organize and bargain collectively. Chavez spent the next eighteen years fighting for civil rights and working to improve the lives of migrant farmworkers in the West. He died in his hometown of Yuma on April 23, 1993.

Sources:

Daniel, Cletus E. "Cesar Chavez and the Unionization of California Farm Workers." In *Labor Leaders in America*. Edited by Melvyn Dubofsky and Warren Van Tine. Champaign: University of Illinois Press, 1987.

Tejada-Flores, Rick. "Cesar Chavez and the UFW," *The Fight in the Fields: Cesar Chavez and the Farmworkers' Struggle*, PBS Documentary, 2004. Available online at http://www.pbs.org/itvs/fightfields/cesarchavez.html.

ment at a time when the unity of all American people is most urgently needed in the face of the Communist threat to world peace and civilization."[7]

The merger was finalized in December 1955, at which time Meany became president of the new AFL-CIO and Reuther took the position of vice president (see "The AFL and CIO Reunite," p. 193). With 15 million members, the new organization was far larger and more powerful than any previous labor federation in American history. Over the next several years, it would use this power not only to defend the interests of working-class Americans, but to support major changes to the very fabric of American society.

Organized Labor and Social Change

In 1947, only one year after assuming the presidency of the UAW, Walter Reuther described the labor movement in a speech to union rank-and-file as "the vanguard in America" and the "architects of the future" who would build a better world founded on principles of social justice and respect for working men and women.[8] Reuther and many other labor leaders of the postwar era believed that the key to building that better world was to pass new laws that would help the most vulnerable members of American society, from the poor and uneducated to the old and sickly. This liberal political activism, which was rooted in the labor movement's historical status as America's leading defender of poor and disadvantaged working men and women, became one of the defining characteristics of unions of the 1950s and 1960s (see "Walter Reuther Discusses Labor's Role in Building a Better Society," p. 188).

American labor supported a wide range of social welfare legislation during this period. Union locals and national organizations alike expressed their support for legislation raising the minimum wage. They also applauded the passage of new federal programs for children, such as the National School Lunch Program (launched in 1946) and the School Milk Program (1954). In addition, organized labor—and the AFL-CIO in particular—energetically lobbied for Medicare and other federal programs that expanded America's social "safety net."

By contrast, organized labor did not speak with one voice on African-American civil rights, which emerged as a major political and social issue in the 1950s. During the early years of the civil rights movement, many labor leaders remained on the sidelines or extended only token support. The only exceptions to this general rule were unions of black workers like the Brotherhood of Sleeping Car Porters, an AFL group headed by A. Philip Randolph. Many other unions within the AFL-CIO had long and sordid histories of racial discrimination. Their white leaderships were slow to recognize the moral force behind the civil rights demonstrations that were spreading like wildfire across the United States.

Given this state of affairs, the stance of Walter Reuther and the United Auto Workers was all the more remarkable. At a time when other majority-

In August 1963 President John F. Kennedy met with leaders of the March on Washington civil rights rally. Attendees included (left to right) Martin Luther King Jr., Rabbi Joachim Prinz, A. Philip Randolph, President Kennedy, Walter Reuther, and Roy Wilkins.

white unions were hanging back, Reuther used the financial, political, and manpower resources of the UAW on behalf of the civil rights cause on a regular basis. He offered particularly spirited support to the campaigns of Martin Luther King Jr., who by 1960 had become the leading figure in the civil rights movement. "The Labor Movement is about the struggle of the people who are denied their measure of justice," Reuther declared in a letter to Meany, "and if the Labor Movement is not in the front rank then I think the Labor Movement begins to forfeit the loyalty of the people whom I profess to represent and lead."[9]

93

The UAW's support for the civil rights movement reached its greatest heights on August 28, 1963, when the historic March on Washington for Jobs and Freedom took place. Meany and other white labor leaders had shied away from the event out of a fear that the demonstration might erupt into violence and chaos. But Reuther staked out a far different position. Under his direction, the UAW provided financial help for the march, transported thousands of rank-and-file supporters to Washington, and lobbied other white-dominated unions, civic groups, and religious organizations to lend their support. Reuther was also the only white labor leader to address the 300,000 people who attended the August 28 rally. This gathering remains best known as the event at which King delivered his famous "I Have a Dream" speech.

As the civil rights movement gained strength in the 1960s, the AFL-CIO became less cautious about extending its support. It actively pressed for passage of historic laws like the Civil Rights Act of 1964 and the Voting Rights Act of 1965. These laws helped pave the way for steady growth in African-American enrollment in labor unions in the 1960s and 1970s.

Problems on the Horizon

Organized labor's success in improving the financial security of union families and lobbying for social change, however, failed to mask serious problems afflicting the labor movement. One of these problems was corruption and criminal activity. In 1953 the AFL took the drastic step of kicking out one of its member unions—the International Longshoremen's Association—when it became clear that its leadership was engaged in "racketeering," or unlawful activities like fraud or extortion. Four years later, the federation expelled its largest union, the 1.5-million-member Teamsters, in response to congressional hearings revealing that President David Beck and other Teamsters officials had ties to organized crime and engaged in all sorts of criminal activity (see "Confronting Union Corruption," p. 194). Beck was replaced by James R. "Jimmy" Hoffa, even though Hoffa had been implicated in many illegal acts as well.

Over the next several years, Hoffa's alleged racketeering and ties to the criminal underworld made him and the Teamsters an even bigger focus of newspaper stories and federal investigations. The controversy that swirled around Hoffa and the Teamsters from the late 1950s through the mid-1970s—when Hoffa disappeared without a trace—gave a black eye to the entire labor movement. Mounting public concern about union corruption also prompted Congress to pass new labor laws like the Landrum-Griffin Act of 1959. This law, formally called the Labor Management Reporting and Disclosure Act, included many provisions designed to protect rank-and-file union members from corrupt officials.

Industrial automation loomed as another source of growing anxiety for both unionized and non-unionized American workers. As technological advances made it possible for manufacturers and other businesses to be more productive with fewer workers, unions increasingly focused on job security in contract negotiations and strike actions. A nationwide steel strike that took place in 1959, for example, stemmed from fears about automation-related job losses as much as wage demands. As *New York Times* labor journalist A.H. Raskin wrote, "the worker's great worry these days is that he will be cast onto the slag heap by a robot."[10]

Non-unionized industry sectors exchanged workers for machines with the greatest speed. American labor unions were able to negotiate contracts that preserved jobs for their memberships. But even these agreements only slowed the transformation that was taking place. Printers, longshoremen, and other workers with historically strong union ties still saw their jobs disappear due to automation. Even union strongholds like auto manufacturing and steel could not hold back the tide. By the early 1960s, steel companies were producing just as much steel as they were in the late 1940s—but with half as many workers. Similarly, the nation's major car manufacturers were able to produce more automobiles in 1963 than they did in 1955, despite having 17 percent fewer workers.[11]

> *"The worker's great worry these days,"* wrote **New York Times** *journalist A.H. Raskin,* *"is that he will be cast onto the slag heap by a robot."*

Meanwhile, the changing nature of work in America made it more difficult for labor unions to replenish their ranks. Most of the industries that experienced the greatest job growth in the late 1950s and 1960s were in retail, restaurant, or professional sectors, none of which had much of a history of union representation. Finally, some union members seemed to forget the long decades of struggle and poverty that American industrial workers had endured before the reforms of the New Deal era. Rank-and-file complaints about the tedious nature of factory work soared, and many labor leaders displayed a sense of complacency and sluggishness as well. These trends greatly alarmed other labor titans like Reuther, who bluntly warned UAW members in a 1962 speech that "a labor movement can get soft

In the 1950s and 1960s automated machinery emerged as a threat to industrial jobs. In this 1962 photo a lone auto worker spray paints the body of a Hudson automobile coming off the assembly line.

and flabby spiritually. It can make progress materially and the soul of the union can die in the process."[12]

Some labor leaders comforted themselves by pointing to positive trends. They noted that workers employed by federal and state governments were unionizing in greater numbers thanks to new laws. Others claimed that bold activists like Cesar Chavez, who established a migrant farm worker union called the United Farm Workers of America in 1966, proved that the fighting spirit of the American labor movement was still alive and well (see "Cesar Chavez and the California Grape Boycott," p. 90).

But despite these areas of encouragement, the signs of trouble continued to pile up. Organized labor in the 1960s became divided over all sorts of social and political controversies, from women's liberation to the Vietnam War. In 1968, in fact, unhappiness over the AFL-CIO's strong pro-war stance contributed to the UAW's decision to leave the giant labor federation. And the percentage of the American labor force that was unionized dropped steadily, from almost 35 percent of the nation's non-agricultural workers in the mid-1950s to 25 percent by 1965. Less than three decades after the New Deal had sparked its greatest triumphs, the nation's labor movement was in full retreat.

Notes

[1] Blum, John M. *V Was for Victory: Politics and American Culture during World War II*. New York: Harcourt Brace, 1976, p. 140

[2] Dulles, Foster Rhea, and Melvyn Dubofsky. *Labor in America: A History*. 5th ed. Wheeling, IL: Harlan Davidson, 1993, p. 340.

[3] Quoted in Boris, Eileen, and Nelson Lichtenstein, eds. *Major Problems in the History of American Workers: Documents and Essays*. Lexington, MA: Heath, 1991, p. 385.

[4] Truman, Harry S. "Special Message to Congress Urging Legislation for Industrial Peace." May 25, 1946. Harry S. Truman Library and Museum, http://www.trumanlibrary.org/publicpapers/index.php ?pid=1567&st=&st1=.

[5] Dollinger, Genora (Johnson). *Striking Flint: Remembering the Flint Sit-Down Strike, 1936-37*. As told to Susan Rosenthal. 2008. Available online at http://www.susanrosenthal.com/wp-content /uploads/2008/08/coldtype-edition-strikingflint.pdf.

[6] Quoted in Handel, Gerald, and Lee Rainwater. "The Working Classes—Old and New." *Society*, November 1963, p. 25.

[7] Quoted in Dulles, Foster Rhea. *Labor in America: A History*. New York: Crowell, 1966, p. 374.

[8] Quoted in Lichtenstein, Nelson. *Walter Reuther: The Most Dangerous Man in Detroit*. New York: Basic Books, 1995, p. 270.

[9] Quoted in Barnard, John. *American Vanguard: The United Auto Workers during the Reuther Years, 1935-1970*. Detroit: Wayne State University Press, 2004, p. 385.

[10] Quoted in Garraty, John Arthur. *The American Nation: A History of the United States*. New York: Harper and Row, 1966, p. 823.

[11] Dulles, p. 375.

[12] Quoted in Barnard, p. 264.

Chapter Six

DOWN A PATH OF PERMANENT DECLINE?

＜◄〰〰〰〰＞

Our world has changed, our economy has changed, employers have changed.

—Labor leader Andy Stern

Since the 1970s, the victories piled up by the American labor movement during the New Deal and postwar eras have come to seem like distant memories. Many unions have shrunk dramatically in size and influence in the past four decades. Automation, overseas competition, pro-management politicians, and union-busting corporate policies have all taken their toll on these organizations. Internal disputes have also injured the labor movement. Determined to reverse these negative trends, labor leaders and their supporters debated a range of strategies for revitalizing American unions in the twenty-first century.

Turbulent Times for American Labor

The setbacks endured by the labor movement in the 1960s and 1970s were balanced somewhat by positive developments. For example, tens of thousands of union jobs were lost to automated machinery during these decades. But these losses were offset to a degree by increased unionization of government jobs. In fact, public employee unions like the American Federation of Teachers (AFT) and the American Federation of State, County, and Municipal Employees (AFSCME) experienced explosive growth. Since women accounted for many of the nation's teachers, principals, and public officials, the percentage of women in the organized labor movement soared, from an estimated 3.3 million in the late 1950s to more than 6.6 million by the close of the 1970s.

American workers, whether unionized or not, also benefited from new laws like the 1970 Occupational Safety and Health Act. This legislation, which went into effect on April 28, 1971, established the federal Occupational Safety and Health Administration (OSHA). This new agency's mandate was to establish and enforce workplace regulations that would shield employees from toxic chemicals, unsanitary conditions, unsafe machinery, and other threats to their health.

Despite these gains, however, the overall picture for labor dimmed during the 1970s. The U.S. economy was beleaguered by inflation for much of the decade, and as prices for gasoline, groceries, clothing, and other household essentials jumped, wages did not keep up. As the buying power of working families diminished, growing numbers of working-class households had to send both parents into the workforce or take on second jobs in order to make ends meet.

Not surprisingly, many unions responded by demanding wage and benefit hikes that would enable members to maintain the standards of living they had enjoyed back in the 1950s and early 1960s. But employers were hard-pressed to meet these demands. Competition from overseas was on the rise in many industries. Companies that were losing customers to foreign manufacturers offering high-quality, low-cost goods were in no position to offer more generous wage and benefit packages to their employees. In fact, rising levels of foreign competition led U.S. automakers, airlines, and other businesses to demand concessions from unions. Major public sector employers like school systems that were struggling with budgetary problems also pressed for salary cuts and other concessions from unions.

By the late 1970s and early 1980s, many struggling American corporations were not only refusing to increase wages, but were actually shutting down plants and laying off union workers. U.S. Steel, for example, shut down more than 150 mills and dismissed more than 100,000 workers after foreign steel began pouring into the United States. Numerous American companies responded to this rapidly changing business environment by shifting operations to factories in foreign countries, where they could pay workers a fraction of the wages that their U.S. employees earned. Of course, many other employers managed to keep their U.S. facilities open and running. But these companies frequently did so by making increased investments in robotics and other forms of automated machinery that reduced their reliance on human workers.

As all of these factors converged in the early 1980s, America reached a milestone that struck fear in the hearts of millions of workers who had long

School teachers with Detroit Public Schools went on strike in 1973 when the financially ailing city tried to cut teacher salaries.

earned paychecks from Boeing, U.S. Steel, Caterpillar, General Motors, Goodyear, and other venerable giants of mass-production industry. In July 1982 the total number of American workers employed in the manufacturing, mining, and construction sectors was eclipsed by employment in the nation's service, consumer, and financial industries. Fast-food titans like McDonald's and Burger King that offered mostly minimum-wage jobs and few fringe benefits were now employing more Americans than either the steel or automobile industries.[1]

Reagan Fires the Air Traffic Controllers

As the 1980s unfolded, the job losses experienced by unions due to automation and "outsourcing"—the corporate practice of sending work overseas to be done more cheaply by workers in India, China, and other developing countries—were further intensified by other factors. In 1981 Republican Ronald Reagan was sworn in as the 40th president of the United States. During his eight years in office, Reagan's administration became known as a reliable supporter of management over workers in labor disputes.

Reagan was himself a former union member. During his acting career he had even served as president of the Screen Actors Guild trade union from 1947 to 1952 and again in 1959. After leaving acting for politics, however, Reagan became much more sympathetic to corporate interests. By the time he reached the White House, he was convinced that excessive labor demands and intrusive government regulation of business activities accounted for much of America's economic difficulties. Despite his opposition to organized labor and workers' rights, however, Reagan attracted significant support in white working-class communities. He managed this by emphasizing other political themes that resonated in those communities, from patriotism to conservative positions on abortion, welfare, and other social issues.

Reagan established the pro-business, anti-union tone of his eight years in Washington at the very outset of his presidency. In August 1981 most of the country's unionized air traffic controllers went on strike for higher pay, better retirement packages, and relief from grueling working conditions. But their union—the Professional Air Traffic Controllers Organization (PATCO)—was a government union that had a clear no-strike clause in its contract with the Federal Aviation Administration (FAA). In addition, Reagan and many other critics of the strike action charged that PATCO was irresponsibly endangering the safety of air travel in the United States. Reagan demanded that the air traffic controllers return to work, but PATCO refused to obey (see "President Ronald Reagan Comments on the Air Traffic Controller Strike," p. 197). The president promptly told the FAA to fire more than 11,000 strikers and hire replacement workers. Some of the PATCO leadership also faced legal charges for conducting the strike.

PATCO's crushing defeat was a foreboding one for the entire labor movement. Union leaders saw Reagan's actions as evidence that he was hostile to the interests of their memberships. But they had to acknowledge that public opinion polls seemed to show broad American support for Reagan's decision to fire the air traffic controllers. To many Americans, the PATCO strikers were selfish workers who did not care about the impact of their actions on the wider American economy, so they had gotten what they deserved.

Battered by New Pressures and Old Image Problems

Public support for Reagan's stance on the air traffic controllers confirmed that labor still had a serious image problem with non-union Ameri-

In this August 3, 1981, address to reporters, President Ronald Reagan explains why he fired more than 11,000 striking air traffic controllers.

cans. Many people resented the fact that unionized workers with industrial jobs were earning higher—and in some cases much higher—wages than people in "skilled" professions. Other people accepted as fact the big business characterization of unions as collections of lazy and greedy workers who were sapping the nation of its economic vitality. These negative views angered and baffled many union members. They responded that when individual American workers negotiated with employers to secure the best possible compensation packages for themselves, they were applauded for showing initiative and going to bat for their families. But when unions did the very same thing, they were attacked for being selfish.

Still, the pressures on American labor continued to mount. "Right to work" laws were strengthened or expanded in several states, especially in the

South and West. In addition, the American labor market was transformed by growing numbers of illegal immigrants from Mexico and other parts of Central America. These desperate people took all manner of low-paying jobs in agriculture, manufacturing, and service industries. Competition for jobs in some of these sectors was low because the work was exhausting or paid poorly. Nonetheless, the growing presence of these illegal immigrants—as well as legal immigrants from Latin America, Asia, and elsewhere—sparked resentment among many American workers. They charged that the presence of these new immigrants made it harder for them to negotiate good wages and obtain job security from employers.

Meanwhile, the labor movement continued to be beset by internal squabbling over political strategy and policy priorities. These divisions remained evident even after the AFL-CIO and its president, Lane Kirkland, managed to bring the United Auto Workers, Teamsters, and United Mine Workers back into full and active federation membership in the 1980s. As its political influence waned, labor was unable to win even modest legislative reforms. In the 1970s and 1980s, for example, the AFL-CIO lobbied repeatedly for changes to the National Labor Relations Act, including provisions to make union elections easier and measures to more severely punish employers who engaged in unfair labor practices. But these efforts were knocked down again and again by corporate lobbyists and their conservative political allies.

Labor's decline continued in the 1990s, despite the fact that a Democrat, Bill Clinton, occupied the White House for the last eight years of the decade. The percentage of American workers that belonged to unions continued to drop—to 10 percent of all private-sector employees by 1996—even as the American economy added new jobs. Meanwhile, Clinton staked much of his political energy on gaining passage of the North American Free Trade Agreement (NAFTA), a 1994 trade agreement with Canada and Mexico that was supported by corporate America.

NAFTA was touted by Clinton and other proponents as a treaty that would boost the economies of all three nations. Labor leaders, however, criticized the agreement, charging that it would encourage American manufacturers to transfer operations to Mexico, where extremely cheap labor was plentiful. Since its passage, the ultimate impact of NAFTA on American jobs and unions has been hotly debated. But virtually everyone agrees that Clinton's push for the agreement provided clear evidence of labor's diminishing influence on U.S. politics in general and the Democratic Party in particular. As historian Richard Roth-

This 1993 labor rally against NAFTA included a man who costumed himself as "The Death of U.S. Jobs."

stein observed after NAFTA's passage, "it has been a long time since a Democratic president was openly pro-union. The Clinton administration, like [President Jimmy] Carter's before it, is ambivalent about unions, viewing them as a handy source of money and phone banks—but not as a needed ingredient in a strategy to restore wage growth and higher 'middle-class' incomes."[2]

A New Emphasis on Organizing

When John Sweeney became the new president of the AFL-CIO in 1995, he said that the labor federation planned to put greater emphasis on recruiting new workers to its banner. He believed that the labor movement could tap into widespread public anxieties about declining living standards and job security in a multitude of industries. Certainly, Sweeney and other labor leaders were right about the broad economic anxiety that Americans were feeling. "Wage stagnation and rising living costs forced countless workers to moonlight," observed historian Robert Zieger:

> A cartoon in the popular press in the late 1990s captured the situation facing many beleaguered American workers ... at century's end: a haggard looking man in an easy chair scowls as he reads his evening newspaper. The headlines proclaim the government's announcement of "Two Million Jobs Created in the Last Year." "Yeah," he growls ruefully, "I have three of them."[3]

Everywhere they went, labor activists and organizers reminded workers that unions were responsible for many things that employees now took for granted, such as the eight-hour day and the presence of basic workplace safety standards. They also declared that if rates of union membership returned to their former heights, American working families would experience new wage gains, increased job and retirement security, and higher living standards. But private sector union membership remained flat in the late 1990s and early 2000s, despite the return to grassroots organizing. In addition, organized labor endured several highly publicized rejections of union representation by factory workers in various industries in the 1980s and 1990s. Labor critics interpreted this lack of success as an indication that American workers no longer saw unions as effective or relevant.

Defenders, however, charged that pro-business laws and politicians made it exceedingly difficult for organizing drives to succeed. "In the current organizing climate, management routinely violates the spirit of the National Labor Relations Act," wrote Rothstein. "The penalties for harassing and firing pro-union workers are so light and so remote that management views them as a trivial cost of doing business and a small price to pay for union avoidance. Except in the public sector, where managers less frequently mount vicious union avoidance campaigns, the legal right to organize has long been rendered moot."[4]

Unions in the Twenty-First Century

Labor absorbed additional blows in the opening years of the twenty-first century. These included continued job and benefit losses in heavily unionized economic sectors, the successful union busting efforts of powerful employers like Wal-Mart, and the anti-union presidency of George W. Bush. During his eight years (2001-2009) in office, Bush's administration successfully neutralized the historically pro-labor National Labor Relations Board and sided with employers in numerous labor-management clashes. It also issued a number of directives that directly targeted unions, such as a 2001 Bush executive order that made it more difficult for unionized companies to secure federal construction contracts (this executive order was repealed by President Barack Obama in February 2009).[5] By 2005 only 12.5 percent of American workers belonged to a union.

That same year, the labor movement also experienced another highly publicized bout of internal squabbling. Both the 1.3-million member Teamsters Union and the 1.7-million member Service Employees International Union (SEIU) resigned from the AFL-CIO. Both Teamsters president James P. Hoffa Jr. and SEIU President Andy Stern said that the departure was necessary because the federation leadership had failed to stop long-term union losses or make unions more attractive to modern workers. "Our world has changed, our economy has changed, employers have changed," declared Stern. "But the

Workers at a Nissan plant in Tennessee take part in an anti-UAW rally in May 1989. Two months later, the factory's workforce rejected union representation by a vote of 1,622 to 711.

AFL-CIO is not willing to make fundamental changes." The resignations were harshly criticized by AFL-CIO leaders. President Sweeney, for example, called it a "tragedy for working people, because at a time when our corporate and conservative adversaries have created the most powerful anti-worker political machine in the history of our country, a divided movement hurts the hopes of working families for a better life."[6]

The loss of the Teamsters and the SEIU (along with a handful of other smaller labor unions) cost the AFL-CIO almost one-third of its 13 million members. The AFL-CIO partly bandaged this wound the following year, however, when it established a partnership with the National Education Association (NEA), which represented 3.2 million elementary and secondary school teachers, higher education faculty, education support professionals, and school administrators. Since the 1.4-million member American Federation of Teachers (AFT) was already part of the AFL-CIO, this historic agreement lifted educators to a preeminent role in the labor federation.

The AFL-CIO's alliance with the NEA also underscored how the characteristics of the typical union worker have changed since the 1950s, 1960s, and 1970s, when unions were dominated by men who jumped from high school to the industrial assembly line. According to a 2009 report by the Center for Economic and Policy Research, the proportion of unionized workers with college degrees has leaped from 20.4 percent in 1983 to 37.5 percent in 2008. In addition, two out of three union members in 2008 had at least attended college. Moreover, the percentage of female nurses, teachers, and other women union members has jumped from 35 to 45 percent of the union membership total since 1983.[7]

At the same time that the AFL-CIO and NEA got together, the SEIU and the Teamsters joined with three other unions—the United Farmworkers of America (UFW), the Laborers' International Union of North America (LIUNA), and the United Food and Commercial Workers International Union (UFCW)—to form Change to Win, a 5.5-million-member labor coalition with a self-proclaimed mission to "build a new movement of working people equipped to meet the challenges of the global economy and restore the American Dream in the 21st century: a paycheck that can support a family, affordable health care, a secure retirement and dignity on the job."[8]

Finding Solutions to the Labor Movement's Problems

In 2009 only a little more than 12 percent of American workers belonged to a union. The percentage is even lower in the private sector—less than 9 percent. Labor leaders and strategists still believe that these low numbers can be improved, and some even assert that dramatic increases in union membership are possible. But various labor factions support very different prescriptions for returning American labor unions to health, and it is unclear which approach—if any—will ultimately prevail (see "Debating the Future of Unions." p. 199).

The Change to Win Coalition spearheaded by Stern and the SEIU has called for a massive consolidation of the American labor movement from nearly sixty national unions into fifteen or twenty "mega-unions" arranged

After he took the reins at SEIU in the mid-1990s, Andy Stern (second from left) emerged as one of America's most powerful and influential labor leaders.

by industry sector. Supporters of this plan say that these new union organizations would have much more bargaining strength, financial resources, and political clout to stand up against big corporations. This proposal received a great deal of media attention, in large part because of Stern's high profile in the labor movement. After all, during the course of Stern's presidency the SEIU has bucked national trends and *increased* in size from fewer than one million members in 1996 to more than 2.2 million members in 2010.

Stern and the SEIU also provided politically vital support in securing the passage of the Affordable Care Act, a major health care reform act passed in 2010 by President Barack Obama and his fellow Democrats in Congress. Observers noted that passage of the Affordable Care Act, which extends health insurance to 30 million previously uninsured Americans, almost certainly means more jobs for the SEIU's membership in health care fields. But the strong efforts of the SEIU and other unions on behalf of health care reform also reflected a long-range consideration. Stern and other labor leaders are convinced that progressive social change helps all working Americans—and that labor's role in securing those changes will eventually be recognized by workers who are not yet unionized.

Most unions share the SEIU's interest in supporting new social welfare legislation designed to help working families. They also are unified in calling for legislation such as the Employee Free Choice Act, which would strengthen the organizing and bargaining position of unions. This legislation would allow employees to form a union by signing a card rather than going through a multi-month—some times years-long—election for union recognition. But many labor leaders do not agree with Stern's call for bigger unions controlled by fewer numbers of people. These critics charge that the key to revitalizing unions and attracting new members is to empower rank-and-file union members. "Unions work best when they are organized from the workplace up, not the top down," insisted the executive board of Communication Workers of America. "Strengthening the role of stewards and workplace mobilizers is critical for effective collective bargaining, organizing, and political action."[9]

Despite these strategic differences, the millions of men and women who comprise America's labor movement continue to forge ahead, even in the face of decades of disappointment and anxiety. And broadly speaking, they are still working together for the same basic goals—economic security for working-class families and peace and prosperity for the United States as a whole. As labor leader Richard Trumka declared shortly after his 2009 election to the presidency of the AFL-CIO, "Think about the great promise of America and the great legacy we have inherited. Our wealth as a nation and our energy as a people can deliver, in the words of my predecessor Samuel Gompers, 'more schoolhouses and less jails; more books and less arsenals; more learning and less vice; more leisure and less greed; more justice and less revenge; in fact, more of the opportunities to cultivate our better natures.' This is the American future the labor movement is working for."[10] (see "One Labor Leader's Perspective on the Future of American Unions," p. 206).

Notes

[1] Dulles, Foster Rhea, and Melvyn Dubofsky. *Labor in America: A History.* 5th ed. Wheeling, IL: Harlan Davidson, 1993, p. 388.

[2] Rothstein, Richard. "Toward a More Perfect Union: New Labor's Hard Road." *The American Prospect,* May-June 1996, p. 47.

3 Zieger, Robert. *American Workers, American Unions: The Twentieth Century*. 3rd rev. ed. Baltimore: Johns Hopkins University Press, 2002, p. 243.

4 Rothstein, p. 47.

5 Zweig, Michael. *What's Class Got to Do with It: American Society in the 21st Century*. Ithaca, NY: Cornell University Press, 2004, p. 116.

6 Edsall, Thomas B. "Two Top Unions Split from AFL-CIO." *Washington Post,* July 26, 2005. Available online at http://www.washingtonpost.com/wp-dyn/content/article/2005/07/25/AR2005072500251 .html.

7 Schmitt, John, and Kris Warner. *The Changing Face of Labor, 1983-2008.* Center for Economic and Policy Research, November 2009. Available online at http://www.cepr.net/index.php/publications /reports/changing-face-of-labor/.

8 "About Us." *Change to Win: The American Dream for American Workers.* N.d. Available online at http://www.changetowin.org/about-us.html.

9 Quoted in Early, Steve. "Labor Debates How to Rebuild Its House." *Tikkun,* May-June 2005. Available online at http://www.tikkun.org/article.php/Early-labordebateshowtorebuilditshouse.

10 Trumka, Richard. Remarks at National Press Club, January 11, 2010. Available online at http://www .aflcio.org/mediacenter/prsptm/sp01112010.cfm.

BIOGRAPHIES

Eugene V. Debs (1855-1926)
Labor Organizer and Five-Time Presidential
Nominee of the Socialist Party of America

Eugene Victor Debs was born in Terre Haute, Indiana, on November 5, 1855. He was the eldest son of six children born to Marguerite and Jean Debs, French immigrants who had come to America a few years earlier in search of a better life. At age fourteen Debs dropped out of school and secured work at a local rail yard. Two years later he was promoted to the position of fireman.

In 1875 Debs began his long career of labor activism by helping to found a local chapter of the Brotherhood of Locomotive Firemen. Even at this early age he was regarded by his fellow unionists as a smart, dedicated, and charismatic leader, and he rose steadily up the union's organizational ranks. By 1880 he had been appointed editor of *Firemen's Magazine*, the union's main periodical, and elected as the union's national secretary-treasurer.

President of the American Railway Union

Debs's passion for the labor cause led him into local politics as well. After a four-year stint (1879-1883) as Terre Haute's town clerk, Debs was elected as a state representative to the Indiana General Assembly as a Democrat in 1885. The union remained his top priority, however, and his impatience with the slow movings of legislative affairs led him to serve only one term. He also married Kate Metzel on June 9, 1885.

In the early 1890s Debs became convinced that railway workers needed to adopt a more confrontational stance and unite across skilled and unskilled lines if they were to obtain better wages, benefits, and working conditions from the giant rail corporations that employed them. To that end, Debs founded the American Railway Union (ARU) in 1893. This early industrial union made headlines one year later when Debs orchestrated a successful ARU strike against the Great Northern Railway. This 18-day strike ended only after the company agreed to the union's call for better wages and other working improvements.

In 1894 Debs played an important role in maintaining the so-called Pullman Strike, which paralyzed the nation's rail network. The strike initially involved only workers of the Pullman Company, who went on strike to protest steep wage cuts. But when the ARU honored the strike and refused to handle any trains with Pullman cars attached, freight shipments and passenger travel across America slowed to a crawl. Debs and other ARU leaders were jailed for defying court orders to end the union boycott, and Debs eventually served a six-month jail sentence after his conviction on contempt of court charges. This was the first of many stints in prison that Debs endured during his career as a labor leader.

America's Leading Socialist

While incarcerated during the Pullman Strike, Debs studied the writings of Karl Marx, a nineteenth-century German philosopher and economist whose political theories became essential in the development of both socialism and communism. After leaving prison in November 1895, Debs increasingly pursued a Socialist political philosophy. In 1897 he founded the Socialist Democratic Party of the United States, also known as the Social Democratic Party. In 1901 Deb's organization merged with two smaller Socialist groups to form the Socialist Party of America.

In 1900 Debs waged the first of five campaigns for the presidency of the United States. Running on a platform of Socialist principles, he called for a complete reorganization of America's economic and political systems. According to Debs, only socialism and unionism could protect the interests of workers and their families from the predatory behavior of the nation's giant corporate interests and the corruption of its politicians. He also called for a wide range of social reforms, including the abolition of child labor, women's suffrage, direct election of U.S. Senators, workmen's compensation, retirement and unemployment benefits for working men and women, and increased investment in public education. Some of these ideas were regarded as "radical" by mainstream Americans when Debs first championed them, but a number of them became widely accepted during the Progressive Era.

Debs never believed that he had a genuine shot at winning the presidency, but he saw campaigning as a good way of explaining his ideas and beliefs to his fellow Americans. In addition, he became convinced that his successively better showings in each of four elections from 1900 to 1912 had a significant impact on American politics in general. In 1900, for example, Debs earned only 0.6 percent of the vote, but in 1912 more than 900,000 Americans—roughly 6 percent of the total electorate—cast their votes for Debs and the Socialist Party. Debs had secured these votes despite the fact that both Democratic candidate (and eventual winner) Woodrow Wilson and Progressive candidate Theodore Roosevelt (the former Republican president) had "stolen Debs's thunder"—taken some Socialist Party ideas and made them their own.[1]

Debs also joined in 1905 with Daniel De Leon, William "Big Bill" Haywood, and other labor activists to establish the Industrial Workers of the World (IWW). But Debs disapproved when the radical "Wobblies," as IWW members came to be known, began using sabotage and other extreme tactics to advance their goals. Debs drifted away from the group and formally resigned his IWW membership in 1908, though he remained friends with some IWW members for many more years.

Debs expressed his steadfast support for workers' rights and Socialist ideals in countless speeches over his lifetime. But in addition to being a gifted public speaker, he was also a skilled labor journalist and editor. Debs contributed hundreds of tough editorials and news stories to the country's leading labor journals over his lifetime, and he was an important presence on the editorial boards of Socialist magazines like *Appeal to Reason*. By the close of the first decade of the twentieth century, Debs's intelligence, his charisma, and his dedication to improving the lives of America's working men and women had made him an inspiration to labor activists, Socialists, and social reformers alike. "That old man with the burning eyes actually believes that there can be such a thing as the brotherhood of man," said one colleague. "And that's not the funniest part of it. As long as he's around I believe it myself."[2]

Running for President from a Prison Cell

When World War I erupted in 1914, Debs fiercely denounced all calls for the United States to enter the conflict. He believed that the war would merely enrich industrial capitalists at the expense of working families whose fathers and sons would be cast into the meat grinder of war. When America entered the war in April 1917, an outraged Debs spoke out against the war in appearances across the country. Debs's opposition infuriated President Wilson, who called him a traitor to his country. In June 1917 the U.S. Congress passed the Espionage Act into law, making it illegal for anyone to interfere with the war effort or military recruitment. Later amendments to the Espionage Act, most notably the 1918 Sedition Act, even made it illegal to "incite" American citizens to oppose U.S. involvement in the war.

Undaunted, Debs continued to speak out despite an extended bout of poor health (his health problems convinced him to refrain from running for president in 1916). He delivered a particularly famous antiwar speech in Canton, Ohio, on June 16, 1918, urging the gathered crowd to resist the wartime military draft. He was subsequently arrested and convicted of violating the wartime Espionage Act, despite his insistence that his criticisms were protected by the First Amendment's guarantee of freedom of speech. Debs was stripped of his U.S. citizenship and sentenced to ten years in prison. He began his prison sentence in a federal facility in Atlanta, Georgia, on April 13, 1919.

Debs remained in prison with the new year, but he nonetheless announced his intention to campaign for the presidency once again. His candidacy attracted the usual support from Socialist and labor groups that had come to see him as a martyr of sorts, but he also received support from moderate and even conservative Americans who were angered and frightened by the government's disregard for his constitutional rights. Debs received nearly one million votes in the 1920 presidential election, about 3.4 percent of all votes cast.

On Christmas Day 1921 Debs's prison sentence was commuted by President Warren G. Harding and he was released. He arrived home in Terre Haute three days later to a hero's welcome from a massive crowd of admirers. Debs never fully returned to the political arena, though. Dogged by continued poor health, he was forced to limit himself to writing political essays and the occasional public lecture. He died on October 20, 1926, in Elmhurst, Illinois. Debs's death was not universally mourned—his left-wing political beliefs aroused bitter condemnation from Americans who disagreed with his economic and political philosophies. But many other Americans felt a deep sense of loss at his passing.

Sources:

Constantine, J. Robert. "Eugene V. Debs: An American Paradox." *Monthly Labor Review,* August 1991.

Salvatore, Nick. *Eugene V. Debs: Citizen and Socialist.* Champaign, IL: University of Illinois Press, 1982.

Young, Marguerite. *Harp Song for a Radical: The Life and Times of Eugene Victor Debs.* New York: Knopf, 1999.

Notes

[1] Constantine, J. Robert. "Eugene V. Debs: An American Paradox." *Monthly Labor Review,* August 1991.

[2] Broun, Heywood. *It Seems to Me: 1925-1935.* New York: Harcourt, Brace, 1935, p. 38.

Samuel Gompers (1850-1924)
Founder and Longtime President of the American Federation of Labor (AFL)

Samuel Gompers was born in London, England, on January 27, 1850. His parents were Solomon and Sarah (Rood) Gompers. Samuel was the oldest of his family's six children. He received several years of tuition-free education at a Jewish school, but at age ten he went to work as an apprentice shoemaker to help his struggling parents make ends meet. Gompers and his family immigrated to New York City in 1863, where his cigar maker father found work and mentored his son in the trade.

At age fourteen Gompers joined the Cigarmakers' International Union (CIU), a loosely organized brotherhood of men who made their living in that trade. Three years later he married Sophia Julian, with whom he eventually had six children who survived infancy (their marriage lasted until 1920 when Sophia died; Gompers married Grace Gleaves Neuscheler one year later). In the late 1870s the Cigarmakers International Union nearly collapsed when poor economic conditions spurred employers to impose steep wage cuts. The union was completely unprepared for this fight, as Gompers later recalled. "There was a vast difference between those early unions, and the unions of today. Then there was no law or order. A union was a more or less definite group of people employed in the same trade who might help each other out in special difficulties with the employer. There was no sustained effort to secure fair wages through collective bargaining."[1]

Establishing the American Federation of Labor

The cigarmakers' struggles convinced Gompers that a new union model needed to be formed—one that emphasized solidarity and tough-minded negotiating with employers. He helped usher in these internal reforms to the CIU in the early 1880s, when he rose to a leading position in the union (he remained a top CIU official until his death in 1924). But Gompers achieved far greater fame and influence with his founding of the

American Federation of Labor (AFL)—the most powerful labor organization in U.S. history—in 1886.

The roots of the AFL lay in the 1881 founding of the Federation of Organized Trades and Labor Unions, an umbrella organization that included the CIU. In 1886 the organization was reorganized as the AFL, a labor federation dedicated to gathering together skilled tradesmen and developing collective bargaining, strikes, boycotts, and other strategies for negotiating with employers. At the urging of Gompers, who played a pivotal role in founding the organization and was promptly elected its first president, the AFL made a conscious decision to avoid recruiting unskilled workers. Gompers and many other AFL officials believed that unionizing unskilled workers was a wasteful expenditure of time and energy because management could easily replace them with desperate immigrants and other poor workers.

Gompers headed the American Federation of Labor from 1886 to 1924 with only one brief interruption. In 1894 he was ousted from the AFL presidency by Socialist opponents within the group, but Gompers and his allies regained control of the federation one year later and Gompers was reinstated as president. During his remarkable tenure of nearly four decades at the helm of the AFL, Gompers lifted member unions to new heights of economic security and material comfort. Under his direction, numerous trade unions were able to negotiate higher wages, shorter workdays, and better working conditions for their memberships.

The eight-hour workday was a special crusade for Gompers, who decried the crushing daily regimen of the country's "long hour men": "[They] go home, throw themselves on a miserable apology for a bed and dream of work. They eat to work, sleep to work, and dream to work, instead of working to live.... Time is the most valuable thing on earth: time to think, time to act, time to extend our fraternal relations, time to become better men, time to become better women, time to become better and more independent citizens."[2] Gompers's focus on this issue enabled many AFL-affiliated craft unions to eventually secure eight-hour workdays in their employment contracts.

Throughout his tenure, Gompers took great pains to keep the AFL "respectable" and to portray AFL members as solid American citizens. Gompers was fiercely opposed to communism and socialism, and he condemned radical groups like the Industrial Workers of the World (IWW) that preached about the need for a complete social and economic revolution in America. "It is a fact that trade unionism in America moves on its own set and deliberate way," he stated in 1910. "In so doing, it has outlived wave upon wave of hastily conceived so-called 'broad' movements that were to reconstruct society in a single season. And it has sufficiently good cause for continuing its own reasoned-out course."[3]

Gompers also made special efforts to keep the AFL out of messy alliances or disputes with political parties. These strategies helped the AFL enjoy decades of fairly steady growth, and by the time Gompers retired in 1924, the federation's total membership stood at nearly 2.9 million.

The Workers Left Behind

Most of the unionists who marched under the AFL banner during Gompers's years in power were white men of western European stock who made their livings as skilled or semi-skilled craftsmen—printers, shoemakers, carpenters, glassmakers, stonecutters, mechanics, and the like. This was by design, for Gompers believed that workers with specialized skills were in the strongest position to bargain with employers over wages, hours, and other working conditions.

By focusing almost exclusively on these workers, however, Gompers and the rest of the AFL leadership ignored the economic struggles of millions of other American workers. The AFL consciously excluded women and African Americans from membership, and it made virtually no effort to lift the fortunes of the immigrants and native-born Americans who toiled in the great factories, foundries, railroad yards, textile mills, mining districts, and lumber camps of industrial America. In fact, the AFL was actively hostile to immigrants from southern and eastern Europe, who comprised the bulk of the new arrivals to American shores during the many years that Gompers led the organization.

From the 1890s through the 1910s Gompers and other trade unionists consistently expressed their support for legislation that would sharply curtail immigration to America. "The workers of America have felt most keenly the pernicious results of the establishment of foreign standards of work, wages and conduct in American industries and commerce," Gompers wrote in 1916. "Foreign labor has driven American workers out of many trades, callings, and communities, and the influence of those lower standards has permeated widely."[4]

Gompers's anti-immigration stance was in large part based on his belief that new immigrants represented a threat to the job security and economic standing of AFL members. But racial bigotry also accounted for some of the hostility expressed by Gompers and many of his AFL colleagues (who were usually of western European ancestry) toward African Americans, Chinese, and immigrants from southern and eastern Europe.

Gompers's Final Years

Gompers supported America's entrance into World War I in 1917, and the AFL refrained from engaging in strikes and other work stoppages during wartime. In fact, Gompers worked closely with President Woodrow Wilson to prevent labor strikes that might jeopardize the country's wartime industrial production. When the federation pushed for wage hikes and other benefits after the war, however, American business interests united against them. Nearly every AFL-supported strike and boycott ended in defeat, and the reputation of the federation among labor activists suffered accordingly.

By the early 1920s Gompers's health was declining rapidly. In late 1923 he collapsed while presiding over a conference of the Pan-American Federation of Labor in Mexico City. Sensing that the end was near, Gompers asked to be transported back to American soil. He was taken to San Antonio, Texas, where he died on December 13, 1924.

Sources:

Gompers, Samuel. *Seventy Years of Life and Labor: An Autobiography*. New York: Dutton, 1925. Reprint. New York: ILR Press, 1984.

Greene, Julie. *Pure and Simple Politics: The American Federation of Labor and Political Activism, 1881-1917*. New York: Cambridge University Press, 1998.

Samuel Gompers Papers [online]. http://www.history.umd.edu/Gompers/bio.htm.

Taft, Philip. *The A.F. of L. in the Time of Gompers*. New York: Harper & Brothers, 1957.

Notes

[1] Gompers, Samuel. *Seventy Years of Life and Labor: An Autobiography*. New York: Dutton, 1925. Reprint. New York: ILR Press, 1984, p. 16

[2] Quoted in *Seattle Post-Intelligencer,* March 23, 1891. *Samuel Gompers Papers* [online]. Available online at http://www.history.umd.edu/Gompers/bio.htm.

[3] Gompers, Samuel. *Labor and the Common Welfare*. New York: Dutton, 1919, p. 18.

[4] Quoted in *American Federationist,* April 1916. *Samuel Gompers Papers* [online]. Available online at http://www.history.umd.edu/Gompers/bio.htm.

William "Big Bill" Haywood (1869-1928)
Leader of the Western Federation of Miners (WFM) and co-founder of the International Workers of the World (IWW)

William Dudley "Big Bill" Haywood Jr. was born on February 4, 1869, in Salt Lake City, Utah. His father, William Sr., had reportedly worked as a Pony Express rider before turning to silver mining. He died of pneumonia when young Bill was three years old, leaving his wife Henrietta with two small children. She married another miner named William Carruthers four years later. At age nine Haywood accidentally punctured his right eye with a knife while whittling the stock of a slingshot. The injury blinded him for life in that eye, but Haywood effectively used the eye's shocking appearance—it filmed over in a milky glaze—as a tool of intimidation when he reached adulthood.

Haywood also began working in the Utah silver mines when he was nine years old. Laboring in the mines involved long hours of dangerous and exhausting work for little money, but there were few other employment options in the region. Haywood spent most of the next several years toiling in western mines, though he also spent time as a surveyor, homesteader, and cowhand in the late 1880s.

A Radical Voice for Miners

All of these efforts to escape mining failed, either because of punishing economic downturns or governmental policies. In the early 1890s, for example, the federal government seized Haywood's 160-acre homestead and added it to an Indian reservation without providing him with a cent of compensation. Haywood drifted back to the silver mines, but by this time labor uprisings such as the 1886 Haymarket Square riots and the 1894 Pullman Strike had also caught his attention. These explosive confrontations both angered and inspired Haywood. By the mid-1890s he had developed a deep conviction that the men who owned and directed America's railroads, mines, and other industries were perfectly willing to sacrifice the bodies and spirits of workers for profits. He also came to believe that radical—even violent—protest was the surest path to economic and social justice for long-suffering American workers.

In 1896 Haywood formally joined the labor movement as a member of the Western Federation of Miners (WFM). Haywood's enthusiasm for the union cause and his personal charisma enabled him to climb up the union ranks, and by 1900 he was one of the WFM's top officials. In 1902 Haywood became secretary-treasurer, which placed him behind only President Charles Moyer in the WFM. Haywood's volatile personality, unyielding Socialist beliefs, and taste for confrontational tactics clashed with the more cautious and moderate Moyer, and the two soon became bitter rivals.

Haywood emerged as one of the most controversial labor leaders in America over the next few years. The event that first vaulted him into the public eye was the so-called Colorado Labor Wars, a deadly clash that pitted miners against mine operators and Colorado state authorities. This battle, which raged across the state for much of 1903 and 1904, was initially triggered by the refusal of Colorado legislators, who did the bidding of the mine owners, to approve eight-hour-workday legislation. But the conflict worsened when mine operators and state militias resorted to savage displays of violence to crush the WFM and other mining unions. The miners reciprocated with bloody forays of their own, including dynamite attacks on replacement workers and numerous acts of sabotage. Throughout these long months of tension and violence, Haywood urged his fellow miners to stand firm—and to use any means necessary to force management to meet their demands. "He had tremendous magnetism [when he appeared before union audiences]," recalled one labor reporter. "Huge frame, one blazing eye, voice filling the hall. When he shouted, 'Eight hours of work, eight hours of play, eight hours of sleep—*eight dollars a day!*' that last line came like a clap of thunder."[1]

Under Haywood's leadership, the WFM experienced a surge in membership (to reach 30-40,000 by 1903) and expanded beyond its Colorado base into several other states, including Idaho, Arizona, and Nevada. The union even began exploring the idea of pushing into the upper Midwest, where mining was growing by leaps and bounds. The expanding influence of the Haywood and his violent rhetoric alarmed the mining industry. But the

125

union's strike actions were ultimately defeated by the mine owners, who used National Guard troops to arrest union organizers and protect strikebreakers. The WFM's position was also greatly weakened by the American Federation of Labor (AFL), whose trade union membership declined to carry out boycotts or sympathy strikes that might have helped the miners.

Haywood and the Wobblies

The WFM survived its defeat in the Colorado Labor Wars, albeit as a much smaller union (it was eventually absorbed into the United Steelworkers). But the whole affair infuriated Haywood. Convinced that the AFL "aristocrats" cared only for themselves and that America's capitalist system was hopelessly corrupt, he concluded that industrial workers could only remake that system by joining forces in a single great union. With that in mind, Haywood and other WFM officials met in Chicago in June 1905 with labor leaders including Daniel De Leon, Eugene V. Debs, and Mary Harris "Mother" Jones. Led by Haywood, the group formed a radical new organization called the Industrial Workers of the World (IWW). "We are here to confederate the workers of this country into a working-class movement that shall have for its purpose the emancipation of the working-class from the slave bondage of capitalism," Haywood declared in a speech at the outset of the convention. "The aims and objects of this organization shall be to put the working-class in possession of the economic power, the means of life, in control of the machinery of production and distribution, without regard to capitalist masters."[2]

Over the next several years, IWW members—known as Wobblies—established a reputation for themselves as the most militant wing of the entire labor movement. The IWW preached a message of revolution to working-class Americans, and they engineered a series of violent strikes and work stoppages that rocked various mining, logging, and manufacturing outfits.

During the earliest years of the IWW, however, Haywood was mostly relegated to the sidelines. In 1906 he was arrested and charged with ordering the murder of Frank Steunenberg, a former governor of Idaho who had been killed by a dynamite explosion outside his home in late 1905. Steunenberg had been a bitter foe of the WFM and Haywood, and when investigators arrested a former WFM member named Harry Orchard for the murder, Orchard claimed that the assassination had been ordered by Haywood.

Haywood's trial attracted national attention, in part because the famous lawyer Clarence Darrow agreed to defend the IWW leader. As Haywood awaited trial, he corresponded from jail with a variety of WFM, IWW, and Socialist leaders. The Socialists even arranged to get him on the 1906 Colorado ballot as their candidate for governor, and he received 16,000 votes—four times the number that the Socialist nominee had received in the previous election. Once the trial got underway, it was revealed that Orchard had secretly worked for both mine owners and private detective agencies that carried out anti-union activities. Since the prosecution's case against Haywood was based largely on Orchard's testimony, the news that he had been a "double agent" in labor-management clashes severely undermined his credibility. Haywood was acquitted of all charges in July 1906.

After regaining his freedom, Haywood returned to both the WFM and the IWW. Both organizations had become wracked by personality clashes and squabbles over political tactics by this time, and in 1907 the WFM formally withdrew from the IWW. One year later, Moyer managed to push Haywood out of the WFM altogether. Haywood decided to devote all his energies to the Wobblies. Over the next several years he orchestrated a number of successful strikes across the country, including the 1912 "Bread and Roses" textile strike in Lawrence, Massachusetts. In 1915 Haywood was formally appointed the head of the IWW. He remained a fixture in the nation's headlines throughout this period. His continued prominence stemmed mostly from his radical political views, but his fierce attacks on Christianity and the Bible—Haywood was a lifelong atheist—also made him a target of religious leaders around the country.

In 1917 the United States entered World War I, and within a matter of months Congress had passed legislation that made it illegal for American citizens to interfere with military recruitment or otherwise "sabotage" the war effort. These new laws blatantly ignored First Amendment guarantees of first speech, but the Woodrow Wilson administration used them to crack down on the IWW and other leftist groups that opposed American involvement in the war. In 1918 Haywood and dozens of other war critics were arrested. Haywood was convicted and sentenced to twenty years in prison for his "seditious" activities. He served a year in the federal prison in Leavenworth, Kansas, before gaining a temporary release on bail while his appeal was being heard. When the courts upheld his conviction in 1921, Haywood fled to Russia, where he was welcomed by that nation's Communist leadership.

Haywood spent the remaining years of his life in exile. He settled in Moscow, where health problems from diabetes and years of alcoholism severely curtailed his activities. Haywood died in Moscow on May 18, 1928.

Sources:

Carlson, Peter. *Roughneck: The Life and Times of Big Bill Haywood*. New York: W.W. Norton, 1983.

Dubofsky, Melvyn. *"Big Bill" Haywood*. New York: St. Martin's Press, 1987.

Lukas, J. Anthony. *Big Trouble: A Murder in a Small Western Town Sets Off a Struggle for the Soul of America*. New York: Simon and Schuster, 1997.

Notes

[1] Quoted in Carlson, Peter. *Roughneck: The Life and Times of Big Bill Haywood*. New York: W.W. Norton, 1983, p. 147.

[2] Foner, Philip S. *The Industrial Workers of the World, 1905-1917*. Volume Four of *History of the Labor Movement in the United States*. New York: International Publishers, 1965, p. 29.

Jimmy Hoffa (1913-1975)
President of the International Brotherhood of Teamsters

James Riddle Hoffa—known as Jimmy—was born on February 14, 1913, in the rough coal-mining town of Brazil, Indiana. His father, John Cleveland Hoffa, was a coal driller who died of lung disease related to his job when Jimmy was seven years old. His mother, Viola Riddle Hoffa, did laundry, cleaned houses, and worked in a restaurant to support Jimmy and his three siblings. In 1924 the Hoffas moved to Detroit, Michigan. Money remained tight for the family, so Jimmy quit school in the ninth grade in order to get a job.

Hoffa worked on a loading dock, where he moved boxes of produce off of trains to be sold in local grocery stores. The teenager grew frustrated with the long hours, low pay, and poor treatment he and the other dockworkers received from their employer. One day, when a huge shipment of fresh strawberries arrived, Hoffa convinced his fellow workers to go on strike and refuse to move the boxes. Realizing that the fruit would spoil quickly, the management of the grocery chain agreed to a new contract within an hour.

Hoffa's leadership role with the "Strawberry Boys" brought him to the attention of the Teamsters union. Originally formed at the turn of the twentieth century to represent wagon drivers, the International Brotherhood of Teamsters later expanded to include truck drivers, dockworkers, and other laborers who helped move freight across the country. In 1932 Hoffa became a full-time organizer for the Teamsters. He led a membership drive that increased the size of his local union from 40 to 5,000 members. In 1936 Hoffa married Josephine Poszywak. They had a daughter, Barbara Ann, who became a judge, and a son, James Phillip, who followed in his father's footsteps as a union leader and was elected president of the Teamsters in 1999.

Becomes President of the Teamsters

At the time Jimmy Hoffa joined the Teamsters, the labor movement was fighting for legal rights, corporate recognition, and public acceptance across the United States. The management at many companies was determined to resist all efforts to organize their workers. Union organizers often faced the threat of physical violence from corporate security forces and sympathetic law enforcement officials. Hoffa was involved in a number of violent confrontations that erupted during labor strikes. "When you went out on strike in those days, you got your head broken," he recalled. "The cops would beat your brains out if you even got caught talking about unions."[1]

Hoffa moved up steadily through the ranks of the Teamsters. He played an important role in consolidating small, local unions into regional organizations, and then consolidating these groups into a powerful, national body. By 1952, when Hoffa was elected international vice president of the Teamsters, the union had grown to over one million members. Hoffa handled collective bargaining for the entire organization and successfully negotiated the first national freight-hauling agreement.

In 1957 Teamsters President Dave Beck made national headlines as the target of a federal corruption investigation. When he was called to testify before a U.S. Senate committee—known as the McClellan Committee after its leader, Arkansas Senator John Little McClellan—Beck faced accusations of corruption, tax evasion, embezzlement of union funds, and secret deals with organized crime. Beck refused to answer any questions, invoking his Fifth Amendment right to avoid self-incrimination 140 times during the hearing. Beck's standing with rank-and-file Teamsters plummeted, and he decided not to seek re-election in late 1957. Hoffa, who had been openly angling to replace Beck, won the October election and took over as president of the Teamsters union. The AFL-CIO was not happy with this turn of events, for it viewed Hoffa to be just as corrupt as Beck. Increasingly concerned that the Teamsters issue was tainting all of organized labor, the AFL-CIO suspended the Teamsters from their organization after Hoffa's election in 1957. Meany and other AFL-CIO officials stated that the Teamsters could return if Hoffa resigned, but when Hoffa refused, the federation formally expelled the union on December 6, 1957.

Spends Time in Prison

Although Hoffa came under investigation by the McClellan Committee as well, federal officials could not find enough evidence to bring criminal charges against him. He remained popular among rank-and-file members of the Teamsters union throughout this time. Members admired his charismatic leadership, tough negotiating style, and outspoken defense of labor positions.

In fact, Hoffa emerged as one of the most powerful union leaders in the country, even as rumors swirled about his connections with organized crime. Hoffa did not deny that he had formed relationships with mob figures during his career. Although he did not specify the nature of the relationships, he insisted that they were similar to those maintained by many high-profile businessmen and politicians.

Still, Hoffa remained a target of federal investigators and politicians like Senator Robert F. Kennedy—who had served as a lawyer for the McClellan Committee—throughout the first decade of his Teamsters presidency. In 1962 Hoffa finally went on trial for allegedly taking a million-dollar "kickback"— essentially a bribe—from a corporation in exchange for guaranteeing peaceful labor relations. Although the trial ended in his acquittal, Hoffa was then accused of trying to bribe a member of the jury. He was convicted on this charge in 1964, and he later received further convictions for mail fraud and misuse of union pension funds. After exhausting a series of appeals, Hoffa began serving a 13-year sentence at a federal prison in Pennsylvania in 1967. His longtime ally Frank Fitzsimmons became acting president of the Teamsters union in his absence.

Hoffa continued to exert influence over the Teamsters during his time in prison. In 1971, after he had served five years of his sentence, Hoffa received a pardon from President Richard M. Nixon. As a condition of his release, Hoffa was required to refrain from participating in any union activity until at least 1980. Unhappy with this requirement, Hoffa appealed the terms of his pardon all the way to the U.S. Supreme Court, but he lost the legal battle in 1973.

Disappears under Mysterious Circumstances

Despite being forced to resign as president of the Teamsters, Hoffa remained active behind the scenes and continued to plot a return to power. In the meantime, Fitzsimmons solidified his control over the union with the help of organized crime. He allegedly used the Teamsters' billion-dollar pension fund to make large loans to various mob figures. The money was supposedly used to finance drug deals, casino purchases, and other criminal activities.

At some point, federal investigators believe that mob kingpins decided that they preferred working with Fitzsimmons over Hoffa. Investigators believe that the mob became determined to prevent Hoffa from regaining his position as head of the Teamsters union. On July 30, 1975, Hoffa was invited to a meeting with two well-known organized crime figures—Anthony Provenzano and Anthony Giacalone—at the Machus Red Fox restaurant in suburban Detroit. After waiting at the restaurant for half an hour, Hoffa called his wife to complain that the other men had failed to show up. Then Hoffa disappeared and was never heard from again.

Although Hoffa's body was never found, and no one was ever arrested in connection with his mysterious disappearance, the evidence suggests that he was murdered. He was officially declared dead in 1982. Since that time, a variety of rumors, tips, and conspiracy theories have been offered to explain what happened to him. Some people speculate that Hoffa disappeared for his own safety and could still be alive, but most authorities and historians believe that he was murdered. One of the most popular theories is that he was killed and dismembered by mobsters and buried under the Meadowlands football stadium in New Jersey.

Whatever the circumstances of his demise, Hoffa became a legendary figure in the labor movement during his lifetime. He showed tremendous courage in early organizing battles and helped build the Teamsters into one of the nation's most powerful unions. Yet Hoffa's legacy has been forever darkened by his involvement in corruption scandals and connections with organized crime.

Sources:
Hoffa, James R., with Oscar Fraley. *Hoffa: The Real Story.* New York: Stein and Day, 1975.

"Investigations: Hoffa Search 'Looks Bad Right Now.'" *Time,* August 18, 1975. Available online at http://www.time.com/time/magazine/article/0,9171,917718-1,00.html.

James, Ralph, and Estelle James. *Hoffa and the Teamsters: A Study of Union Power.* New York: Van Nostrand, 1965.

Kennedy, Robert F. *The Enemy Within: The McClellan Committee's Crusade against Jimmy Hoffa and Corrupt Labor Unions.* New York: Harper, 1960.

Sloane, Arthur A. *Hoffa.* Boston: MIT Press, 1991.

Notes

[1] James, Ralph, and Estelle James. *Hoffa and the Teamsters: A Study of Union Power.* New York: Van Nostrand, 1965, p. 86.

Mary Harris "Mother" Jones (1837-1930)
Labor Organizer and Activist

Mary Harris "Mother" Jones was born in 1837 in the city of Cork, Ireland. For much of her life, Jones insisted that she had actually been born on May 1, 1830. But scholars have disproved this claim. They say that the false birth date stemmed from Jones's desire to emphasize her ties to the labor movement—May 1 was known to workers around the world as "May Day," a day commemorating labor's fight for an eight-hour workday. Her claim to have been born seven years earlier than her actual birth, meanwhile, apparently was meant to enhance her reputation as the feisty "grandmother" figure of the labor movement.

Jones was the second of five children born to Richard and Ellen Harris, poor Catholic farmers who coaxed a meager living out of a small plot of farmland owned by a wealthy landowner. Ireland was controlled at that time by England, which used a range of discriminatory and punishing laws to pressure Irish Catholics into converting to the Protestant Church of England. Years later, Jones indicated that this family background gave her an early understanding of the many ways in which the rich and powerful took advantage of the poor and weak.

Jones and her family emigrated to North America in the early 1840s, eventually settling in the Canadian city of Toronto, Ontario. Her father supported the family as a railroad worker, and Mary Jones was able to obtain a fairly good public education. Upon reaching adulthood she worked as a seamstress and teacher in several cities in Canada and the northern United States. Around 1860 she took a teaching job in Memphis, Tennessee, where she met and fell in love with an iron worker named George Jones. They were married in 1861 and soon had four young children.

Over the next several years Mary received a crash course in the ideals of organized labor from her husband, who was a devout member of the city's

133

Iron Molders Union. In 1867 a yellow fever epidemic raged through Memphis, claiming the lives of her husband and every one of her children. This devastating event prompted Jones to move to Chicago, where she and a friend opened a small dressmaking shop. Four years later, however, the shop burned to the ground—along with much of the rest of the city—in the Great Chicago Fire of 1871.

Birth of a Labor Activist

Chicago was rebuilt quickly by industrialists who poured money into creating a "second city" and immigrant laborers who supplied the muscle and sweat that went into construction of new office buildings, bridges, roads, homes and apartments, and railroad depots. Jones witnessed the city's rebirth at the same time that she was undergoing a transformation of her own. By the mid-1870s she was spending many of her evenings at meetings of the Knights of Labor and other early union organizations, where labor organizers preached of workers' rights and radical social change.

Jones became a committed labor activist, and by the late 1870s her daily life pivoted around union organizing and social justice campaigns. She later characterized this period of her life as one in which she gained a much greater understanding of the political and social challenges facing poor American workers. In 1877, for example, she participated in a nationwide railroad strike for better wages and working conditions that was eventually crushed by industrial executives and their allies in government. The defeat was tough for Jones to accept, especially because labor received the lion's share of public blame for violence that had actually been sparked by corporate thugs, police, and state militias. "Then and there I learned in the early part of my career that labor must bear the cross for others' sins," she later wrote in her autobiography. "Hand in hand with the growth of factories and the expansion of railroads, with the accumulation of capital and the rise of banks, came anti-labor legislation. Came strikes. Came violence. Came the belief in the hearts and minds of the workers that legislatures but carry out the will of the industrialists."[1]

Jones worked as a labor organizer all across the country over the last two decades of the nineteenth century. She spent the majority of this time working with impoverished miners in Colorado, Pennsylvania, West Virginia, and other coal mining regions of the United States. As an official representative of the United Mine Workers of America, she pushed tirelessly to convince unorganized miners to join the union. And once they organized, Jones delivered fiery speeches to inspire them and stood at their side through dozens of dangerous marches and strike actions. She also helped workers to organize in the textile, steel, railroad, and brewery industries over the course of her career, but she remained most famous for her efforts on behalf of coal mining families. In many coal towns, in fact, she became known as the "miners' angel."

Jones acquired another nickname—"Mother"—in the late 1890s from unionized workers who enjoyed the fact that one of the labor movement's leading figures looked like a kindly and harmless old lady. Jones enjoyed the nickname as well, and she took maximum advantage of it. "The way Mother Jones lived her life was breathtaking," wrote one biographer. "She tailored her appearance to match every sentimental notion about mothers. Then she subverted the very idea of genteel womanhood upon which such stereotypes were based with her vituperative, profane, electric speeches. Women—especially old women—were not supposed to have opinions about politics and economics; they were not supposed to travel alone; they were too delicate for controversy. Yet there she was, haranguing workers, berating politicians, attacking the 'pirates' [of business], and telling women to take to the streets, all under the cover of sacred motherhood."[2]

Lifelong Belief in the Power of Unions

Jones's life in the labor movement contained many frustrations. Many union fights to obtain better wages and living conditions ended in failure, and she knew that her gender limited her advancement through the official ranks of the United Mine Workers. She watched time and again as she was passed over for official leadership positions in favor of men with less talent and dedication. But Jones comforted herself with the knowledge that the inspirational role she played was an important one. She also knew that she wielded considerable influence over the attitudes of working men and women, even if she did not have a fancy title. Her support for bringing African Americans and immigrants into the union fold, for example, helped pave the way for their acceptance in many unions.

Jones remained a giant of the labor movement as America entered the twentieth century. She continued to organize workers in strikes and boycotts, and she championed the value of unions in countless speeches. "[The union] is the school, the college," she said in a 1901 address to mine workers. "It is where you learn to know and to love each other and learn to work with each other and bear each other's burdens, each other's sorrows and each other's joys."[3]

In 1905 Jones helped found the Industrial Workers of the World (IWW) or Wobblies, a radical organization dedicated to replacing America's capitalist society with a Socialist model. She was the only woman among twenty-seven persons who signed the IWW's founding documents, and she spent several years working on behalf of the group. In 1911 she left the Wobblies and returned to organizing work with the United Mine Workers, but she remained a friend and confidante to many IWW leaders.

By the 1910s Jones was in her seventies, making her far older than most other union activists roaming the countryside. But her appetite for organizing and confrontation remained undiminished. In 1913, for example, she spent three months in a West Virginia jail on charges that her angry speeches to striking miners were inciting them to violence. One West Virginia official went so far as to call her the most dangerous woman in America. Her imprisonment, however, triggered such national outrage and controversy that the new state governor decided to release her. Jones then made her way to Ludlow, Colorado, where—despite being arrested on several occasions—she helped striking coal miners seeking better wages and safer working conditions from John Rockefeller Sr.'s Colorado Fuel and Iron (CFI), the largest coal operator in the state.

Jones was far from Ludlow in April 1914, however, when the Ludlow strike erupted in bloodshed. On April 20 guards hired by CFI murdered nineteen men, women, and children in an attack on the miners' tent colony. Afterward, Jones helped raise funds for the Ludlow miners and testified before Congress about the deplorable conditions in America's coal fields. She also met with John D. Rockefeller Jr., whose family owned CFI. Jones found him to be a pleasant enough fellow, but completely clueless about the struggles and hopes of working-class Americans. "He was alien as is one species from another; as alien as is stone from wheat," she declared.[4]

Jones finally began slowing down in the early 1920s. Suffering from rheumatism and other frailties of old age, she ended her wanderings and settled in Chicago, where she wrote her autobiography. In 1929 she moved to Silver Spring, Maryland. She died on November 30, 1930. Her funeral attracted labor officials and rank-and-file union members from all across the country, and her casket was carried by representatives from eight different trade unions that she had helped over the years. Fittingly, she was buried among generations of miners in the Union Miners Cemetery in Mount Olive, Illinois.

Sources:

Gorn, Elliott J. *Mother Jones: The Most Dangerous Woman in America.* New York: Hill and Wang, 2001.

Kraft, Betsy Harvey. *Mother Jones: One Woman's Fight for Labor.* New York: Clarion Books, 1995.

Notes

[1] Jones, Mother. *The Autobiography of Mother Jones.* Chicago: Kerr, 1925, p. 4.

[2] Gorn, Elliott J. *Mother Jones: The Most Dangerous Woman in America.* New York: Hill and Wang, 2001, p. 302.

[3] Quoted in Gorn, p. 89.

[4] Jones, p. 202.

John L. Lewis (1880-1969)
President of the United Mine Workers of America (UMWA) and Founder of the Congress of Industrial Organizations (CIO)

John Llewellyn Lewis was born on February 12, 1880, in Lucas, Iowa. He was the first of seven children born to Welsh immigrants Tom Lewis and Ann (Watkins) Lewis. John's father, who worked as a coal miner, introduced him to the principles of trade unionism. His mother was a homemaker who encouraged him to read widely. He credited her influence for helping him build the extensive vocabulary and knowledge of quotations that he later showcased in his speeches.

Lewis quit school around the age of sixteen to begin working in area coal mines. In 1901 he hopped on a train headed west and spent the next four years traveling and working at mines in Montana, Utah, Colorado, Arizona, and Wyoming. In 1905 an explosion killed 236 workers at a coal mine in Wyoming. This incident, combined with the hardships he witnessed among fellow miners across the country, contributed to Lewis's lifelong dedication to the labor movement and pursuit of mine-safety legislation.

In 1907 Lewis married Myrta Edith Bell, with whom he eventually had three children. A short time later his extended family moved to Springfield, Illinois, in the middle of the state's coalfields. With help from his five younger brothers, Lewis was elected president of the local branch of the United Mine Workers of America (UMWA). His first task involved lobbying the state legislature to pass new laws to increase mine safety and provide compensation to miners who were injured on the job. Lewis's energy and dedication brought him to the attention of Samuel Gompers, president of the American Federation of Labor (AFL). Lewis served as a national organizer for the AFL from 1910 to 1916 while also continuing his work with the UMWA.

Takes Control of the UMWA

Lewis quickly moved up through the ranks of the UMWA. In 1917 he became the union's lead negotiator. During World War I, he worked closely with federal officials to help regulate mining production and maintain good labor relations. After the war ended, he successfully negotiated wage increases for miners in bituminous coalfields. In 1920, at the age of forty, Lewis took over as president of the UMWA. It was the largest and most influential union in the country at that time, with 500,000 members.

Lewis immediately took steps to solidify his control over the union. He expelled several of his political rivals, for instance, and banned radicals and Communists. His ruthless tactics alienated some union members, but his colorful personality, bold strategies, and strong public speaking skills made him a formidable presence in the labor movement. During the early 1920s he led the nation's miners in a successful five-month strike to preserve the wage gains they had won after World War I.

When the U.S. economy spiraled downward into the Great Depression, however, the mining industry declined. The UMWA faced stiff competition from non-union mine operators, and union membership dropped steadily to reach 75,000 in 1933. Lewis met with President Franklin D. Roosevelt to ask him to protect workers' right to organize as part of his New Deal package of economic relief programs. The 1935 passage of the National Labor Relations Act or Wagner Act addressed many issues of concern to the labor movement. Most importantly, it guaranteed workers' right to organize unions and bargain collectively over the terms and conditions of their employment.

Launches the CIO

The passage of the Wagner Act gave added legitimacy to the American labor movement, and Lewis took advantage of the situation. He led an all-out membership drive that succeeded in organizing 92 percent of the nation's coal miners by 1937. Lewis also launched unionization drives in other mass-production industries. His efforts helped create such major unions as the United Auto Workers (UAW) and the United Steel Workers of America (USWA).

Lewis initially tried to add the new industrial unions to the AFL, which consisted mostly of skilled craftsmen and other professionals at that time. Although Lewis had been named to the AFL's executive council in 1934, his plan to include unskilled industrial workers met with fierce resistance from other AFL leaders. During a heated debate at the AFL's 1935 national convention, Carpenters Union President William Hutcheson used an unflattering term in reference to Lewis. Lewis responded by leaping over a row of chairs and punching Hutcheson in the nose.

This violent incident deepened the divide between the AFL and the growing number of industrial unions. In 1938 Lewis resigned from the AFL and formed the Congress of Industrial Organizations (CIO), a new federation of unions from mass-production industries. As the first president of the CIO, Lewis became one of the most powerful figures in the labor movement. He inspired working Americans with rousing speeches and bold initiatives. Thanks in part to his efforts, four million workers joined unions that year.

Increases Safety and Benefits for Miners

In 1940 Lewis had a falling out with Roosevelt over the president's economic programs and foreign policy. Lewis endorsed Republican candidate Wendell Willkie for president and made a national radio speech encouraging American workers to vote Republican in that year's elections. Most workers ignored his advice, however, and instead showed their support for Roosevelt. Following this blow to his leadership stature, Lewis resigned as president of the CIO but remained head of the UMWA. In 1942 he withdrew the UMWA from the CIO.

After the United States entered World War II, most union leaders pledged not to organize labor strikes in the interest of national defense. Lewis bucked this trend in 1943, when he called a mine strike that idled half a million workers. Subsequent shortages of coal led to power outages and factory shutdowns in several industries that were vital to wartime production. Lewis's actions met with a great deal of criticism from people who felt that he and the miners were putting their own interests above that of the nation at a time of crisis. This strike action also contributed to the eventual passage of anti-labor legislation like the 1947 Taft-Hartley Act.

Once the war ended in 1945, Lewis negotiated big wage and benefit increases for miners. In fact, Lewis managed to obtain one of the first employer-paid health insurance and retirement programs ever granted to industrial workers. The UMWA Welfare and Retirement Fund provided medical and pension benefits for miners and constructed hospitals and health clinics in mining towns. In 1952 Lewis saw one of his lifelong goals become reality with the passage of the Federal Mine Safety Act.

Not all UMWA members received improved wages, benefits, and working conditions, however. Many of them, in fact, saw their jobs eliminated.

The contracts Lewis negotiated for the benefit of some miners also gave employers greater freedom to automate mining operations and close unprofitable mines. Increased mechanization and a decline in the overall mining industry due to the rise of oil use caused the number of employed miners to fall by two-thirds by 1965.

Lewis retired as president of the UMWA in 1960. Four years later he received the nation's highest civilian honor, the Presidential Medal of Freedom, from Lyndon B. Johnson. The citation described him as an "eloquent spokesman of labor who has given voice to the aspirations of the industrial workers of the country and led the cause of free trade unions within a healthy system of free enterprise." Lewis died in 1969 at his home in Alexandria, Virginia.

Sources:

Dubofsky, Melvyn, and Warren Van Tine. *John L. Lewis: A Biography.* Champaign: University of Illinois Press, 1977.

"History of John L. Lewis." Coal Mining Labor Museum, n.d. Available online at http://www.coalmining labormuseum.com/lewis.html.

"John L. Lewis." AFL-CIO, n.d. Available online at http://www.aflcio.org/aboutus/history/history /lewis.cfm.

Laslett, John H. M. *The United Mine Workers of America.* University Park, PA: Pennsylvania State University Press, 1998.

Zieger, Robert H. *John L. Lewis: Labor Leader.* New York: Twayne, 1989.

George Meany (1894-1980)
President of the American Federation of Labor-Congress of Industrial Organizations (AFL-CIO)

George Meany was born on August 16, 1894, in the Bronx section of New York City. He grew up in an Irish Catholic family. His father, Michael Meany, worked as a plumber and served as president of the local plumbers' union. The elder Meany often discussed the importance of trade unions with his son. Around 1910 George dropped out of high school and sought employment to help support his family. After completing a five-year apprenticeship under an experienced plumber, he received his plumber's certificate in 1915.

Around 1920 Meany married Eugenia McMahon, with whom he eventually had three daughters. In 1922 Meany was elected business manager of the local plumbers' union. He immediately set out to expand the union to include members from other building trades. In 1929 the Great Depression washed over American and the rest of the world, triggering massive economic upheaval. This horrible downturn crushed business owners and workers alike. But the bleak economic conditions did not stop Meany's rise through the union ranks. In 1934 he was elected president of the New York State Federation of Labor. Under his leadership, the federation became a powerful political organization that helped secure passage of several pro-labor laws, including one of the first state laws to provide unemployment insurance for workers.

In 1939 Meany was elected secretary-treasurer of the American Federation of Labor (AFL), an organization made up of labor unions representing teachers, airline pilots, firefighters, and other skilled workers. Once the United States entered World War II in 1941, Meany served on the War Labor Board and various presidential committees that helped focus American industries on wartime production. He also helped arrange wage controls in industries that were vital to the war effort, such as the automobile, shipping, railroad, and telegraph industries. After the war ended in 1945, Meany helped establish the International Confederation of Free Trade Unions. This organization sought to protect the rights of workers around the world. It also played a role in implementing the Marshall Plan, which provided U.S. assistance to help the war-torn nations of Europe rebuild their economies and infrastructure.

Becomes President of the AFL-CIO

In 1947 Meany led the AFL's opposition to the Taft-Hartley Act, which was passed by Congress over President Harry S. Truman's veto. The act placed new restrictions on the activities of labor unions. It labeled a number of common union tactics as "unfair labor practices"—such as wildcat strikes (strikes not officially sanctioned by a union), solidarity strikes (strikes called in sympathy for other workers on strike), and closed shops (workplaces that do not allow non-union employees). It also gave the federal government new strike-breaking powers in situations when a strike was determined to pose a risk to national health or safety.

Meany and other union leaders complained that the Taft-Hartley Act rolled back many of the gains made by the labor movement during the New Deal era. They also charged that the act gave too much power to employers and the government. To coordinate labor's response, Meany established the League for Political Education, which led a major effort to register, educate, and mobilize union members. This effort played an important role in helping Truman win the 1948 presidential election.

In 1952, upon the death of AFL President William Green, Meany took over as leader of the organization. He soon gained a reputation as a tough but fair president who attacked union corruption, established a code of ethical practices, and expelled radicals and Communists. He also took steps to expand the organization and increase its influence. In 1955 Meany negotiated a merger between the AFL and the Congress of Industrial Organizations (CIO), a federation of industrial labor unions led by Walter P. Reuther. Meany became president of the combined AFL-CIO. He and Reuther had frequent disagreements about the organization's direction and strategy, however, and Reuther withdrew the United Auto Workers (UAW) union from the AFL-CIO in 1968.

Makes Gains in the 1960s and 1970s

As president of the AFL-CIO, Meany was one of the leading spokesmen for the interests of working Americans throughout the social protests of the 1960s and 1970s. He supported the passage of the Social Security Act of 1965, which created Medicare to provide health care for elderly Americans, and the passage of the Occupational Safety and Health Act of 1970, which protected workers from unsafe or unhealthy working conditions. Meany also emerged as a prominent anti-Communist and a strong supporter of U.S. involvement in the Vietnam War during this time. In 1963 he received the prestigious Presidential Medal of Freedom from President Lyndon B. Johnson.

Meany stepped down as president of the AFL-CIO in 1979 and handed the reins of the organization over to Lane Kirkland. At the time of his retirement, Meany was widely hailed for effectively representing the interests of working Americans within the corridors of power in Washington, D.C. He also came under some criticism, however, for failing to inspire passion among rank-and-file union members. Critics also asserted that the AFL-CIO's ability to attract new members fell off during Meany's tenure. They pointed out that union membership declined during his long reign as head of the AFL-CIO. Defenders of Meany's record argued that this decline was mostly attributable to rising automation of industrial production and increased competition from overseas manufacturers.

Meany died on January 10, 1980, at the age of 86. Supporters argued that he had achieved his stated goal of improving the lives of working people. "The basic goal of labor will not change," Meany once declared. "It is—as it has always been, and I am sure always will be—to better the standards of life for all who work for wages and to seek decency and justice and dignity for all Americans."[1]

Sources:

Buhle, Paul. *Taking Care of Business: Samuel Gompers, George Meany, Lane Kirkland, and the Tragedy of American Labor.* Monthly Review Press, 1999.

Finke, Blythe F. *George Meany: Modern Leader of the American Federation of Labor.* Charlottesville, NY: Samhar Press, 1972.

"George Meany." AFL-CIO, n.d. Available online at http://www.aflcio.org/aboutus/history/meany.cfm.

Robinson, Archie. *George Meany and His Times: A Biography.* New York: Simon and Schuster, 1981.

Notes

[1] Robinson, Archie. *George Meany and His Times: A Biography.* New York: Simon and Schuster, 1981, p. 405.

Walter P. Reuther (1907-1970)
President of the United Auto Workers (UAW)

Walter Philip Reuther was born in Wheeling, West Virginia, on September 1, 1907. He was the second of five children born to Valentine and Anna (Stocker) Reuther. Walter's parents were German immigrants who held Socialist political views. His father was a member of the Brewery Workers union and often discussed labor issues with his children. "I was raised in a trade union family," Walter recalled. "At my father's knee we learned the philosophy of trade unionism. We got the struggles, the hopes, and the aspirations of working people every day."[1]

Reuther dropped out of Wheeling High School at the age of sixteen. He spent the next three years serving as an apprentice to a tool and die maker. He learned how to mold hardened steel into forms or dies that are used in factory machinery to stamp out metal parts. Those skills came in handy when he moved to Detroit, Michigan, in 1927 to look for work in the rapidly expanding automobile industry. Reuther quickly found a job as a die maker at the Ford Motor Company's River Rouge assembly plant. In those days, most factory workers toiled long hours in difficult or hazardous working conditions for low wages. Reuther felt as if Ford's management viewed him and other assembly-line workers as nameless, faceless, replaceable parts of its industrial operation rather than as individual human beings.

During his years at Ford, Reuther earned his high school diploma and took classes at Wayne State University. Once his younger brothers Victor and Roy joined him on campus, they formed a Socialist group with fellow students and campaigned for Socialist Party candidate Norman Thomas in the 1932 presidential election. When Reuther's political activism cost him his job at Ford, he and his brother Victor decided to take a bicycle tour of Europe. They visited nine countries, including Nazi Germany, and spent two years in the Soviet Union training workers at the Gorky automobile factory. Reuther returned to the United States in 1935. The following year he married May Wolf, a physical education teacher. They eventually had two daughters, Linda and Lisa.

Becomes a Labor Union Organizer

As soon as he returned to the United States, Reuther became an active organizer in the labor movement that was sweeping through American industry. He joined the United Auto Workers (UAW), a new labor union for workers in the automobile industry. Reuther met with leaders of several small local unions and convinced them to join forces to form one large local group within the UAW. In 1936 he represented his local group at the UAW's first national convention and was elected to the union's executive board.

In early 1937 the UAW organized a major sit-down strike against General Motors (GM), the largest and most powerful American automobile manufacturer. During this protest, thousands of GM factory workers occupied the Fisher Body assembly plant in Flint, Michigan. They halted production at the factory and refused to leave the premises until GM management officially recognized the UAW as the exclusive bargaining agent for its factory workers. After forty-four days and several violent confrontations with police and corporate security forces, the Flint Sit-Down Strike finally ended in triumph for the labor movement. GM agreed to recognize the UAW and negotiate with union leaders to increase wages and improve working conditions. The successful conclusion to the strike gave the fledgling UAW instant legitimacy on the national stage.

The UAW then turned its attention to the Ford Motor Company, which had staunchly resisted all efforts to unionize its workforce. On May 26, 1937, Reuther and three other UAW leaders stood on a bridge outside Ford's River Rouge plant handing out union pamphlets to factory workers as they arrived for their shift. Approximately forty Ford security agents confronted the UAW organizers and delivered a vicious beating. "They picked me up about eight different times and threw me down on my back on the concrete, and while I was on the ground they kicked me in the face, head, and other parts of my body," Reuther remembered. "After they kicked me for a while, one fellow would yell, 'All right, let him go now.' Then they would raise me up, hold my arms behind me, and begin to hit me some more."[2] Photographs of the violent assault appeared in newspapers across the country. Reuther gained national recognition and respect for his courage in this incident, which became known as the Battle of the Overpass. The event also provoked a barrage of negative publicity for Ford. Nonetheless, Henry Ford and his lieutenants continued to vow that they would never allow unionization in their plants. But the union continued to apply relentless pressure, and in 1941

Ford gave in and recognized the UAW as the legitimate bargaining agent for its factory workers.

Elected President of the UAW

In 1942 Reuther was elected as the first vice president of the UAW. During World War II he helped retool automobile assembly plants to produce tanks, airplanes, and other machinery to support the war effort. Reuther and other UAW leaders agreed to maintain industrial production and not organize any labor strikes while the nation was at war. In 1946, after the war ended, Reuther was elected president of the UAW. He then led union members in a 116-day strike against GM, arguing that workers deserved a greater share of the automaker's record profits. Reuther demanded that the company increase wages by 30 percent without raising the retail price of cars. He invited GM to "open its books" and prove that his request was financially unreasonable. Although the company refused to reveal its finances, GM and the UAW eventually settled on an 18 percent wage increase.

Reuther's collective bargaining successes continued in 1948. He negotiated a historic deal with GM that linked wage increases for factory workers to productivity improvements and cost-of-living expenses. The UAW eventually made similar contract arrangements with the other domestic auto companies. Over the next decade, Reuther also secured a number of other benefits that improved the lives of autoworkers, such as safety measures, grievance procedures, health insurance, retirement pensions, paid vacation time, and supplemental unemployment payments. Reuther's success in gaining benefits for workers did not always make him popular with management, and on a few occasions it put his life in danger. One night in 1948, as he was eating dinner in his kitchen, an unknown assailant fired a shotgun through the window. The blast caused serious damage to his right arm.

In 1952 Reuther became president of the Congress of Industrial Organizations (CIO), a federation of industrial labor unions that included the UAW. In 1955 he negotiated a merger with the American Federation of Labor (AFL), the nation's other major labor coalition. The head of the AFL, George Meany, became president of the combined AFL-CIO. Reuther was named second-in-command. Before long, however, Reuther became frustrated with Meany's conservative leadership style. Complaining that the organization "lacks the social vision, the dynamic thrust, the crusading spirit that should characterize the progressive modern labor movement,"[3] Reuther withdrew the UAW from the AFL-CIO in 1968.

Fights for Civil Rights and Social Justice

During the 1960s Reuther emerged as a prominent supporter of social and political protest movements that worked to improve the lives of the urban poor and end discrimination against women and minorities. He believed that labor unions should play an important role in promoting the public welfare. Reuther fought for programs to alleviate poverty, renew urban areas, build low-income housing, protect the environment, promote universal health care, and secure civil rights. Reuther's contributions to the fight for African-American equality earned him a coveted spot on the podium next to Martin Luther King Jr. when the civil rights leader made his famous "I Have a Dream" speech during the 1963 March on Washington.

Reuther also continued to work to obtain a higher standard of living for UAW members. As part of this mission, he oversaw the construction of an education and recreation center for union members in northern Michigan. On May 9, 1970, Reuther was on his way to this facility in a private plane when it crashed in a rainstorm near Pellston, Michigan. Everyone on board was killed, including Reuther and his wife, May.

By the time of his death, Reuther had served as president of the UAW for twenty-five years. Under his leadership, the union became one of the largest and most influential labor organizations in the United States, with more than 1.5 million members. Even people who sat across from Reuther at the bargaining table acknowledged his contributions to increasing the status of industrial workers. "Walter Reuther was an extraordinarily effective advocate of labor's interest," said Henry Ford II of Ford Motor Company. "His tough-minded dedication, his sense of social concern, his selflessness and his eloquence all mark him as a central figure in the development of modern industrial history."[4] In 1995 Reuther was awarded the Presidential Medal of Freedom—the nation's highest civilian honor—in recognition of his accomplishments.

Sources:

Barnard, John. *Walter Reuther and the Rise of the Autoworkers.* Boston: Little, Brown, 1983.

Bluestone, Irving. "Walter Reuther: Working-Class Hero." *Time,* December 7, 1998. Available online at http://www.time.com/time/magazine/article/0,9171,989782,00.html.

Featherstone, Thomas. "No Greater Calling: The Life of Walter Reuther." Detroit: Walter P. Reuther Library, Wayne State University, n.d. Available online at http://reuther100.wayne.edu/bio.php.

Lichtenstein, Nelson. *Walter Reuther: The Most Dangerous Man in Detroit.* New York: Basic Books, 1995.

Smith, Mike. "Labor of Love." *Michigan History for Kids Magazine,* Summer 2003, p. 8.

"Walter Reuther (1907-1970)." AFL-CIO Labor History Biographies, n.d. Available online at http ://www.aflcio.org/aboutus/history/history/reuther.cfm.

Notes

[1] Quoted in Carew, Anthony. *Walter Reuther.* Manchester University Press, 1993, p. 2.

[2] Quoted in Lichtenstein, Nelson. *Walter Reuther: The Most Dangerous Man in Detroit.* New York: Basic Books, 1995, p. 82.

[3] Quoted in Featherstone, Thomas. "No Greater Calling: The Life of Walter Reuther." Detroit: Walter P. Reuther Library, Wayne State University, n.d. Available online at http://reuther100.wayne.edu /bio.php.

[4] Quoted in Featherstone, "No Greater Calling."

PRIMARY SOURCES

A Textile Mill Worker Mourns the Hardships of the Factory System, 1845

As the Industrial Revolution spread across America in the nineteenth century, many factories became notorious for mistreating and taking advantage of workers. This grim state of affairs triggered the first rumblings of unionization in numerous industries—including textiles, which was one of the first manufacturing sectors to be transformed by industrialization. By the 1840s, in fact, efforts to organize the New England-based industry's workforce, which was composed primarily of young single women, were underway in several cities.

These campaigns to enlist textile workers in the union cause and boost public support for social reforms made extensive use of pamphlets and other propaganda. In the mid-1840s, for example, a group called the Female Labor Reform Association published a series of anonymously written "Factory Tracts" that sought to expose the ways in which women textile workers were being exploited by factory owners. This document, originally published in 1845 by an "operative" or worker known only as Amelia, was the first of these "Factory Tracts."

For the purpose of illustration, let us go with that light-hearted, joyous young girl who is about for the first time to leave the home of her childhood; that home around which clusters so many beautiful and holy associations, pleasant memories, and quiet joys; to leave, too, a mother's cheerful smile, a father's care and protection; and wend her way toward this famed "city of spindles," this promised land of the imagination, in whose praise she has doubtless heard so much.

Let us trace her progress during her first year's residence, and see whether she indeed realizes those golden prospects which have been held out to her. Follow her now as she enters that large gloomy looking building—she is in search of employment, and has been told that she might here obtain an eligible situation. She is sadly wearied with her journey, and withal somewhat annoyed by the noise, confusion, and strange faces all around her. So, after a brief conversation with the overseer, she concludes to accept the first situation which offers; and reserving to herself a sufficient portion of time in which to obtain the necessary rest after her unwonted exertions, and the gratification of a stranger's curiosity regarding the place in which she is now to make her future home, she retires to her boarding house, to arrange matters as much to her mind as may be. The intervening time passes rapidly away, and she soon finds herself once more within the confines of that close noisy apartment, and is forthwith installed in her new situation—first, however, premising that she has been sent to the Counting-room, and receives therefrom a Regulation paper, containing the rules by which she must be governed while in their employ; and lo! Here is the beginning of mischief; for in addition to the tyranous and oppressive rules which meet her astonished eyes, she finds herself compelled to remain for the space of twelve months in the very place she then occupies, however reasonable and just cause of complaint might be hers, or however strong the wish for dismission; thus, in fact, constituting herself a slave, a very slave to the caprices of him for whom she labors. Several incidents coming to the knowledge of the writer, might be somewhat interesting in this connection, as tending to show the prejudicial influence exerted upon the interests of the operative by this unjust requisition. The first is of a lady who has been engaged as an operative for a number of years, and recently entered a weaving room on the Massachusetts Corporation; the overseer having assured her previous to her entrance, that she should receive the sum of $2.25 per week, exclusive of board; which she finding it impossible to do, appealed to the Counting-room for a line enabling her to engage elsewhere, but it was peremptorily refused.

The next is of a more general bearing, concerning quite a number of individuals employed on the Lawrence Corporation, where the owners have recently erected and put in motion a new mill, at the same time stopping one of the old, in which said persons were employed. Now as they did not voluntarily leave their situations, but were discharged therefrom on account of suspension of operations by the company; they had an undoubted right to choose their own place of labor; and as the work in the new mill is vastly more laborious, and the wages less than can be obtained in many parts of the city, they signified their wish to go elsewhere, but are insolently told that they shall labor there or not at all: and will not be released until their year has expired, when if they can *possibly* find *no* further excuse for delay, they *may* deign to bestow upon them what is in common parlance termed, a "regular discharge;" thus enabling them to pass from one prison house to another. Concerning this precious document, it is only necessary to say, that it very precisely reminds one of that which the dealers in human flesh at the South are wont to give and receive as the transfer of one piece of property from one owner to another.

Now, reader, what think you? is not this the height of the beautiful? and are not we operatives an ungrateful set of creatures that we do not properly appreciate, and be highly thankful for such unparalleled generosity on the part of our employers!

But to return to our toiling Maiden,—the next beautiful feature which she discovers in this *glorious* system is, the long number of hours which she is obliged to spend in the above named close, unwholesome apartment. It is not enough, that like the poor peasant of Ireland, or the Russian serf who labors from sun to sun, but during one half of the year, she must still continue to toil on, long after Nature's lamp has ceased to lend its aid—nor will even this suffice to satisfy the grasping avarice of her employer; for she is also through the winter months required to rise, partake of her morning meal, and be at her station in the mill, while the sun is yet sleeping behind the eastern hills; thus working on an average, at least twelve hours and three fourths per day, exclusive of the time allotted for her hasty meals, which is in winter simply one half hour at noon,—in the spring is allowed the same at morn, and during the summer is added 15 minutes to the half hour at noon. Then too, when she is at last released from her wearisome day's toil, still may she not depart in peace. No! her footsteps must be dogged to see that they do not stray beyond the corporation limits, and she *must*, whether she will or no, be subjected to the manifold inconveniences of a large crowded boarding-house, where too, the price paid for her accommodation is so utterly insignificant, that it will not ensure to her the common comforts of life; she is obliged to sleep in a small comfortless, half ventilated apartment containing some half a dozen occupants each, but no matter, *she is an operative*—it is all well enough for her; there is no "abuse" about it; no, indeed; so think our employers,— but do we think so? time will show. Here, too, comes up a case which strikingly illustrates the petty tyranny of the employer. A little girl, some 12 or 13 years of age, the daughter of a poor widow, dependent on her daily toil for a livelihood, worked on one of the Corporations, boarding with her mother; who dying left her to the care of an aunt, residing but a few steps from the Corporation—but the poor creature all unqualified as she was, to provide for her own wants, was *compelled* to leave her home and the motherly care bestowed upon her, and enter one of these same large crowded boarding-houses. We do but give the facts in this case and they need no comment for every one must see the utter heartlessness which prompted such conduct toward a mere child.

Reader will you pronounce this a mere fancy sketch, written for the sake of effect? It is not so. It is a real picture of "Factory life;" nor is it one half so bad as might truthfully and justly have been drawn. But it has been asked, and doubtless will be again, why, if these evils are so aggravating, have they been so long and so peacefully borne? Ah! and why have they? It is a question well worthy of our consideration, and we would call upon every operative in *our* city, aye, throughout the length and breadth of the land, to awake from the lethargy which has fallen upon them, and assert and maintain their rights. We will call upon you for action—*united and immediate action*. But, says one, let us wait till we are stronger. In the language of one of old, we ask, when shall we be stronger? Will it be the next week, or the next year? Will it be when we are reduced to the servile condition of the poor operatives of England? for verily we shall be and that right soon, if matters be suffered to remain as they are. Says another, how shall we act? we are but one amongst a thousand, what shall we do that our influence may be felt in this vast multitude? We answer, there is in this city an Association called the Female Labor Reform Association, having for its professed object, the amelioration of the condition of the operative. Enrolled upon its records are the names of five hundred members—come then, and add thereto five hundred or rather five thousand more, and in the strength of our united influence we will soon show these *drivelling* cotton lords, this mushroom aristocracy of New England, who so arrogantly aspire to lord it over God's heritage, that our rights cannot be trampled upon with impunity; that we WILL no longer submit to that arbitrary power which has for the last ten years been so abundantly exercised over us.

One word ere we close, to the hardy independent yeomanry and mechanics, among the Granite Hills of New Hampshire, the woody forests of Maine, the cloud capped mountains of Vermont, and the busy, bustling towns of the old Bay State—ye! who have daughters and sisters toiling in these sickly prison-houses which are scattered far and wide over each of these States, we appeal to you for aid in this matter. Do you ask how that aid can be administered? We answer through the Ballot Box. Yes! if you have one spark of sympathy for our condition, carry it *there*, and see to it that you send to preside in the Councils of each Commonwealth, men who have hearts as well as heads, souls as well as bodies; men who will watch zealously over the interests of the laborer in every department; who will protect him by the strong arm of the law from the encroachments of arbitrary power; who will see that he is not deprived of those rights and privileges which God and Nature have bestowed upon him—yes,

From every rolling river,
From mountain, vale and plain,

We call on you to deliver
Us, from the tyrant's chain:
And shall we call in vain? we trust not. More anon.
AMELIA.

Source: Amelia. "Some of the Beauties of Our Factory System—Otherwise, Lowell Slavery." In *Factory Tracts: Factory Life as It Is. By an Operative.* Lowell, MA: Female Labor Reform Association, 1845, pp. 4–7.

The Knights of Labor Explain Their Cause and Issue Demands, 1878

One of the first truly national labor unions in the United States was the Knights of Labor. Founded by a group of Philadelphia tailors in 1869, the Knights managed to survive the economic turmoil of the 1870s. By 1878, when the union approved a formal constitution at its general assembly in Rochester, New York, the Knights were poised for a decade of steady growth under the leadership of Terence Powderly. Following is the preamble from the 1878 constitution, which lays out the philosophy and priorities of Powderly and his fellow Knights.

The recent alarming development and aggression of aggregated wealth, which, unless checked, will invariably lead to the pauperization and hopeless degradation of the toiling masses, render it imperative, if we desire to enjoy the blessings of life, that a check should be placed upon its power and upon unjust accumulation, and a system adopted which will secure to the laborer the fruits of his toil; and as this much-desired object can only be accomplished by the thorough unification of labor, and the united efforts of those who obey the divine injunction that "In the sweat of thy brow shalt thou eat bread," we have formed the [Knights of Labor] with a view of securing the organization and direction, by co-operative effort, of the power of the industrial classes; and we submit to the world the objects sought to be accomplished by our organization, calling upon all who believe in securing "the greatest good to the greatest number" to aid and assist us:—

I. To bring within the folds of organization every department of productive industry, making knowledge a stand-point for action, and industrial and moral worth, not wealth, the true standard of individual and national greatness.

II. To secure to the toilers a proper share of the wealth that they create; more of the leisure that rightfully belongs to them; more societary advantages; more of the benefits, privileges, and emoluments of the world; in a word, all those rights and privileges necessary to make them capable of enjoying, appreciating, defending, and perpetuating the blessings of good government.

III. To arrive at the true condition of the producing masses in their educational, moral, and financial condition, by demanding from the various governments the establishment of bureaus of Labor Statistics.

IV. The establishment of co-operative institutions, productive and distributive.

V. The reserving of the public lands—the heritage of the people—for the actual settler;—not another acre for railroads or speculators.

VI. The abrogation of all laws that do not bear equally upon capital and labor, the removal of unjust technicalities, delays, and discriminations in the administration of justice, and the adopting of measures providing for the health and safety of those engaged in mining, manufacturing, or building pursuits.

VII. The enactment of laws to compel chartered corporations to pay their employees weekly, in full, for labor performed during the preceding week, in the lawful money of the country.

VIII. The enactment of laws giving mechanics and laborers a first lien on their work for their full wages.

IX. The abolishment of the contract system on national, State, and municipal work.

X. The substitution of arbitration for strikes, whenever and wherever employers and employees are willing to meet on equitable grounds.

XI. The prohibition of the employment of children in workshops, mines and factories before attaining their fourteenth year.

XII. To abolish the system of letting out by contract the labor of convicts in our prisons and reformatory institutions.

XIII. To secure for both sexes equal pay for equal work.

XIV. The reduction of the hours of labor to eight per day, so that the laborers may have more time for social enjoyment and intellectual improvement, and be enabled to reap the advantages conferred by the labor-saving machinery which their brains have created.

XV. To prevail upon governments to establish a purely national circulating medium, based upon the faith and resources of the nation, and issued directly to the people, without the intervention of any system of banking corporations, which money shall be a legal tender in payment of all debts, public or private.

Source: Preamble to the Constitution of the Knights of Labor, 1878. In Powderly, T.V. *Thirty Years of Labor, 1859-1889.* Columbus, OH: Excelsior, 1889, pp. 243-45.

Eugene Debs Asks "What Can We Do for Working People?" 1890

Labor unions began to emerge as a significant part of America's economic and social landscape in the late nineteenth century. Organizations such as the Knights of Labor came to prominence at this time, as did legendary union organizers like Eugene Debs. The following essay was written by Debs in 1890, a few years before the founding of the American Railway Union (in 1893) and the events of the Pullman Strike (1894) made him a national figure. But Debs returned to the themes of this essay again and again over the course of his career.

In one form or another certain persons are continually asking, "What can we do, or, What can be done for working people?" Why should such a question be asked at all in the United States? What gives rise to it? Are there circumstances and conditions warranting such an interrogatory? Who propounds it?

In old slave times there were men who counted their human chattels by the hundred, and the question was common among them, "What can we do for these people?" They said, "by virtue of the mysterious ways of providence these descendents of Ham have been committed to our care. It is a great responsibility," and some of the more pious owners of "these people" thought that they would have to give an account at the Day of Judgment for the way they treated "these people." But the slaves were kept at work raising cotton, sugar, tobacco, peanuts, hemp, etc. They went on multiplying. The slave whip, the slave pens and the slave blocks maintained their places, and the prices of "niggers" fluctuated little. The "nigger," male or female, was a valuable piece of property, and something had to be done for him. What? Simply clothe, feed and shelter him. Keep him at work. If he was refractory, whip him; if funds were wanted, sell him. The question, what can we do for "these people?" was easily answered. The slave owner owned his labor—owned his workingmen. The slave market was the *labor market*. The "labor market" was never over-stocked. A "nigger" would always sell for something.

Negro slavery has been abolished in the United States, but according to some writers on labor questions we still have the "labor market." And now the question is asked "up North" as well as "down South," continually, by certain persons, in a kind of a slobbering, deprecatory way, "What can we do, or, What can be done for working people?" In religious circles, in the pulpit, the question is asked, "What can be done to get nearer working people?" Is the question answered by building palatial church edifices, for the display of pomp and pride and fashion? Is it answered by paying "fat salaries," and to raise the funds sell the seats to the highest bidder and institute an aristocracy of piety?

Philanthropists of a certain type ask, "What can be done for working people?" and recommend soup houses, free baths, and more stringent laws against idleness and tramping, together with improved machinery in penitentiaries.

Another class devote time and investigation to diet, to show if wages decline that a man can live on ten cents a day and keep his revolting soul within his wretched body.

Another class, in answering the question, "What can we do for working people?" reply by saying, "We will organize an Insurance Bureau which shall insure workingmen against accident, sickness and death. We will supply them with medicine, doctors and hospitals, taking so much from their wages to maintain the Bureau, and then, by compelling them to sign a contract which virtually reduces them to chattels, and makes them a part of our machinery, we will permit them to work for such pay as we choose to determine."

Another class answer the question, "What can we do for working people?" by telling them that unless they consent to abandon their labor organizations, absolve themselves from all obligations to such organizations, so far as they are concerned they shall have no work at all.

There are others, still, who discuss schemes for doing great and good things for working people, excepting, so far as it has come under the notice of the writer, to pay fair, honest wages.

This whole business of doing something for working people is disgusting and degrading to the last degree. It is not desirable to deny that in some quarters the question is asked honestly, but in such cases it is always in order to manifest pity for the questioner. He is not inconvenienced by a surplus of brains. The question, "What can we do for working people?" as a general proposition, finds its resemblance in a question that might be asked by the owner of a sheep ranch, "What can I do for these sheep?" The reply would be, doubtless, "shear them." The ranch man takes care of the sheep that he may shear them, and it will be found that the men who ask with so much pharisaical solicitude, "What can we do for working men?" are the very ones who shear them the closest when opportunity offers—strip them of everything of value that they may the more easily subjugate them by necessities of cold and hunger and nakedness, degrade and brutalize them to a degree that they become as fixed in their servitude as the wheels, cogs, cranks and pins in the machinery they purchase and operate.

The real question to be propounded is, "What can workingmen do for themselves?" The answer is ready. They can do all things required, if they are independent, self-respecting, self-reliant men.

Workingmen can organize. Workingmen can combine, federate, unify, cooperate, harmonize, act in concert. This done, workingmen could control governmental affairs. They could elect honest men to office. They could make wise constitutions, enact just laws and repeal vicious laws. By acting together they could overthrow monopolies and trusts. They could squeeze the water out of stocks, and decree that dividends shall be declared only upon cash investments. They could make the cornering of the food products of the country a crime, and send the scoundrels guilty of the crime to the penitentiary. Such things are not vagaries. They are not Utopian dreams. They are practical. They are honest, they are things of good report.

Workingmen are in the majority. They have the most votes. In this God favored land, where the ballot is all powerful, peaceful revolutions can be achieved. Wrongs can be crushed—sent to their native hell, and the right can be enthroned by workingmen acting together, pulling together.

What can workingmen do for themselves? They can teach capitalists that they do not want and will not accept their guardianship; that they are capable of self-management, and that they simply want fair pay for an honest day's work, and this done, "honors are easy." Fidelity to obligation is not a one-sided affair. Mutual respect is not the offspring of arrogance. There may have been a time when it was proper for the Southern slave owner to ask himself, "What can I do to better the condition of my slaves?" He owned them, they were his property; he controlled their destiny. He made them work as he did his cattle, mules and horses, and appropriated all their earnings. Their children were his property as were the calves and colts of his cows and mares. But there never was a time beyond the dark boundary line of slavery when an employer of American workingmen could ask himself such a question without offering a degrading insult to every self-respecting workingman, and when a workingman hears it or anything like it and his cheek does not burn with righteous indignation he may know that he is on the road to subjugation, and if there exists a more humiliating spectacle within the boundaries of all the zones that belt the earth, what is it?

At every turn the question recurs, "What can workingmen do for themselves?" The question demands an answer, and unbidden a thousand are ready. We have not space for them. Let each workingman answer for himself. For one, we say the workingman can educate himself. He can read, study, and vote. He can improve his time and perfect his skill. He can see as clearly as others coming events, and prepare for their advent.

Source: Debs, Eugene V. "What Can We Do for Working People?" *Locomotive Firemen's Magazine,* vol. 14, no. 4, April 1890, pp. 291-293.

Samuel Gompers Answers the Question, "What Does Labor Want?" 1893

In 1886 the American Federation of Labor (AFL) was established under the guidance of Samuel Gompers, a London-born cigar maker and dedicated unionist. Under Gompers's leadership, the AFL added unions at a rapid rate, and by the 1890s it was the most important labor organization in the country. In the following excerpt from an 1893 address to fellow labor activists, Gompers portrays the AFL in particular—and organized labor in general—as a perfectly reasonable response to decades of mistreatment at the hands of America's capitalist class. But he also takes special care to assure the American public that the labor movement "entertains no desire for revenge or retaliation" against the nation's ruling class.

The separation between the capitalistic class and the laboring mass is not so much a difference in industrial rank as it is a difference in social status, placing the laborers in a position involving a degradation of mind and body.

This distinction, scarcely noticeable in the United States before the previous generation, rapidly became more and more marked, increasing day by day, until at length it has widened into a veritable chasm—economic, social, and moral. On each side of this seemingly impassable chasm, we see the hostile camps of rich and poor. On one side, a class in possession of all the tools and means of labor; on the other, an immense mass begging for the opportunity to labor. In the mansion, the soft notes betokening ease and security; in the tenement, the stifled wail of drudgery and poverty. The arrogance of the rich ever mounting in proportion to the debasement of the poor.

From across the chasm we hear the old familiar drone of the priests of Mammon [money], called "political economists." The words of the song they sing are stolen from the vocabulary of science, but the chant itself is the old barbaric lay. It tells us that the present absolute domination of wealth is the result of material and invariable laws, and counsels the laborers, whom they regard as ignorant and misguided, to patiently submit to the natural operations of the immutable law of "supply and demand." The laborers reply: They say that the political economists never learned sufficient science to know the difference between the operation of a natural law and the law on petty larceny. The day is past when the laborers could be cajoled or humbugged by the sacred chickens of the augers, or by the bogus laws of the political economists....

The laborers know that the capitalist class had its origin in force and fraud, that it has maintained and extended its brutal sway, more or less directly through the agency of specified legislation, most ferocious and barbarous, but always in cynical disregard of all laws save its own arbitrary will.

The first things to be recognized in a review of the capitalistic system are that the possessors of the tools and means of labor have not used their power to organize industry so much as to organize domestic and international industrial war, and that they have not used the means in their possession to produce utilities so much as to extract profits. The production of profits, instead of the production of honest goods, being the primary and constant object of the capitalistic system. We have a waste of labor appalling in its recklessness and inhumanity, a misuse of capital that is really criminal and a social condition of cheerless drudgery and hopeless poverty, of sickening apprehension and fathomless degradation almost threatening the continuance of civilization.

The state of industrial anarchy produced by the capitalist system is first strongly illustrated in the existence of a class of wealthy social parasites; those who do no work, never did any work, and never intended to work. This class of parasites devours incomes derived from many sources; from the stunted babies employed in the mills, mines, and factories, to the lessees of the gambling halls and the profits of fashionable brothels; from the lands which the labor of others has made valuable; from royalties on coal and other minerals beneath the surface, the rent paying all cost of the houses many times over and the houses coming back to those who never paid for them. Then we have the active capitalists—those engaged in business. This number must be divided into two classes; the first consisting of those legitimately using their capital in the production of utilities and honest goods. The second, those misusing their capital in the production of "bogus" imitations of luxuries; of adulterations, and of useless goods, the miserable makeshifts specially produced for the consumption of underpaid workers. With this "bogus" class must be included not only the jerry builders and the shoddy clothiers, but also the quack doctors and the shyster lawyers, also the mass of insurance and other agents and middlemen. Coming to the laborers, we must regard them not only according to their technical divisions as agricultural, mechanical, commercial, literary and domestic, with numerous subdivisions, but also as economically divided in three classes — those engaged in the production of utilities, those engaged in all other pursuits, and those constituting the general "reserve army" of labor....

While failing to protect society in its consumptive capacity, the capitalist class has shamed and degraded society in its productive capacity.

It has accomplished this result by establishing alternating periods of enervating idleness and debilitating overwork, by undermining the very foundation of society, the family life of the workers, in reducing the wages of the adult male workers below the cost of family maintenance and then employing both sexes of all ages to compete against each other.

> "Our fathers are praying for pauper pay.
> Our mothers with death's kiss are white;
> Our sons are the rich man's serfs by day,
> Our daughters his slaves by night."

And finally, by refusing to recognize the workers in a corporate capacity, and by invoking the collusion of their dependents, the judges and the legislators, to place the organized outside the pale of the law.

Nevertheless, in spite of all opposition, the Trade Unions have grown until they have become a power that none can hope to annihilate.

To-day modern society is beginning to regard the Trade Unions as the only hope of civilization; to regard them as the only power capable of evolving order out of the social chaos. But will [organized labor's] demand be regarded or heeded before it is too late? Let us hope so. The Trade Unions having a thorough knowledge of the origin and development of the capitalist class, entertains no desire for revenge or retaliation. The Trade Unions have deprecated the malevolent and unjust spirit with which they have had to contend in their protests and struggles against the abuse of the capitalist system, yet while seeking justice have not permitted their movement to become acrid by a desire for revenge. Their methods were always conservative, their steps evolutionary.

One of the greatest impediments to a better appreciation by the capitalists of the devoted efforts of the Trade Unions to establish harmony in the industrial relations, has been the perverted view taken by capitalists in regarding their capital as essentially if not absolutely their own; whereas, the Trade Unions, taking a more comprehensive and purer view, regard all capital, large and small, as the fruits of labor economics and discoveries, inventions and institutions of many generations of laborers and capitalists, of theoreticians and practitioners, practically as indivisible as a living man....

166

In order to understand the wants of labor, it is essential to conceive the hypothesis upon which the claims are based, hence the necessity of presenting the foregoing.

What does labor want? It wants the earth and the fullness thereof. There is nothing too precious, there is nothing too beautiful, too lofty, too ennobling, unless it is within the scope and comprehension of labor's aspirations and wants. But to be more specific: The expressed demands of labor are, first and foremost, a reduction of the hours of daily labor to eight hours today, fewer to-morrow.

Is labor justified in making this demand? Let us examine the facts: Within the past twenty-five years more inventions and discoveries have been made in the method of producing wealth than in the entire history of the world before. Steam power has been employed on the most extensive scale. The improvement of tools, the consequent division and subdivision of labor; and the force of electricity, so little known a few years ago, is now applied to an enormous extent. As a result the productivity of the toiler with these new improved machines and forces has increased so manifold as to completely overshadow the product of the joint masses of past ages. Every effort, every ingenious device has been utilized to cultivate the greater productivity of the worker.

The fact that in the end the toilers must be the great body of the consumers, has been given little or no consideration at all. The tendency to employ the machines continuously (the worker has been made part of the machines) and the direction has been in the line of endeavoring to make the wealth producers work longer hours.

On the other hand, the organized labor movement, the Trade Unions, have concentrated all their forces upon the movement to reduce the hours of daily toil not only as has been often said to lighten the burdens of drudgery and severe toil, but also to give the great body of the people more time, more opportunity, and more leisure, in order to create and increase their consumptive power; in other words, to relieve the choked and glutted condition of industry and commerce....

Millions of willing heads, hands, and hearts are ready to frame and to fashion the fabrics and supply the necessities as well as the desires of the people. There are hundreds of thousands of our fellow men and women who can not find the opportunity to employ their powers, their brain and brawn, to satisfy their commonest and barest necessities to sustain life. In every city and town of this broad land of plenty, gaunt figures, hungry men, and women with blanched faces, and children having the mark of premature age, and emaciated conditions indelibly impressed upon their countenances, stalk through the streets and highways. It does not require a philanthropist, nor even a humanitarian, to evidence deep concern or to give deep thought, in order to arrive at the conclusion that in the midst of plenty, such results are both unnatural and wrong. The ordinary man may truly inquire why it is that the political economist answers our demand for work by saying that the law of supply and demand, from which they say there is no relief, regulates these conditions. Might we not say fails to regulate them? …

We demand a reduction of the hours of labor, which would give a due share of work and wages to the reserve army of labor and eliminate many of the worst abuses of the industrial system now filling our poor houses and jails.…

Labor demands and insists upon the exercise of the right to organize for self and mutual protection. The toilers want the abrogation of all laws discriminating against them in the exercise of those functions which make our organizations in the economic struggle a factor and not a farce.

That the lives and limbs of the wage-workers shall be regarded as sacred as those of all others of our fellow human beings; that an injury or destruction of either by reason of negligence or maliciousness of another, shall not leave him without redress simply because he is a wageworker. We demand equality before the law, in fact as well as in theory.

The right to appear by counsel guaranteed by the Constitution of our country is one upon which labor is determined.… The court our counsels file their briefs in and make their pleas for justice, right, and equality, are in the offices of the employers. The denial to labor of the right to be heard by counsel—their committees—is a violation of the spirit of a fundamental principle of our Republic.

And by no means the least demand of the Trade Unions is for adequate wages.

The importance of this demand is not likely to be under estimated. Adam Smith says: "It is but equity that they who feed, clothe, and lodge the whole body of the people, should have such a share of the produce of their labor as to be themselves tolerably well fed, clothed, and lodged." But the Trade Unions' demand is for better pay than that which Adam Smith deemed equitable. The Trade Unions, taking normal conditions as its point of view, regards the workman as the producer of the wealth of the world, and demands that wages (as long as the wage system may last) shall be sufficient to enable him to support his family in a manner consistent with existing civilization, and all that is required for maintaining and improving physical and mental health and the self respect of human beings; render our lives while working as safe and healthful as modern science demonstrates it is possible; give us better homes—just as potent a cry to-day as when Dickens voiced the yearnings of the people a generation ago; save our children in their infancy from being forced into the maelstrom of wage slavery; see to it that they are not dwarfed in body and mind, or brought to a premature death by early drudgery; and give them the sunshine of the school and playground instead of the factory, the mine, and the workshop.

We want more school houses and less jails; more books and less arsenals; more learning and less vice; more constant work and less crime; more leisure and less greed; more justice and less revenge; in fact, more of the opportunities to cultivate our better natures, to make manhood more noble, womanhood more beautiful, and childhood more happy and bright.

These, in brief, are the primary demands made by the Trade Unions in the name of labor.

These are the demands made by labor upon modern society, and in their consideration is involved the fate of civilization; for

> There is a moving of men like the sea in its might.
> The grand and resistless uprising of labor;
> The banner it carries is justice and right,
> It aims not the musket, it draws not the sabre.

> But the sound of its tread, o'er the graves of the dead,
> Shall startle the world and fill despots with dread;
> For 'tis sworn that the land of the Fathers shall be
> The home of the brave and the land of the free.

Source: Gompers, Samuel. "What Does Labor Want?" An address before the International Labor Congress, August 28, 1893. Reprinted in *Lowell: A City of Spindles.* Lowell (Mass.) Trades and Labor Council. Lowell, MA: Lawler, 1900, pp. 201-211.

Clarence Darrow Defends Unions in the "Trial of the Century," 1907

In 1907 America was spellbound by the murder trial of "Big Bill" Haywood, who had been charged with ordering the assassination of former Idaho governor Frank Steunenberg two years earlier. By the time Haywood was brought to trial on May 9, 1907, he ranked as one of the country's most controversial public figures. An avowed labor radical and co-founder of the Industrial Workers of the World, Haywood was known not only for his Socialist beliefs, but also for his claims that violence, sabotage, and other forms of "direct action" were legitimate tools for labor to use in its struggles against the owners of the country's mines and factories.

Haywood was represented at the trial by famed defense attorney Clarence Darrow, a strong union supporter. As the trial progressed, much of the prosecution's case fell apart. Darrow used his closing argument—excerpted here—to argue that the true target of prosecutors was not Haywood, but rather the labor movement as a whole. This speech is one of the most famous of Darrow's entire career. On July 29, the jury announced its verdict after nine hours of deliberations: Haywood was acquitted of all charges. The only person who was found guilty of murdering Steunenberg was Harry Orchard, the admitted assassin. He was initially sentenced to death, but his sentence was later commuted to life in prison.

Let me tell you, gentlemen, if you destroy the labor unions in this country, you destroy liberty when you strike the blow, and you would leave the poor bound and shackled and helpless to do the bidding of the rich.… It would take this country back … to the time when there were masters and slaves.

I don't mean to tell this jury that labor organizations do no wrong. I know them too well for that. They do wrong often, and sometimes brutally; they are sometimes cruel; they are often unjust; they are frequently corrupt.… But I am here to say that in a great cause these labor organizations, despised and weak and outlawed as they generally are, have stood for the poor, they have stood for the weak, they have stood for every human law that was ever placed upon the statute books. They stood for human life, they stood for the father who was bound down by his task, they stood for the wife, threatened to be taken from the home to work by his side, and they have stood for the little child who was also taken to work in their places—that the rich could grow richer still, and they have fought for the right of the little one, to give him a little of life, a little comfort while he is young. I don't care how many wrongs they committed, I don't care how many crimes these weak, rough, rugged, unlettered men who often know no other power but the brute force of their strong right arm, who find themselves bound and confined and impaired whichever way they turn, who look up and worship the god of might as the only god that they know—I don't care how often they fail, how many brutalities they are guilty of. I know their cause is just.

I hope that the trouble and the strife and the contention have been endured. Through brutality and bloodshed and crime has come the progress of the human race. I know they may be wrong in this battle or that, but in the great, long struggle they are right and they are eternally right, and that they are working for the poor and the weak. They are working to give more liberty to the man, and I want to say to you, gentlemen of the jury, you Idaho farmers removed from the trade unions, removed from the men who work in industrial affairs, I want to say that if it had not been for the trade unions of the world, for the trade unions of England, for the trade unions of Europe, the trade unions of America, you today would be serfs of Europe, instead of free men sitting upon a jury to try one of your peers. The cause of these men is right....

I have known Haywood. I have known him well and I believe in him. I do believe in him. God knows it would be a sore day to me if he should ascend the scaffold; the sun would not shine or the birds would not sing on that day for me. It would be a sad day indeed if any calamity should befall him. I would think of him, I would think of his mother, I would think of his babes, I would think of the great cause that he represents. It would be a sore day for me.

But, gentlemen, he and his mother, his wife and his children are not my chief concern in this case. If you should decree that he must die, ten thousand men will work down in the mines to send a portion of the proceeds of their labor to take care of that widow and those orphan children, and a million people throughout the length and the breadth of the civilized world will send their messages of kindness and good cheer to comfort them in their bereavement. It is not for them I plead.

Other men have died, other men have died in the same cause in which Bill Haywood has risked his life, men strong with devotion, men who love liberty, men who love their fellow men have raised their voices in defense of the poor, in defense of justice, have made their good fight and have met death on the scaffold, on the rack, in the flame and they will meet it again until the world grows old and gray. Bill Haywood is no better than the rest. He can die if die he needs, he can die if this jury decrees it; but, oh, gentlemen, don't think for a moment that if you hang him you will crucify the labor movement of the world.

Don't think that you will kill the hopes and the aspirations and the desires of the weak and the poor, you men, unless you people who are anxious for this blood—are you so blind as to believe that liberty will die when he is dead? Do you think there are no brave hearts and no other strong arms, no other devoted souls who will risk their life in that great cause which has demanded martyrs in every age of this world? There are others, and these others will come to take his place, will come to carry the banner where he could not carry it.

Gentlemen, it is not for him alone that I speak. I speak for the poor, for the weak, for the weary, for that long line of men who in darkness and despair have borne the labors of the human race. The eyes of the world are upon you, upon you twelve men of Idaho tonight. Wherever the English language is spoken, or wherever any foreign tongue known to the civilized world is spoken, men are talking and wondering and dreaming about the verdict of these twelve men that I see before me now. If you kill him your act will be applauded by many. If you should decree Bill Haywood's death, in the great railroad offices of our great cities men will applaud your names. If you decree his death, amongst the spiders of Wall Street will go up paeans of praise for those twelve good men and true who killed Bill Haywood. In every bank in the world, where men hate Haywood because he fights for the poor and against the accursed system upon which the favored live and grow rich and fat—from all those you will receive blessings and unstinted praise.

But if your verdict should be "Not Guilty," there are still those who will reverently bow their heads and thank these twelve men for the life and the character they have saved. Out on the broad prairies where men toil with their hands, out on the wide ocean where men are tossed and buffeted on the waves, through our mills and factories, and down deep under the earth, thousands of men and of women and children, men who labor, men who suffer, women and children weary with care and toil, these men and these women and these children will kneel tonight and ask their God to guide your judgment. These men and these women and these little children, the poor, the weak, and the suffering of the world will stretch out their hands to this jury, and implore you to save Haywood's life.

Source: "Excerpt from Darrow's Summation in the Haywood Trial." *Famous American Trials: Bill Haywood Trial, 1907.* University of Missouri-Kansas City Law School. Available online at http://www.law.umkc.edu/faculty/projects/ftrials/haywood/HAY_SUMD.HTM.

Investigating the Ludlow Massacre, 1915

In September 1913 the United Mine Workers of America (UMWA) organized a strike of Colorado coal miners against Colorado Fuel and Iron (CFI), which was owned by famous industrialist John D. Rockefeller Sr., and other major western coal companies. Sick of enduring low wages, horrible working and living conditions, and other types of mistreatment at the hands of employers, the striking workers issued demands for higher wages, an eight-hour workday, and other changes. They also insisted that CFI and other coal companies recognize the UMWA as the legitimate bargaining agent of the workers in future negotiations.

CFI turned down these demands and evicted many mining families from their rental housing. The UMWA relocated the families into a series of tent colonies, the largest of which was established outside of the town of Ludlow. The standoff continued until April 20, 1914, when Colorado National Guardsmen staged a vicious attack on the Ludlow colony that claimed the lives of six miners, two women, and eleven children.

Reports of the "Ludlow Massacre" sparked explosions of new violence between miners and company guards and state troopers throughout the state. News of the attack also prompted the federal government to launch investigations into the incident. One of the most critical of the resulting reports, published mere months after the battered UMWA called off the strike and the mines reopened, was authored by George P. West of the U.S. Committee on Industrial Relations. According to West, the strike had been rooted in decades of worker frustration about the "tyrannical" behavior of the mine owners. In addition, the investigator strongly implied that state guardsmen had actually murdered unarmed strike leaders in cold blood. The following is an excerpt from West's report.

The struggle in Colorado was primarily a struggle against arbitrary power, in which the question of wages was Secondary, as an immediate issue. And the merits of the strikers' cause must be judged by an answer to the question of whether they and their representatives demanded arbitrary and tyrannical power for their collective organization, or whether they sought only that measure of control over their own lives that is guaranteed by the spirit and letter of American constitutions and statutes.

Involving as its major issue the demand of the miners for a voice in determining the conditions under which they worked, the Colorado conflict was also a struggle for a voice in determining political and social conditions in the communities where they and their families lived. The strikers passionately felt and believed that they were denied, not only a voice in fixing working conditions within the mines, but that political democracy, carrying with it rights and privileges guaranteed by the laws of the land, had likewise been flouted and repudiated by the owners. It was this latter belief that gave to the strikers that intensity of feeling which impelled them to suffer unusual hardships during their stay in the tent colonies, and which gave to the strike the character more of a revolt by entire communities than of a protest by wage earners only....

Assuming, as we must, that the miners of southern Colorado are capable of exercising the rights guaranteed every man by the laws of the land, the question remains whether or not they have hitherto submitted to the industrial, political and social domination of the companies without protest. If this were the fact, then the revolt of 1913-14 might more easily be attributed to agitation by union officials from other districts and not to the miners' deep-seated resentment and their determination to obtain their rights and liberties.

The history of the coal mining industry shows that, far from living complacently under company rule, the Colorado miners have revolted time and again during the past thirty years. Strikes have occurred each ten years since 1883. In 1903, during John Mitchell's incumbency as president of the United Mine Workers, miners in the same camps affected by the recent strike quit work for similar reasons and under circumstances very much resembling those of the 1913 strike. The report of the United States Bureau of Labor shows that the history of this earlier strike was almost identical with the history of the strike of 1913. Strikers and their leaders were deported from the state by the military authorities of Colorado; large numbers of armed guards in the employ of the companies terrorized the strikers' communities and ruthlessly disregarded their civil rights. The strike was defeated by these methods, and the mines were re-opened with strikebreakers recruited from the immigrant population of non-union eastern coal mining towns. Lacking as they were in radical or revolutionary background, these strike breakers themselves struck ten years later.

The recurrence of these strikes as evidence of the miners' intense dissatisfaction is strengthened by the difficulties that attended their efforts to organize and the hardships that inevitably were to be faced by those who quit work....

CAUSES OF THE STRIKE

The Colorado strike was a revolt by whole communities against arbitrary economic, political and social domination by the Colorado Fuel & Iron Company and the smaller coal mining companies that followed its lead. This domination has been carried to such an extreme that two entire counties of southern Colorado for years have been deprived of popular government, while large groups of their citizens have been stripped of their liberties, robbed of portions of their earnings, subjected to ruthless persecution and abuse, and reduced to a state of economic and political serfdom. Not only the government of these counties, but of the state, has been brought under this domination and forced or induced to do the companies' bidding, and the same companies have even flouted the will of the people of the nation as expressed by the President of the United States.

Economic domination was achieved by the Colorado Fuel & Iron Co. and its followers through the ruthless suppression of unionism, accomplished by the use of the power of summary discharge, the black list, armed guards, and spies, and by the active aid of venal state, county and town officials, who placed the entire machinery of the law at the disposal of the companies in their persecution of organizers and union members.

This economic domination was maintained by the companies in order that they might be free to obey or disregard state laws governing coal mining as they pleased; arbitrarily determine wages and working conditions; and retain arbitrary power to discharge without stated cause. The power to discharge was in turn used as a club to force employees and their families to submit to company control of every activity in the mining communities, from the selling of liquor and groceries to the choice of teachers, ministers of the gospel, election Judges, and town and county officials. In the cases of several companies, the suppression of unionism was used also to deny checkweighmen to the men in order that the miners might be cheated of part of their earnings.

Political domination was achieved by the companies by the use of their monopoly of employment to suppress free speech, free press and free assembly, by the appointment of company officials as election judges, by the formation of a political partnership with the liquor interests, and, in the case of the Colorado Fuel & Iron Company, also by the expenditure of large sums of money to influence votes during campaigns, and by resort to other forms of fraud and corruption. Where a public official refused to do their bidding, he was whipped into line through pressure from interests that responded to the economic power of the Colorado Fuel & Iron Company and its followers.

This political domination was maintained by the companies in order that they might ignore or defy state laws enacted to safeguard the interests of their employees, prevent legislation by state or county unfavorable to their interests and obtain such legislation as they wished, control coroners and judges and thus prevent injured employees from collecting damages; and flagrantly disregard the constitutional and statutory guarantees that otherwise would have prevented them from procuring the imprisonment, deportation or killing of union organizers and strikers.

The policies and acts of the executive officials of the Colorado Fuel & Iron Company, and of the other companies that acted with them, had the hearty support and endorsement of the greatest and most powerful financial interest in America, that of John D. Rockefeller, and his son, John D. Rockefeller, Jr., who controlled the company through ownership of approximately 40 per cent of its stocks and bonds. Letters from Mr. Rockefeller, Jr., heartily approving of his company's refusal to meet representatives of the strikers, of the measures taken to suppress the strike, and of the coercion of the governor that resulted in throwing the state troops on the side of the owners, were shown not only to executive officers of his company, but to other operators who followed its lead, and his support contributed largely to the unyielding and lawless policy that finally resulted in the horrors of the Ludlow massacre and the intervention of the federal government....

THE COLORADO MILITIA AND THE STRIKE

By April 20th the Colorado National Guard no longer offered even a pretense of fairness or impartiality, and its units in the field had degenerated into a force of professional gunmen and adventurers who were economically dependent on and subservient to the will of the coal operators. This force was dominated by an officer whose intense hatred for the strikers had been demonstrated, and who did not lack the courage and the belligerent spirit required to provoke hostilities. Although twelve hundred men, women and children remained at the Ludlow Tent Colony and [Lieutenant K.E.] Linderfelt's immediate force consisted of not more than thirty-five men, the militiamen were equipped with machine guns and high powered repeating rifles and could count on speedy reinforcement by the members of Troop "A", which numbered about one hundred. The Ludlow Colony had been repeatedly searched during the preceding weeks for arms and ammunition, and Major Boughton's testimony before this Commission indicates that Linderfelt believed the strikers to be unarmed.

Mrs. Helen Ring Robinson, a member of the Colorado State Senate and a distinguished citizen of the State, testified that while visiting the strike zone just before the Ludlow affair she heard reports and threats that the Ludlow Colony was to be wiped out. Similar testimony was given at the Coroner's inquest by Miss Susan Hollearin, postmistress and school teacher at Ludlow.

On April 20th militiamen destroyed the Ludlow Tent Colony, killing five men and one boy with rifle and machine gun fire and firing the tents with a torch.

Eleven children and two women of the colony who had taken refuge in a hole under one of the tents were burned to death or suffocated after the tents had been fired. During the firing of the tents, the militiamen became an uncontrolled mob and looted the tents of everything that appealed to their fancy or cupidity.

Hundreds of women and children were driven terror stricken into the hills or to shelter at near-by ranch houses. Others huddled for twelve hours in pits underneath their tents or in other places of shelter, while bullets from rifles and machine guns whistled overhead and kept them in constant terror.

The militiamen lost one man. He was shot through the neck early in the attack.

Three of the strikers killed at Ludlow were shot while under the guard of armed militiamen who had taken them prisoners. They included Louis Tikas, a leader of the Greek strikers, a man of high intelligence who had done his utmost that morning to maintain peace and prevent the attack and who had remained in or near the tent colony throughout the day to look after the women and children. Tikas was first seriously or mortally wounded by a blow on the head from the stock of a Springfield rifle in the hands of Lieutenant K. E. Linderfelt of the Colorado National Guard, and then shot three times in the back by militiamen and mine guards.

Accounts vary as to who fired the first shot on the morning of the tragedy, but it is established that the first offensive movement was the occu-pation of a hill near the tent colony by militiamen in full view of the strikers, the planting of a machine gun there, and the exploding of two dynamite bombs by the militia. These bombs had been made by Linderfelt to be used as signals to call the militia and mine guards from near-by mines and camps, but the strikers did not know their purpose. They streamed out of the colony, and about sixty who had rifles took up a position in a railroad out. Many of the women and children ran from the colony in another direction and took shelter in ranch houses or the open hill country before the destruction began.

The investigating committee of national guard officers charged the strikers with deliberate intent to attack the militia and with starting the fight. Undoubtedly the excitable Greeks hastened the attack by seizing their rifles and streaming from the colony when they saw the militiamen advancing and planting a machine gun; but from the testimony of witnesses, the known attitude of the militia and from the events that followed, it is reasonable to suspect that the militia was not averse to seizing upon the slightest pretext to start their work of destruction.

Fifteen or twenty of the women and children who were caught in the tent colony when the firing began escaped during the morning to a pump house near the tents. There they hid in a deep well, while bullets whistled overhead. A ladder extended down the side of the well to a landing where the terror-stricken refugees remained huddled. At 7 o'clock in the evening, a freight train pulled into the station between the pump house and the soldiers, who were directing a heavy fire into the tent colony. The women and children took advantage of the shelter its steel coke cars afforded to climb from the well and make a dash for shelter in an arroyo. The conductor and brakeman of the freight train testified at the inquest that they saw about fifteen women and children, crying and whimpering, scurrying along a fence near the railroad track. The trainmen testified that twelve militiamen covered the engineer with revolvers and ordered him to pull his train out and do it "damn quick," or they would shoot him. The engineer obeyed, although he had orders to take a side track at Ludlow in order to let a passenger train pass.

After the women and children had escaped from the pump house, militiamen took possession of it and there captured Louis Tikas, leader of the Greek strikers. According to the testimony of women who remained in the tent colony, Tikas with James Fyler, Secretary Treasurer of the Union, remained in the colony all day looking after the many women and children who had been unable to escape. Affidavits from women survivors attached hereto agree that he busied himself in saving women and children from the flames after the tents were set on fire, and took refuge in the pump house only when it was too late to be of further service. Fyler was captured near the colony a few minutes after the capture of Tikas. He was shot to death a short time later.

Tikas was taken before Lieutenant Linderfelt. About Linderfelt at the time stood fifty or seventy-five militiamen, most of them members of Troop "A" and acting in their double capacity as militiamen and mine guards. Hot words ensued, and although Tikas was absolutely defenseless, Linderfelt grasped his Springfield rifle by the barrel and broke the stock over Tikas' head. Linderfelt then strode away, and a few moments later there was a fusillade of shots. R. J. McDonald, stenographer for the militia officers, testified at the inquest that Linderfelt did not look around when he heard the shots. Tikas was shot three times in the back. The doctors who testified at the inquest said that he had been literally "shot to pieces inside." ...

Source: West, George P., U.S. Commission on Industrial Relations. *Report on the Colorado Strike.* Washington, DC: Commission on Industrial Relations, 1915, pp. 5-6, 12-13, 15-17, 126-29.

Laying the Groundwork for the National Labor Relations Act, 1935

In 1935 Congress passed the National Labor Relations Act (NLRA), a sweeping new labor law that had been crafted and sponsored by Democratic Senator Robert Wagner of New York. The legislation was then signed into law by President Franklin D. Roosevelt on July 5, 1935. The NLRA—also known as the Wagner Act in recognition of the New York senator's role in its creation—aimed to correct problems that had cropped up with an earlier major piece of New Deal legislation—the 1933 National Recovery Act. It gave the American labor movement important new legal rights and changed the landscape of worker-management relations. But the act almost died before it even came to a vote. In this excerpt from her memoir The Roosevelt I Knew, *Secretary of Labor Frances Perkins recalls the political hurdles that Wagner faced in advancing the NLRA through Congress.*

The NRA [National Recovery Act] became ... one of the most vital causes of the revival of the American spirit, and signalized emergence from the industrial depression. Industry after industry, beginning with textiles—often regarded as a model code—set up codes of fair practice. These provided for fair competition and honorable practices in industry, and every code called for limitation of hours, minimum wage regulations, limitation or abolition of child labor, and other labor standards....

After a few months of experience with NRA, it was evident that its operation had led to improvements in working conditions and the status of labor. Through NRA codes the regulation of hours of labor of men and women alike were undertaken for the first time in our history. Whereas state laws regulated only the hours of labor of women, some permitting women to work as many as ten hours a day, under NRA most of the codes prescribed forty hours a week as the standard, and about twenty-five per cent required a limit of eight hours or less as the hours to be worked any one day. Thus we came practically to a five-day, forty-hour week as standard in the United States.

This was accompanied by an increase rather than a decrease of hourly wages and weekly earnings. From June 1933 to June 1934 the average hourly earnings in manufacturing increased thirty-one per cent. The downward spiral of hourly earnings was checked and an upward spiral set in motion. The per capita weekly earnings in manufacturing increased fourteen per cent in the same period, while the cost of living increased less than seven per cent....

Under the protection of Section 7A [of the NRA] the trade unions started to organize in earnest. The rapid growth of membership when workers were relieved of the fear of being fired if they joined a union was evidence that there was a real trade union movement in the making in the United States. It was evidence too that trade unions could function effectively in determining some economic factors for the protection of their members and for the general welfare of their industries.

NRA was enormously popular. The Blue Eagle spread everywhere, and in some people's minds the New Deal and NRA were almost the same thing....

By late summer of 1933 there was restiveness in other places. Workers in some plants were complaining to the NRA that codes were not being complied with and that employers were refusing to meet with committees of workers as the latter believed they should under Section 7A. There were grievances that foremen were requiring tasks beyond the capacity of an individual to perform. The stretch-out, this was called.

The conciliators of the Department of Labor hurried here and there. The Labor Department set up special boards to deal with worker-employer relationships in particular industries; we were gradually thrashing out the threatened disputes and making adjustments. There were not many difficult strikes, but strike talk was everywhere. I suppose this is characteristic of a period after depression when times are, or look, better. Labor then seeks to correct in one drive all abuses and difficulties that have grown up in depression times. No doubt an enormous number of grievances had accumulated during the depression....

It must be remembered that the NRA itself created grievances between labor and employers which had not existed previously. Publicity led working people to believe that a code was their salvation if they were going to have the protection and advantages everyone else was getting. While the terms of the code, particularly for minimum wages and maximum hours, might be more favorable than anything the union had been able to achieve in an industry, workers were aggrieved if their wage rates did not match those of some other industry....

[Perkins goes on to explain how these problems led the administration to form a mediation board headed by Senator Wagner, who also began work on a bill—the National Labor Relations Act—that would address gaps in the NRA and provide additional protections to labor.]

Wagner was powerful in the Senate at the time because he had foresight and had been successful. The measures he had stood for through the years, sometimes unsuccessfully, were now the most popular the country had seen. A movement grew in the Senate to support his bill.

It ought to be on the record that the President did not take part in developing the National Labor Relations Act and, in fact, was hardly consulted about it. It was not a part of the President's program. It did not particularly appeal to him when it was described to him. All the credit for it belongs to Wagner.

The proposed bill, it must be remembered, was remedial. Certain unfair practices which employers had used against workers to prevent unionization and to cripple their economic strength had been uncovered by Wagner in the administration of Section 7-A of NRA. The bill sought to correct these specific, known abuses, and did not attempt to draw up a comprehensive code of ethical behavior in labor relations. Such a comprehensive code, however, was needed. Roosevelt supported my suggestion that labor leaders who wanted to distinguish themselves should draw up such a code and let us take a look at it. A code developed by labor itself even now might be both knowing and practice and might evoke the adherence of the great body of labor people. Principles so arrived at might be added to the National Labor Relations Act in the future.

Since Senator Wagner was going to introduce a bill anyhow, we wanted it to be a good practical bill....

I had thought originally, and so reported to the President, that the National Labor Relations bill was unlikely to become law. I felt sure that labor would object, for the recognition of a union under the NLRA would depend upon the counting of noses. A labor union would have to prove it had the backing of a majority of the workers in a plant. This was certainly new doctrine in 1934.

It had not been AF of L policy in the past to count noses before a committee went in to see the boss to demand better wages, hours, working conditions. No labor union had ever asked a government board to tell it whether they could represent a whole factory or one department or one craft. That was the union leader's judgment. Closed shops had been gained by bold methods at times. This bill would make that impossible. A union would have to prove majority support.

I expected Matthew Woll and William Green of the AF of L to tell me that they were opposed to the Wagner bill. They were enthusiastically in favor of it. I remember Woll saying with a superior smile, "My dear Miss Perkins, times have changed and we must change with them." …

The bill was passed in the form Wagner desired on June 19, 1935. Roosevelt signed it on July 5.

Source: Perkins, Frances. *The Roosevelt I Knew.* New York: Viking Press, 1946, pp. 208, 210, 235-36, 239-40, 243-44.

Remembering the Flint Sit-Down Strike, 1937

The 1936-37 Flint Sit-Down Strike was one of the great victories in the history of the American labor movement. When members of the United Automobile Workers (UAW) occupied one of General Motors's key manufacturing facilities in Flint, Michigan, on December 29, 1936, they managed to stop GM's operations in its tracks. Six weeks later, on February 11, 1937, GM's leadership formally recognized the UAW, which was part of the larger Congress of Industrial Organizations (CIO), as the exclusive bargaining representative for the company's factory workers.

One of the strike participants was Bob Stinson, who worked in the automotive industry from 1917 to 1962 before retiring. In this excerpt from an interview with historian Studs Terkel, Stinson recalls the daily grind of the sit-down strike. He also compares the joyful atmosphere at the end of the strike to the celebrations that washed over the United States when the Armistice agreement ending World War I was announced.

I was in Detroit, playing Santa Claus to a couple of small nieces and nephews. When I came back [to Flint], the second shift [men who worked from 4:30 p.m. to 12:30 a.m.] had pulled the plant. It took about five minutes to shut the line down. The foreman was pretty well astonished. (Laughs.)

The boys pulled the switches and asked all the women who was in Cut-and-Sew to go home. They informed the supervisors they could stay, if they stayed in their office. They told the plant police they could do their jobs as long as they didn't interfere with the workers.

We had guys patrol the plant, see that nobody got involved in anything they shouldn't. If anybody got careless with company property—such as sitting on an automobile cushion without putting burlap over it—he was talked to. You couldn't paint a sign on the wall or anything like that. You used bare springs for a bed. 'Cause if you slept on a finished cushion, it was no longer a new cushion.

Governor [Frank] Murphy said he hoped to God he would never have to use National Guard against people. But if there was damage to property, he would do so. This was right down our alley, because we invited him to the plant and see how well we were taking care of the place.

From *Hard Times: An Oral History of the Great Depression.* Copyright © 1970, 1986 by Studs Terkel. Reprinted by permission of The New Press. www.thenewpress.com.

They'd assign roles to you. When some of the guys at headquarters wanted to tell some of the guys in the plant what was cookin', I carried the message. I was a scavenger, too.

The merchants cooperated. There'd be apples, bushels of potatoes, crates of oranges that was beginnin' to spoil. Some of our members were also little farmers, they come up with a couple of baskets of junk.

The soup kitchen was outside the plant. The women handled all the cooking, outside of one chef who came from New York. He had anywhere from ten to twenty women washing dishes and peeling potatoes in the strike kitchen. Mostly stews, pretty good meals. They were put in containers and hoisted up through the window....

Most of the men had their wives and friends come down, and they'd stand inside the window and they'd talk. Find out how the family was. If the union supplied them with enough coal....

We had a ladies' auxiliary. They'd visit the homes of the guys that was in the plant. They would find out if there was any shortage of coal or food. Then they'd maneuver around amongst themselves until they found some place to get a ton of coal. Some of them even put the arm on Consumers Power if there was a possibility of having her power shut off.

Any of the wives try to talk the guys into coming out?

Some of 'em would have foremen come to their homes: "Sorry, your husband was a very good operator. But if he don't get out of the plant and away from the union, he'll never again have a job at General Motors." If this woman was the least bit scared, she'd come down and cry on her husband's shoulder. He'd more than likely get a little disturbed, get a hold of his strike captain.... Maybe we'd send a couple of women out there. Sometimes you just had to let 'em go. Because if you kept them in there, they'd worry so damn much over it, that'd start ruinin' the morale of the rest of the guys.

Morale was very high at the time. It started out kinda ugly because the guys were afraid they put their foot in it and all they was gonna do is lose their jobs. But as time went on, they begin to realize they could win this darn thing, 'cause we had a lot of outside people comin' in showin' their sympathy.

Time after time, people would come driving by the plant slowly. They might pull up at the curb and roll down the window and say, "How you guys doin'?" Our guys would be lookin' out the windows, they'd be singin' songs and hollerin'. Just generally keeping themselves alive....

Nationally known people contributed to our strike fund. Mrs. [Eleanor] Roosevelt for one. We even had a member of Parliament come from England and address us.

Lotta things worked for the union we hadn't even anticipated. Company tried to shut off the heat. It was a bluff. Nobody moved for half an hour, so they turned it back on again. They didn't want the pipes to get cold. (Laughs.) If the heat was allowed to drop, then the pipes will separate—they were all jointed together—and then you got a problem.

Some of the time you were scared, because there was all kinds of rumors going around. We had a sheriff—he came in one night at Fisher One and read the boys the riot act. He told 'em they had to leave. He stood there, looked at 'em a few minutes. A couple of guys began to curse 'im, and he turned around and left himself....

The men sat in there for forty-four days. Governor Murphy—I get emotional over him (laughs)—was trying to get both sides to meet on some common ground. I think he lost many a good night's sleep. We wouldn't use force. Mr. Knudsen was head of General Motors and, of course, there was John L. Lewis. They'd reach a temporary agreement and invariably the Flint Alliance or GM headquarters in Detroit would throw a monkey wrench in it. So every morning, Murphy got up with an unsolved problem.

John L. was as close to a Shakespearean actor as any I've ever listened. He could get up there and damn all the adversaries—he had more command of language. He made a speech that if they shoot the boys out at the plant, they'd have to shoot him first.

There were a half a dozen false starts at settlement. Finally, we got the word: THE THING IS SETTLED. My God, you had to send about three people, one right after the other, down to some of those plants because the guys didn't believe it. Finally, when they did get it, they marched out of the plants with the flag flyin' and all that stuff.

You'd see some guys comin' out of there with whiskers as long as Santa Claus. They made a rule they wasn't gonna shave until the strike was over. Oh, it was just like—you've gone through the Armistice delirium, haven't you? Everybody was runnin' around shaking everybody by the hand, sayin',

"Jesus, you look strange, you got a beard on you now." (Laughs.) Women kissin' their husbands. There was a lotta drunks on the streets that night.

When Mr. Knudsen put his name to a piece of paper and says that General Motors recognizes the UAW—CIO—until that moment, we were non-people, we didn't even exist. (Laughs.) That was the big one. (His eyes are moist.)

Source: Terkel, Studs. Interview with Bob Stinson. *Hard Times: An Oral History of the Great Depression.* New York: New Press, 2000, pp. 129-133.

Walter Reuther Discusses Labor's Role in Building a Better Society, 1952

During the 1940s and 1950s, the American labor movement became a formidable force in U.S. politics. In addition to influencing labor and business laws and regulations, unions played a major role in pushing Washington lawmakers to support and pass ambitious social reform measures designed to help reduce poverty, increase educational opportunity, protect the environment, and care for elderly and infirm members of society.

United Auto Workers (UAW) President Walter Reuther was among the most dedicated of the labor leaders who used their union's political clout to press for wider reforms in American society. And in 1952, when he was elected to head the Congress of Industrial Organizations (CIO), Reuther became an even more powerful architect of social change. In the following address accepting the presidency of the CIO, Reuther discusses both his vision of union solidarity and his beliefs about labor's duties and obligations to the citizenry of the United States.

In the halls of government we shall speak with one voice. We shall stand together at the collective bargaining tables, doing the practical work on the bread-and-butter front. If and when reactionary managements are unwilling to give the workers of America the things to which they are entitled, we shall exhaust every means of resolving these issues across the bargaining table through the use of logic and reason, but, failing to get economic justice through that process, we shall march together on the picket lines of America to win what is rightfully ours.

There has been some talk that we have division in the CIO between the big unions and small unions. Nothing could be further from the truth. I think the majority of little unions maybe felt that this was their first opportunity to stand up and have their say—and, God bless them—they have that right. But what we need to do is to weld together the kind of practical, effective, working teamwork between all the unions, large and small and those in between. No one, not the biggest union down to the smallest union, can get along without being a part of the family of CIO. We want to help build the little unions. We want to help them do the practical job of organizing the unorganized in their fields so that they, too, can spread the good work that they are doing for their membership on the countless thousands of workers yet unorganized in their respective jurisdictions....

We need each other. The Auto Workers need the Steelworkers. The Steelworkers need the Auto Workers. I say nothing, nothing, no matter where it comes from, and no one is going to divide either the leadership or the rank and file of the Steelworkers and the Auto Workers. We are going to work at this job together, because we need to. We have a slogan in the UAW—"Teamwork in the leadership and solidarity in the ranks." That is precisely what we are going to do inside the CIO.

There are many practical jobs ahead, jobs that will test the best that is in all of us. There is the job of organizing the unorganized. No union, no movement that rests upon past achievements will have the drive and the energy and the power without which we cannot succeed. We must recapture the crusading spirit we had in the early days, and we need to take on some of the areas of the unorganized and begin to do the kind of job that I know we are capable of doing if we pull together in the days ahead. But, our job is more than just organizing the unorganized. I think if we are going to be realistic, we must recognize the fact that when you sign up a worker in a union and he pays his dues, his obligation and his responsibilities do not end there. They just begin. All of our unions have too many people who are just card-carrying members. They pay their dues. They come to a meeting occasionally. Yes, they walk the picket lines when they are called upon. We have the job, not only to organize the unorganized, but we have the job of educating and unionizing the organized. We need to give our members a sense of participating in a great human crusade. We need to make them conscious of the fact that the free labor movement for the first time in the history of human civilization is trying consciously to give direction in the shaping of history. We are trying to participate in the great social changes that are taking place in the world in which we live.

When you belong to a union, when you understand where we are going and how we hope to get there, what tools free people have to use in the building of that better world that we dream about, then you have the satisfaction of knowing that as a free human being you have something to say about the kind of tomorrow that your children will grow up in. Until we do a better job of educating and unionizing the people whom we have organized, we will not have mobilized the real potential power and the spiritual strength of our great, free labor movement....

I take no credit in a personal sense for the fact that I am a trade unionist. I was raised in a trade union family. My father was an international representative of the Brewery Workers Union. He was President of the Central Trades and Labor Assembly in our home town when he was twenty-three years old.

189

Along with my brothers at my father's knee, we learned the philosophy of trade unionism, we got the struggles, the hopes, and aspirations of working people every day. I was raised in the kind of trade union atmosphere that said to me when I was a boy that a trade union movement based upon the principles of pure and simple trade unionism could not adequately deal with the complex problems of the working people in the world in which we live. Our labor movement is a labor movement which integrates our efforts with the efforts of the whole people to move ahead in finding a practical and democratic solution to the complex problems that beset us. In a free and interdependent society, labor can make progress only to the extent that it helps to provide leadership in solving the problems of all the people. We have a job as free labor, of doing much more than just bargaining for our membership. We have to assume ever-increasing social responsibilities. We have a practical job of completing the task of organizing the unorganized, of unionizing the organized through educational work, and we must apply ourselves to the difficult, long-range program of finding a way ultimately, in a free society, to raise collective bargaining above the level of a continuing struggle between competing economic pressure groups. A free society cannot solve its basic economic problems unless free labor and free management can find the common denominators through good faith and understanding by which both can meet their joint moral and social responsibilities to the whole community. Collective bargaining must be based upon acceptance of and extension of the democratic processes in our industrial and economic life. Basic collective bargaining decisions must be based upon economic facts and not dictated by the use of economic power.

These are the basic factors that should influence our collective bargaining attitudes and in a large measure will control the destiny of free men in the challenging years that lie ahead. We must work for the complete destruction of the economic and moral double standards that certain industries bring to the bargaining table.

They gave their high-paid officials fat pensions when they didn't need them, while they denied pensions to working people who did need them. We have problems like the guaranteed annual wage. They pay the people who get more than they need by the year, and they pay the people who get too little by the hour. These are not just matters of economic justice to the worker, but they are matters of economic survival for a free society. That is why we are compelled to work and if need be fight for objectives such as the guaranteed annual wage, no matter how great the opposition. The future of peace and the future of freedom in the world in which we live cannot be made secure if we go on trying to divide up economic scarcity in the world. Freedom and peace are possible only if their future is made secure by the economics of abundance. We must fight the forces of monopoly and scarcity in their opposition to the expansion of our productive capacity and the full development of our material resources. We must create the maximum economic abundance and then translate that abundance into tangible human values. The world is going to judge America not by how many tons of steel we produce or what our material wealth is. America will be judged by the real standards by which a civilization should be judged. The real measurement of the greatness of a civilization is its ability to demonstrate the sense of social and moral responsibility needed to translate material values into human values, technological progress into human progress, human happiness, and human dignity. That is the job that we in the CIO are working on....

There is a revolution going on in this world. The Communists didn't start the revolution. It is a revolution of hungry men to get the wrinkles out of their empty bellies. It is a revolution of people who have been exploited by imperialism and who are trying to throw off the shackles of imperialism and colonialism, and who want to march forward in freedom and independence. It is a struggle of the have-nots to get something for themselves. The Communists didn't start it. They are riding its back. What we have to do is to answer the Communist propaganda not with slogans; we must expose the hypocrisy of Communist propaganda which offers these hungry and desperate people the promise of economic security with a price tag.

We need to answer the reactionaries in Wall Street who play the other side of that Communist record. The Communists would have people trade freedom for bread and the reactionaries would have you believe that if you want to be free you have to be economically insecure. And we say to the Communists and the reactionaries, "You are both wrong. In the world that we are trying to help build, people can have both bread and freedom."

Man is an economic being and needs food, clothing, housing, medical care, and all of the other material needs, and we struggle to make that possible. But man is more than just an economic being. He is a social and spiritual being, and just as food is needed for the economic man so the spiritual man needs food, and freedom is the food of the soul. The great challenge in the world is to find a way so that men can so arrange their relationship of one to the other within a free society, and one nation to another in a free world, so that we can live at peace and harness the power of our advancing technology, develop our resources, and translate this abundance into a good life for everyone.

Source: Reuther, Walter. "We Shall March Together." Address accepting the Presidency of the Congress of Industrial Organizations, December 4, 1952. In *Walter Reuther: Selected Papers*. Edited by Henry M. Christman. New York: Macmillan, 1961, pp. 47-49, 53-55, 56.

The AFL and CIO Reunite, 1955

In 1955 the American labor movement's two largest organizations, the American Federation of Labor (AFL) and the Congress of Industrial Organizations (CIO), reunited almost two decades after the CIO left the AFL over a range of strategic and philosophical issues. This merger, which created a fifteen-million-member AFL-CIO, was hailed by AFL President George Meany and CIO President Walter Reuther as a landmark event in American history. The following is the preamble to the AFL-CIO constitution that was approved in 1955.

The establishment of this Federation through the American Federation of Labor and Congress of Industrial Organizations is an expression of the hopes and aspirations of the working people of America.

We seek the fulfillment of these hopes and aspirations through democratic processes within the framework of our constitutional government and consistent with our institutions and traditions.

At the collective bargaining table, in the community, in the exercise of the rights and responsibilities of citizenship, we shall responsibly serve the interests of all the American people.

We pledge ourselves to the more effective organization of working men and women; to the securing to them of full recognition and enjoyment of the rights to which they are justly entitled; to the achievement of ever higher standards of living and working conditions; to the attainment of security for all the people; to the enjoyment of the leisure which their skills make possible; and to the strengthening and extension of our way of life and the fundamental freedoms which are the basis of our democratic society.

We shall combat resolutely the forces which seek to undermine the democratic institutions of our nation and to enslave the human soul. We shall strive always to win full respect for the dignity of the human individual whom our unions serve.

With Divine Guidance, grateful for the fine traditions of our past, confident of meeting the challenge of the future, we proclaim this constitution.

Source: *Report of the Constitutional Convention Proceedings*, Vol. 1. AFL-CIO, 1955, p. xxxviii. Reprinted in Goldberg, Arthur J. *AFL-CIO: Labor United.* New York: McGraw-Hill, 1956, p. 235.

Confronting Union Corruption, 1957

The reputation of the American labor movement took a significant hit in the 1950s with revelations of criminal conduct and corruption among some of its unions. The most heavily publicized of these scandals surrounded the Teamsters Union, which was led by President Dave Beck and Vice President James "Jimmy" Hoffa. In 1956 AFL-CIO President George Meany launched a campaign to expel the Teamsters, which had become a massive embarrassment, from his federation.

The AFL-CIO launched internal investigations into Beck, Hoffa, and the Teamsters, even as Congressional inquiries into the union intensified. In December 1957 the Ethical Practices Committee of the AFL-CIO, which was chaired by Alex Rose, completed its investigation of the Teamsters. The AFL-CIO leadership followed the committee's recommendation and formally expelled the Teamsters on December 5. The following excerpts from the Ethical Practices Committee report detail the corrupt activities of Beck and Hoffa and also include Rose's remarks to the leadership upon delivering the report.

The Committee found that President Beck had in many ways used his official union position for his own substantial personal profit and advantage, many times at the expense of the Teamsters Union. Included in these activities were loans for $200,000 from the Fruehauf Trailer Company after President Beck, as Chairman of the International Brotherhood's Finance Committee, had loaned $1,500,000 of Teamsters' Funds to that Company; a whole series of dealings with Nathan Shefferman by virtue of which Beck and his relatives received substantial sums of money and Shefferman and his relatives received substantial sums of Teamsters Union money; and control of the investment of Teamsters Union funds in such a manner as to advance the private business interests of Beck, members of his family and his associates.

The Committee found that typical of this latter category was a transaction by which President Beck, as a trustee of a memorial fund for the widow of a Teamster official, enriched himself out of the investment of the trust in a mortgage.

Vice President Hoffa similarly used his official union position, the Committee found, for personal profit and advantage, frequently to the direct detriment of the membership of the Teamsters Union. Typical of the findings with respect to Vice president Hoffa was the finding of the Committee with respect to Test Fleet Corporation. Test Fleet Corporation was established for the benefit of Vice President Hoffa and Bert Brennan by Commercial Carriers, a trucking company whose employees were represented by the Teamsters Union. Shortly after Vice President Hoffa terminated a strike of the employees of Commercial Carriers, Commercial Carriers established Test Fleet as a corporation, transferred trucks which it already owned to Test Fleet and leased back those same trucks from Test Fleet. Test Fleet, whose stock was held in the names of Brennan's and Hoffa's wives, had no employees and did no business other than to receive rentals from Commercial Carriers. The total investment of Hoffa and Brennan in Test Fleet was, at most, $4,000 and they expended no actual effort or direction in the company's business. But, over a period of years, Commercial Carriers paid enough money to Test Fleet so that Brennan and Hoffa derived $125,000 in income from it.

Similar use of union position for personal advantage was demonstrated by Hoffa's borrowing $18,000 from eleven different Teamster business agents and at least $20,000 from employers under contract with the Teamsters Union. The final item found by the Ethical Practices Committee in this category was Vice President Hoffa's relationship with a real estate promoter whose subdivision was "sponsored" by the Teamsters Union at a time when Hoffa secretly held an option to participate in the profits of the enterprise and had borrowed $25,000 from the promoter.

COMMITTEE CHAIRMAN ROSE: Mr. President and fellow delegates, I want to begin by saying that I consider myself a friend of the Teamsters and that every member of our Committee considers himself a friend of the Teamsters. I believe that every delegate at this Convention considers himself a friend of the Teamsters.

Many of us have received benefits from the cooperation of the Teamsters' organization. I can tell you that right now, at this very minute, my Union is conducting a strike in Louisville, Kentucky, and we are getting splendid cooperation from the Teamsters local organization and its officers.

Because—and precisely because—we know the great role that the Teamsters Union can perform in cooperation with the entire trade union movement, precisely because we know the great record of the Teamsters and the contribution which they can make to the labor movement, we want to see a fraternal, clean Teamsters organization as part of the labor movement....

Let me turn now to an appeal to the Teamsters. Don't waste time; act quickly. Restore the good name of the Teamsters Union, because involved in this appeal and in this proceeding today is not only the fate of 1,400,000 members of the Teamsters Union—involved also is the fate of 15 million organized workers and the fate of 30 million unorganized workers. Involved also is our whole democratic way of life, because in the struggles that are now going on in the world all democracy will be judged by the kind of labor movement we possess. We here this morning are about to make a historic decision on which will depend not only the fate of the organized workers and unorganized workers, but also the good name of our democracy and the role we can play in the events of the world.

The organized labor movement in every single modern civilized country stands in the forefront in fighting for social betterment. They are not merely an economic group, confined to their own economic interests. The labor movement is a moral force, must be a moral force, and it needs the cooperation and the good will of people outside the ranks of the organized labor movement in order to prevail....

This is a very historic decision that we are to make this morning. It is a decision of morality versus cynicism and of honesty versus corruption. It is because of this that I urge you, on behalf of our Committee, to adopt our Committee's Report.

Source: "Use of Official Union Position for Personal Profit and Advantage—President Beck and Vice President Hoffa." *Proceedings of the Second Constitutional Convention of the AFL-CIO*. Volume 1, Daily Proceedings, Atlantic City, NJ, December 5-12, 1957. Supplementary Report, pp. 80-89. Reprinted in *American Labor: A Documentary Collection*. Edited by Melvin Dubofsky and Joseph A. McCartin. New York: Palgrave Macmillan, 2004, pp. 225-27.

President Ronald Reagan Comments on the Air Traffic Controller Strike, 1981

On August 3, 1981, air traffic controllers across the United States went on strike to pressure the federal government for better pay, scheduling reforms, and other benefits. But the Professional Air Traffic Controllers Organization (PATCO) to which these workers belonged was a government union that had a clear no-strike clause in its contract with the Federal Aviation Administration (FAA). A few hours after PATCO began its strike, President Ronald Reagan held a question-and-answer session with reporters on the strike. During the course of this session, which is excerpted here, Reagan announced that if the 11,000 striking workers did not quickly return to work, he would fire them and replace them. When PATCO refused to obey, Reagan followed through on his promise and fired them. He also imposed a lifetime ban on rehiring the strikers.

The President: This morning at 7 a.m. the union representing those who man America's air traffic control facilities called a strike. This was the culmination of seven months of negotiations between the Federal Aviation Administration and the union. At one point in these negotiations agreement was reached and signed by both sides, granting a $40 million increase in salaries and benefits. This is twice what other government employees can expect. It was granted in recognition of the difficulties inherent in the work these people perform. Now, however, the union demands are seventeen times what had been agreed to—$681 million. This would impose a tax burden on their fellow citizens which is unacceptable.

I would like to thank the supervisors and controllers who are on the job today, helping to get the nation's air system operating safely. In the New York area, for example, four supervisors were scheduled to report for work, and seventeen additionally volunteered. At National Airport a traffic controller told a newsperson he had resigned from the union and reported to work because, "How can I ask my kids to obey the law if I don't?" This is a great tribute to America.

Let me make one thing plain. I respect the right of workers in the private sector to strike. Indeed, as president of my own union, I led the first strike ever called by that union. I guess I'm maybe the first one to ever hold this office who is a lifetime member of an AFL-CIO union. But we cannot compare labor-management relations in the private sector with government. Government cannot close down the assembly line. It has to provide without interruption the protective services which are government's reason for being.

It was in recognition of this that the Congress passed a law forbidding strikes by government employees against the public safety. Let me read the solemn oath taken by each of these employees, a sworn affidavit, when they accepted their jobs: "I am not participating in any strike against the Government of the United States or any agency thereof, and I will not so participate while an employee of the Government of the United States or any agency thereof."

It is for this reason that I must tell those who fail to report for duty this morning they are in violation of the law, and if they do not report for work within 48 hours, they have forfeited their jobs and will be terminated....

Q: Mr. President, will you delay your trip to California or cancel it if the strike is still on later this week?

The President: If any situation should arise that would require my presence here, naturally I will do that. So, that will be a decision that awaits what's going to happen. May I just—because I have to be back in there for another appointment—may I just say one thing on top of this? With all this talk of penalties and everything else, I hope that you'll emphasize, again, the possibility of termination, because I believe that there are a great many of those people—and they're fine people—who have been swept up in this and probably have not really considered the result—the fact that they had taken an oath, the fact that this is now in violation of the law, as that one supervisor referred to with regard to his children. And I am hoping that they will in a sense remove themselves from the lawbreaker situation by returning to their posts.

I have no way to know whether this had been conveyed to them by their union leaders, who had been informed that this would be the result of a strike....

Q: Mr. President, why have you taken such strong action as your first action? Why not some lesser action at this point?

The President: What lesser action can there be? The law is very explicit. They are violating the law. And as I say, we called this to the attention of their leadership. Whether this was conveyed to the membership before they voted to strike, I don't know. But this is one of the reasons why there can be no further negotiation while this situation continues. You can't sit and negotiate with a union that's in violation of the law.

Source: Reagan, Ronald. "Remarks and a Question-and-Answer Session with Reporters on the Air Traffic Controllers Strike," August 3, 1981. Ronald Reagan Presidential Library Archives. Available online at http://www.reagan.utexas.edu/archives/speeches/1981/80381a.htm.

Debating the Future of Unions, 2009

As American labor unions move deeper into the twenty-first century, defenders and critics have entered into contentious debates about the present character and future prospects of organized labor. Advocates acknowledge that unions have been under extended siege from an array of political and economic forces, but they assert that unions remain a viable—and even essential— component of America's overall vitality and long-term future. Detractors, on the other hand, argue that poor leadership and unreasonable expectations have turned unions into albatrosses around the neck of American business.

In 2009 the Los Angeles Times *published a four-part debate about the future of the American union between David Madland, director of the American Worker Project for the Center for American Progress Action Fund, and Shikha Dalmia, a senior analyst with the Reason Foundation. Following are two segments from that debate. In the first segment, Madland and Dalmia discuss the future impact of unions on the wider American economy. In the second segment, they debate the merits of the Employee Free Choice Act, a proposal to make significant changes in the way union elections are held.*

After the U.S. Recovers, Will Unions?

Healthy unions pump money into the economy

Point: David Madland

The future of labor unions is very much in doubt, but the need for them continues to grow. The essence of what labor unions do—give workers a stronger voice to get a fair share of the economic growth they help create—is and has always been important to making our economy work properly for all Americans. The worse our economy gets, the more important this function becomes.

Even when times were relatively good, workers were getting squeezed. The real median income for working-age households—those headed by someone younger than 65—fell between 2000 and 2007 by about $2,000. Though workers helped the economy grow during this time period by becoming ever more productive—increasing productivity by 18%—they did not receive a share of the new wealth they helped create, and instead fell further behind. As a result, 2000-2007 was a period of growth in which the nation's middle-class families had less real income at the end than when they started.

One of the primary reasons for why our current recession endures is the fact that workers do not have the purchasing power needed to drive our economy. Consumer activity accounts for about 70% of our nation's economic activity, and for a while, workers used debt to sustain their consumption. Yet, as we are plainly seeing, debt-driven consumption is not sustainable.

What is sustainable is an economy in which workers are adequately rewarded and have the income they need to purchase goods—which is where unions come in.

Unions raise wages for their members by about 12% compared with similar nonunion workers, according to the Center for Economic and Policy Research. And when unions are strong and able to represent the people who want to join them, these gains spread throughout the economy; nonunion companies increase their wages, and all workers have more purchasing power, producing a "virtuous circle of prosperity and jobs," according to UC Berkeley professor Harley Shaiken.

Less than 8% of today's private-sector workers are unionized—even though polls show that more than half of Americans would join a union if they could—because the union selection process is broken, exposing workers to the aggressive tactics of anti-union employers and endangering workplace democracy. It will take substantial legislative changes—such as the Employee Free Choice Act—to allow all Americans a stronger voice on the job and a true opportunity to unionize.

If the Employee Free Choice Act becomes law, it is likely that the number of workers in unions will grow. It is impossible to predict by how much or what industries will grow the most, though it seems likely that organizing efforts would focus on fast-growing sectors of the economy such as healthcare, alternative energy and education, as well as the very large service sector, which accounts for about 70% of the country's gross domestic product. New research from the Economic Policy Institute estimates that if 5 million service workers joined unions, these workers would get a $7,000 annual raise on average, and $34 billion in total new wages would flow into the economy. These working-class employees would be more likely to spend their money during an economic downturn than CEOs—who can afford to save during lean economic times—and thus provide a significant boost to the economy. There is both a moral and economic argument for empowering workers and their unions.

Whatever industry workers choose to organize, it is key for our economy that they do so.

If unions are so good for the economy, how do you explain Michigan?

Counterpoint: Shikha Dalmia

David, I agree with your opening comment that the future of labor unions in this country is bleak—at least in the private sector. The public sector is another story.

Before getting into that, however, let me address some outstanding issues from Tuesday. I can't correct all of your claims here, but you allege that I oppose "workers joining together in unions to better themselves." That is a total strawman argument. I support the right of workers to use any and all forms of collective or non-collective action to get the best possible deal from employers, even, as I indicated Monday, wildcat strikes that are currently illegal.

What I don't support are unions that are accountable neither to their own members nor to market realities. Regrettably, organized labor in this country is guilty on both counts. And that is the major reason for its decline.

Only 8% of private-sector employees are unionized today, as you point out, compared with 35% in the 1950s. However, citing unnamed polls, you suggest that this dwindling membership is the result not of employee choice but some insidious anti-union plot by employers. Employers may indeed have such a plot (although James Sherk of the Heritage Foundation examined this claim in his 2007 brief, "The Truth About Improper Firings and Union Intimidation," and found less than compelling evidence for it). But that's not why unions are going kaput; it's because they offer a poor "value proposition."

Successful clubs constantly look for ways to offer their members better services for lower fees. Not so with unions. Once they set up shop, they gain the right to collect membership dues in perpetuity without giving most workers any say in how this money is spent. An analysis by the Mackinac Center for Public Policy in 2006 found that Michigan unions on average spent only 43.5% of these dues on workplace representation issues, with much of the rest going toward political activism. Most workers want "paycheck protection" laws that would require unions to obtain their approval before diverting their hard-earned dollars toward candidates and causes they may not always support. But union bosses have fought tooth-and-nail against even such elementary accountability measures. This can hardly be a selling point during unionization drives.

David, you claim that the key to reviving the U.S. economy is boosting worker wages by strengthening unions. By that logic, Michigan, where I live, should be the economic superstar of the nation. After all, its unionized autoworkers earn three times more in wages and benefits than the average private-sector worker. Sadly, the opposite is the case: Michigan has been in a single-state recession for years, even when the rest of the country was booming. Its home foreclosure rates are among the highest in the nation, and its unemployment rate—10.6%—is the highest. And much of its auto industry—the mainstay of its economy—might have been dead were it not for the grace of federal taxpayers.

Nor is Michigan an anomaly. States with the heaviest union presence tend to perform far worse in nearly every economic measure—job growth, cost of living, entrepreneurial activity and tax rates—than those with a lower union presence.

The reality is that companies can't afford to pay their workers more in wages and benefits than these workers produce in value. When unions insist they do, they make these companies less able to compete and usher in their decline. And dying companies don't make good candidates for unionization.

The only entity that can ignore this reality is the government, because it doesn't have to compete for its survival. It has been the main growth industry for unions in the past, and it is likely to an even bigger one in the future, given the big boost Uncle Sam will likely give it through the $800-billion-plus "stimulus" spending bill.

Things might be different if unions manage to get more powers to coax, cajole and coerce private-sector workers into joining through the so-called card-check legislation. More on that tomorrow.

Card Check: Unions' Salvation?

When unions win, we all win

Point: David Madland

Nearly three in five American workers say they would vote to join a union if they could, according to a poll done by Peter D. Hart Research Associates. Yet only 8% of private-sector workers are union members—down from about one-third in the middle of the 20th century—because existing laws make organizing a union a Herculean task that few want to undertake.

Unionizing workers face an undemocratic system that allows them to be intimidated by their employers. Bosses can legally force workers to attend anti-union meetings and have "one-on-one conversations" about the union, which happens in more than 90% of all organizing campaigns, according to a Cornell University study. Workers often are pressured by employers to reveal their private preferences for joining a union, and thus the current process does not truly keep "secret ballots" a secret.

When employers cross the line and actually break the law, penalties are weak and insufficient. In about 25% of all organizing campaigns, workers are illegally fired and can at best hope to recover their lost wages and get reinstated in their jobs, often after several years of legal battles. And even if workers prevail against these odds, employers often refuse to negotiate with the union.

Unfairly preventing workers from organizing is a violation of basic human rights; it is also bad for the economy. Without strong unions, our entire community pays a heavy price: Wages lag and workers don't have the purchasing power needed to drive the economy; race and gender pay gaps widen; and insecurity, poverty and inequality increase.

The Employee Free Choice Act would promote free and fair union elections by making it harder for employers to intimidate workers. The bill would increase penalties for employers who break the law, allow an employee to choose to join a union by signing a membership card (a system that works well at the small number of workplaces that permit it) and encourage good-faith bargaining so employees can collectively negotiate a first contract. The act would not deny workers their right to vote in a union election, as some conservatives maintain; rather, if 30% of workers were to say they wanted an election, they would get one.

If the Employee Free Choice Act becomes law, union members will likely grow. Though it is hard to say by how much, the bill holds the potential of improving millions of Americans' economic standing and workplace conditions. Workers in the public sector, where government employers typically remain neutral in union elections, are four times more likely to be unionized than those in the private sector. But no matter how many more workers join unions, the bill's impact would be profound because it would make clear that employers can no longer deny workers the right to join a union.

The rights of workers versus the rights of union bosses

Counterpoint: Shikha Dalmia

David, you keep insisting that the misleadingly titled Employee Free Choice Act is about protecting workers who wish to unionize from employer intimidation. However, you fail to explain how taking away the right of workers to a secret ballot election would accomplish this. I worked for a corporation, so I am well aware of the subtle tactics that companies can use to influence workers. But that's all the more reason to keep a worker's final decision private.

Let's be honest: The purpose of card check is not to protect workers from employer intimidation, but to expose them to union coercion. How many late-night home visits by local union bosses will a worker be able to resist before signing on the dotted line? Which worker will refuse to check a card if accosted in his company locker room by union supporters? It is precisely because of such concerns that even staunch labor supporters such as the Rev. Al Sharpton and former Sen. George McGovern are fighting this bill and urging fellow Democrats to oppose it. Secret ballots are the pillar of democratic self-governance.

David, you note that 60% of private-sector workers said in a poll that they want a union yet only 8% of the private workforce is unionized. This, to you, is proof positive that employer coercion is preventing widespread unionization. But there is nothing inconsistent about workers wanting a union in theory (I want one too) but rejecting the one being offered to them in practice because it would force them to pay dues without giving them any say in how their money is spent. Yet that's what unions currently do.

Resorting to coercive tactics such as eliminating secret ballots is not the right way to restore flagging union membership. This won't sit well with workers. (A 2004 Zogby poll conducted for the Mackinac Center for Public Policy found that between 53% and 84% of union workers prefer secret ballots.) The more enlightened approach would be to accept reforms that make unions more accountable, such as paycheck protection that would require written approval from members before their dues are diverted toward political activity.

You are right, however, that card-check coercion might well boost union membership. Unionization rates in Canada, where many provinces allow card check, are three times those in the United States. Many U.S. service industries such as pharmacies, day-care centers and hotels might well become targets of unionization drives under a card-check regime.

However, if the historic performance of unionized states in this country is any indication, the Employee Free Choice Act wouldn't restore the great American middle class—as you claim—but would instead do the opposite. Unions certainly extract great wages and benefits for their workers; witness the life-long healthcare coverage that members of the United Auto Workers get. But the price is paid by the rest of the economy. According to the Mackinac Center, seven of the eight states that experienced nonfarm employment growth of 3% or better in 2006 were right-to-work states that prohibit forced union dues. Similarly, between 1970 and 2000, manufacturing employment grew by 1.43 million jobs in right-to-work states but declined by 2.18 million in closed-shop states.

This is not to suggest that unions shouldn't drive a tough bargain on behalf of their workers. David, you previously mentioned the obscene paychecks received by the CEOs of U.S. automakers even as their companies are going bankrupt. In fact, the problem of overpaid management is not limited to the top rungs of American automakers; it is endemic throughout the ranks of management. So there is absolutely nothing wrong in unions trying to get more parity. However, they cannot ignore market realities and raise labor costs to such an extent that companies can't compete.

Yet that's what American unions have done. Finding the right balance that serves both workers and employers is what will ultimately secure the long-term health of unions—not undemocratic, strong-arm tactics against their own members.

Source: Madland, David, and Shikha Dalmia. "After the U.S. Recovers, Will Unions?" *Los Angeles Times*, Feb. 4, 2009, http://www.latimes.com/news/opinion/la-oew-dalmia -madland4-2009feb04,0,4345012.story; and Madland and Dalmia, "Card Check: Unions' Salvation?" *Los Angeles Times*, Feb. 6, 2009, http://www.latimes.com/news /opinion/la-oew-dalmia-madland6-2009feb06,0,5917880.story.

One Labor Leader's Perspective on the Future of American Unions, 2010

In September 2009 Richard L. Trumka was elected president of the AFL-CIO. A veteran labor organizer and activist who started working in Pennsylvania coal mines as a teenager and became head of the United Mine Workers of America at age thirty-three, Trumka has seen the overall health and vitality of the labor movement decline during his lifetime. But Trumka believes that despite its current troubles—and larger problems within the nation's political and economic systems—organized labor is still capable of charting a new path of prosperity for union members and America alike. He explains his position in the following remarks, excerpted from a January 11, 2010, speech in Washington, D.C.

Ten days into the new decade, and one year into the Obama Administration, our nation remains poised between the failed policies of the past and our hopes for a better future. This is a moment that cries out for political courage—but it is not much in evidence.

I spent the first week of this year traveling on the west coast. In San Francisco, I was arrested with low-wage hotel workers fighting to protect their health care and pensions from leveraged buyouts gone bad. In Los Angeles and San Diego, I talked with working Americans moved to tears by foreclosure and unemployment, outsourcing and benefit cuts.

Everywhere I went, people asked me, why do so many of the people we elect seem to care only about Wall Street? Why is helping banks a matter of urgency, but unemployment is something we just have to live with? Why don't we make anything in America anymore? And why is it so hard to pass a health care bill that guarantees Americans healthy lives instead of guaranteeing insurance companies healthy profits?

As I travelled from city to city, I heard a new sense of resignation from middle class Americans, people laid off for the first time in their lives asking, "What did I do wrong?"

I came away shaken by the sense that the very things that make America great are in danger. What makes us unique among nations is this: In America, working people are the middle class. We built our middle class in the

20th century through hard work, struggle and visionary political leadership. But a generation of destructive, greed-driven economic policies has eroded that progress and now threatens our very identity as a nation....

At this moment, the voices of America's working women and men must be heard in Washington—not the voices of bankers and speculators for whom it always seems to be the best of times, but the voices of those for whom the New Year brings pink slips and givebacks, hollowed-out health care, foreclosures and pension freezes—the roll call of an economy that long ago stopped working for most of us.

Today I want to talk to you about the labor movement's vision for our nation.

Working people want an American economy that works for them—that creates good jobs, where wealth is fairly shared, and where the economic life of our nation is about solving problems like the threat of climate change rather than creating problems like the foreclosure crisis. We know that growing inequality undermines our ability to grow as a nation—by squandering the talents and the contributions of our people and consigning entire communities to stagnation and failure.

If we are going to make our vision real, we must challenge our political leaders, and we must also challenge ourselves and our movement.

Workers formed the labor movement as an expression of our lives—a chain of responsibility and solidarity, making millions of people here in America and around the world into agents of social change—able to accomplish much more together than as isolated individuals. That movement gives voice to the hopes, values and interests of working people every day. But despite our best efforts, we have endured a generation of stagnant wages and collapsing benefits—a generation where the labor movement has been much more about defense than about offense, where our horizons are shrinking rather than growing.

But the future of the labor movement depends on moving forward—on innovating and changing the way we work, on being open to all working people and giving voice to all workers, even when our laws and employers seek to divide us from each other. And that is something we are working on every day....

I grew up in a small town in western Pennsylvania, and I was surrounded by the legacy of my parents and grandparents. My grandfather and my father and their fellow workers went into mines that were death traps, to work for wages that weren't enough to buy food and clothes for their families. They and the union they built made those jobs into middle class jobs. When I went into the mine, it was a good job. A good job meant possibilities for me—possibilities that my mother moved heaven and earth to make real—that took me to Penn State and to law school and to this podium.

What is our legacy—the legacy of those of us who are shaping the world our children and grandchildren will inhabit? Is our government laying the foundations young people need? Do workplaces offer hope? Do they even offer work? Are we building a world we will be proud to hand over to our children? Are the voices of the young, of the future, being heard?

In September, I was elected President of the AFL-CIO together with Secretary Treasurer Liz Shuler and Executive Vice President Arlene Holt Baker, both of whom are here today. Liz Shuler is the youngest principal officer of the AFL-CIO in our history, and I asked her to lead a program of outreach to young workers. As part of that effort, the AFL-CIO conducted a study of young adults between the ages of 18 and 34, comparing their economic standing, attitudes and hopes with those from a similar survey conducted 10 years ago. The findings are shocking. They reveal a lost decade for young workers in America. Lower wages. Education deferred. Things are so bad that one in three of these 18–34-year-olds is currently living at home with their parents.

The desperation I heard in this survey and in the voices of proud, hard-working Americans fills me with an enormous sense of urgency, an urgency that should be shared by every elected official here in Washington and across this country.

As a country and a movement, our challenge is to build a new economy that can restore working people's expectations and hope. If you were laid off because of what Wall Street did to our economy, it's not your fault. A dead end job with no benefits is not the best our country can do for its citizens.

What went wrong with our economy? You could say it is as simple as we built a low-wage, high consumption economy and tried to bridge the contradiction with debt. And there's a lot of truth in that simplicity. But if we are going to understand what is wrong in a way that will help us understand how to fix it, we need a little more detail.

A generation ago, our nation's policymakers embarked on a campaign of radical deregulation and corporate empowerment—one that celebrated private greed over public service.

The AFL-CIO warned of the dangers of that path—trade policies that rewarded and accelerated outsourcing, financial deregulation designed to promote speculation and the dismantling of our pension and health care systems. We warned that the middle class could not survive in such an economy, that growing inequality would inevitably shrink the American pie, that we were borrowing from the rest of the world at an unsustainable pace, that busts would follow bubbles and that our country would be worse off in the end.

These policies culminated in the worst economic decade in living memory—we suffered a net loss of jobs, the housing market collapsed, real wages fell and more children fell into poverty. And the enormous growth in inequality during that decade yielded mediocre growth overall. This is not a portrait of a cyclical recession, but of a nation with profound, unaddressed structural economic problems on a long-term, downward slide....

First, we have underinvested in the foundations of our economy—including the transportation and communications infrastructure that are essential to a middle-class society and a dynamic, competitive high-wage economy. But the most important foundation of our economy is education and training. We simply cannot continue to skimp on the quality of education we provide to all of our children and expect to lead in the global economy. Likewise, we need to provide opportunities for lifelong skills upgrading to workers—through both private and public sector initiatives.

Second, we have failed over a long period of time to create enough good jobs at home to maintain our middle class—and we have allowed corporate hacks to whittle away at workers' bargaining power to undermine the quality of the remaining jobs.

Finally, the structural absence of good jobs means a shortage of sustainable demand to drive our economy....

Some in Washington say when it comes to jobs: Go slow—take half steps. These voices are harming millions of unemployed Americans and their families—but they are also jeopardizing our economic recovery. It is responsible to have a plan for paying for job creation over time. But it is bad economics and suicidal politics not to aggressively address the job crisis at a time of double-digit unemployment. In fact, budget deficits over the medium and long term will be worse if we allow the economy to slide into long job stagnation—unemployed workers don't pay taxes and they don't go shopping; businesses without customers don't hire workers, they don't invest and they also don't pay taxes.

Our economy does not work without good jobs, so we must take action now to restore workers' voices in America. The systematic silencing of American workers by denying our right to form unions is at the heart of the disappearance of good jobs in America. We must pass the Employee Free Choice Act so that workers can have the chance to turn bad jobs into good jobs, and so we can reduce the inequality which is undermining our prospects for stable economic growth. And we must do it now—not next year, not even this summer. Now....

Beyond the short-term jobs crisis, we must have an agenda for restoring American manufacturing—a combination of fair trade and currency policies, worker training, infrastructure investment and regional development policies targeted to help economically distressed areas. We cannot be a prosperous middle class society in a dynamic global economy without a healthy manufacturing sector.

We must have an agenda to address the daily challenges workers face on the job—to ensure safe and healthy workplaces and family-friendly work rules.

We also need comprehensive reform of our immigration policy—based on shared prosperity and fairness, not cheap labor.

And we must take on the retirement crisis. Too many employers have replaced the system of pensions we used to have with underfunded savings accounts fully exposed to everything that is wrong with Wall Street. Today, the median balance in 401K accounts is only $27,000—nowhere near enough to fund a secure retirement. We need to return to a policy of employers sharing responsibility for retirement security with employees, while also bolstering and strengthening Social Security....

Too often Washington falls into the grip of ambivalence about the fundamental purpose of government. Is it to protect wealthy elites and gently encourage them to be more charitable? Or is it to look after the vast majority of the American people?

Government in the interests of the majority of Americans has produced our greatest achievements. The New Deal. The Great Society and the Civil

Rights movement—Social Security, Medicare, the minimum wage and the forty-hour work week, the Civil Rights Act and the Voting Rights Act. This is what made the United States a beacon of hope in a confused and divided world.

But too many people now take for granted government's role as protector of Wall Street and the privileged. They see middle-class Americans as over-paid and underworked. They see Social Security as a problem rather than the only piece of our retirement system that actually works. They feel sorry for homeless people, but fail to see the connections between downsizing, out-sourcing, inequality and homelessness.

This world view has brought Democrats nothing but disaster. The Republican response is to offer the middle class the false hope of tax cuts. Tax cuts end up enriching the rich and devastating the middle class by destroying the institutions like public education and Social Security that make the middle class possible.

But no matter what I say or do, the reality is that when unemployment is 10 percent and rising, working people will not stand for tokenism. We will not vote for politicians who think they can push a few crumbs our way and then continue the failed economic policies of the last 30 years.

Let me be even blunter. In 1992, workers voted for Democrats who promised action on jobs, who talked about reining in corporate greed and who promised health care reform. Instead, we got NAFTA, an emboldened Wall Street—and not much more. We swallowed our disappointment and worked to preserve a Democratic majority in 1994 because we knew what the alternative was. But there was no way to persuade enough working Americans to go to the polls when they couldn't tell the difference between the two parties. Politicians who think that working people have it too good—too much health care, too much Social Security and Medicare, too much power on the job—are inviting a repeat of 1994.

Our country cannot afford such a repeat.

President Obama said in his inaugural address, "The state of the economy calls for action, bold and swift, and we will act—not only to create new jobs, but to lay a new foundation for growth." Now is the time to make good on these words—for Congress, for President Obama and for the American people.

These are big challenges. But it is long past time to take them on. And for those members of Congress who think maybe taking on big challenges is not their job, and who want to keep offering working people tokenism while they govern in the interests of the people who trashed our economy, I have a suggestion for how to spend your weekends.

Go sit with the unemployed. Talk to college students looking at tuition hikes, laid-off professors, and no jobs at graduation. Talk to workers whose jobs are being offshored. Ask what these Americans think about their future. Ask them what they think of Wall Street, of health insurance companies, of big banks. Ask them if they want a government that is in partnership with those folks, or a government that stands up for working people.

Then think about the great promise of America and the great legacy we have inherited. Our wealth as a nation and our energy as a people can deliver, in the words of my predecessor Samuel Gompers, "more schoolhouses and less jails; more books and less arsenals; more learning and less vice; more leisure and less greed; more justice and less revenge; in fact, more of the opportunities to cultivate our better natures."

This is the American future the labor movement is working for. Our political leaders have a choice. They can work with us for a future where the middle class is secure and growing, where inequality is on the decline and where jobs provide ladders out of poverty. Or they can work for a future where the profits of insurance companies, speculators and outsourcers are secure. There is no middle ground. Working America is waiting for an answer. We are in a "show me" kind of mood, and time is running out.

Source: Trumka, Richard. Remarks at National Press Club, January 11, 2010. Available online at http://www.aflcio.org/mediacenter/prsptm/sp01112010.cfm.

IMPORTANT PEOPLE, PLACES, AND TERMS

AFL-CIO
Acronym for American Federation of Labor-Congress of Industrial Organizations, the largest labor organization in U.S. history.

American Federation of Labor (AFL)
Major labor organization first established by Samuel Gompers in 1886.

Apprentice
An employee who receives on-the-job training to learn a skilled trade.

Arbitration
A method of settling disputes between employers and workers in which an impartial person or panel decides the issue.

Boycott
Organized campaign that focuses on refusing to buy goods or services from a targeted employer as a way to pressure that employer to accede to worker demands regarding wages or other workplace conditions.

Brotherhood
A term used by unions of the nineteenth century to refer to their organizations.

Closed shop
A workplace in which employment is limited to workers who belong to the union that is in place there.

Collective bargaining
A type of labor negotiation in which authorized union representatives bargain with management over wages, hours, and work rules applicable to all union members for a specified length of time.

Company union
A labor group established and usually controlled by the employer itself as a way to prevent regular unions from taking hold in the company's workplace.

Congress of Industrial Organizations (CIO)
Major industrial trade union founded by John Lewis and other dissident AFL leaders in 1935.

Craft union
A labor organization that limits membership to persons with specific and valuable skills, such as electricians, glassmakers, nurses, carpenters, and plumbers.

Debs, Eugene V. (1855-1926)
Labor organizer and five-time presidential nominee of the Socialist Party of America.

Gompers, Samuel (1850-1924)
Founder and long-time president of the American Federation of Labor (AFL).

Haywood, William "Big Bill" (1869-1928)
Leader of the Western Federation of Miners (WFM) and co-founder of the International Workers of the World (IWW).

Hoffa, Jimmy (1913-1975)
President of the Teamsters Union who disappeared without a trace in 1975.

Industrial union
Labor organization composed of all or most hourly workers within an industry, both skilled and unskilled.

Industrial Workers of the World (IWW)
Radical organization that urged workers of all industries to join together to remake American society along Socialist lines.

Injunction
An order from a judge that legally requires the target of the order to refrain from carrying out a given activity. In the realm of labor law, injunctions have been usually used to stop unions or individual labor

leaders from picketing, striking, conducting boycotts, or engaging in other protest actions.

Jones, Mary Harris "Mother" Jones (1837-1930)
Labor organizer and activist.

Knights of Labor
Leading labor union of the late nineteenth century.

Lewis, John L. (1880-1969)
President of the United Mine Workers of America (UMWA) and founder of the Congress of Industrial Organizations (CIO).

Lockout
Suspending a plant's operations and idling its workers as a strategy for forcing workers to accept the employer's terms of employment.

Meany, George (1894-1980)
President of the AFL-CIO from 1955 to 1979.

Open shop
Technically, a place of business where both union and non-union employees can work, but in actuality, a term that has come to mean a workplace that is closed to union members.

Picketing
A strategy employed by workers during labor disputes in which representatives march and carry signs at the entrance of a targeted workplace as a way of informing the public and members of other unions that they are locked in a disagreement with that employer. The goal is to get sympathetic customers and union allies to "honor" their picket line and refuse to do business with the targeted workplace.

Radical
Revolutionary or extreme political and social change.

Reuther, Walter P. (1907-1970)
President of the United Auto Workers (UAW) from 1946 to 1970.

Right-to-work laws
State labor laws that exempt employees from joining a union as a condition of employment.

Scab

Derogatory term for a worker who continues to work during a strike action or who accepts work where a union strike action is taking place.

Socialism

A political and economic system based on government or community-wide ownership of industry and resources rather than private ownership.

Strikebreaker

Replacement worker hired by a company to fill the jobs of striking workers.

Union shop

Places of employment in which the employer and union agree that all employees have to be members of that union.

Wobbly

Slang term for a member of the Industrial Workers of the World (IWW).

CHRONOLOGY

1619
American colonists begin importing slaves to serve as manual labor. *See p. 12.*

1718
Parliament passes the Transportation Act, which paves the way for exiling criminals to the colonies to provide labor. *See p. 11.*

1775
American Revolution begins. *See p. 12.*

1786
Philadelphia printers conduct one of the first successful strikes for higher wages. *See p. 18.*

1794
The Federal Society of Journeymen Cordwainers, cited by many historians as America's first genuine trade union, is founded by shoemakers in Philadelphia. *See p. 18.*

1827
The Mechanics' Union of Trade Associations, the first American union to bring together workers from more than one trade, is established. *See p. 19.*

1861
The American Civil War begins. *See p. 24.*

1866
National Labor Union is founded in Baltimore. *See p. 28.*

1867
Reconstruction policies are enacted across the American South. *See p. 24.*

1869
Knights of Labor union is organized in Philadelphia. *See p. 24.*

1877
A nationwide rail strike paralyzes the American economy. *See p. 29.*

Nineteen members of the notorious Molly Maguires are executed for murder and other crimes. *See p. 27.*

1886

> The Haymarket tragedy erupts in the streets of Chicago on May 3-4. *See p. 31.*
>
> The American Federation of Labor (AFL) is founded. *See p. 32.*

1892

> Pennsylvania's Homestead Steel Strike ends in a crushing defeat for organized labor. *See p. 36.*

1894

> The American Railway Union leads a major strike against the Pullman Palace Car Company. *See p. 38.*

1902

> The United Mine Workers of America achieves a landmark victory over coal companies in the Anthracite Coal Strike after President Theodore Roosevelt refuses to side with industry in the dispute. *See p. 47.*

1903

> A violent two-year clash between the Western Federation of Miners and mine operators erupts in Colorado. *See p. 46.*

1905

> Labor activists establish the Industrial Workers of the World in Chicago. *See p. 50.*

1907

> "Big Bill" Haywood goes on trial for arranging the murder of former Idaho Governor Frank Steunenberg. He is eventually acquitted of all charges. *See p. 54.*

1911

> The Triangle Shirtwaist Fire claims the lives of 146 workers in New York City. *See p. 58.*

1912

> The successful "Bread and Roses" Strike is waged against the textile mills of Lawrence, Massachusetts. *See p. 58.*
>
> Socialist Eugene Debs wins 6 percent of the vote in the 1912 presidential election. *See p. 53.*

1914

> Thirteen women and children of mining families are slaughtered by Colorado state troops in the Ludlow Massacre. *See p. 59.*

1917

> The United States enters World War I and passes various legislative acts to criminalize antiwar activity. *See p. 65.*

1918

> Labor leader Eugene Debs is sent to prison for violating the Espionage Act. *See p. 65.*

1919

A "Great Strike" of labor unions in numerous industries takes place across the country. *See p. 66.*

1924

American Federation of Labor President Samuel Gompers dies. *See p. 123.*

1929

The Great Depression begins with a stunning stock market crash in October. *See p. 69.*

1933

President Franklin D. Roosevelt is sworn in and immediately launches his New Deal policies for economic recovery and expanded worker rights. *See p. 70.*

The National Industrial Recovery Act is passed. *See p. 71.*

1934

Violent labor strikes erupt in several major cities across the country. *See p. 72.*

1935

The National Labor Relations Act, also known as the Wagner Act, becomes law. *See p. 75.*

The labor federation that eventually becomes known as the Congress of Industrial Organizations (CIO) is established. *See p. 76.*

1936

The Flint Sit-Down Strike begins, concluding in early 1937 with a resounding victory for the United Auto Workers (UAW). *See p. 77.*

1937

The Little Steel Strike ends in defeat for striking steelworkers. *See p. 79.*

1938

The Fair Labor Standards Act is passed. *See p. 75.*

The Congress of Industrial Organizations formally leaves the American Federation of Labor. *See p. 77.*

1941

The United States enters World War II after a December 7 Japanese sneak attack on the U.S. Naval Base at Pearl Harbor in Hawaii. *See p. 81.*

1947

The Taft-Hartley Act is passed, placing new limits on union activities. *See p. 85.*

1950

The Congress of Industrial Organizations (CIO) formally expels eleven unions for being under Communist influence. *See p. 86.*

1955

    The American Federation of Labor (AFL) and the Congress of Industrial Organizations (CIO) formally join together as the AFL-CIO. *See p. 88.*

1957

    The AFL-CIO expels the Teamsters Union in response to revelations of widespread corruption. *See p. 94.*

1959

    The Labor Management Reporting and Disclosure Act, also known as the Landrum-Griffin Act, is passed. *See p. 95*

1966

    United Farm Workers of America is established. *See p. 96.*

1968

    The United Auto Workers leave the AFL-CIO. *See p. 97.*

1970

    The Occupational Safety and Health Act is passed into law. *See p. 100.*

1975

    Former Teamsters President Jimmy Hoffa disappears. *See p. 94.*

1981

    President Ronald Reagan fires striking air traffic controllers. *See p. 102.*

1994

    The North American Free Trade Agreement (NAFTA) is passed. *See p. 104.*

2005

    A coalition of labor groups known as Change to Win is established under the direction of Andy Stern, President of the Service Employees International Union (SEIU). *See p. 108.*

2010

    Major health reform legislation known as the Affordable Care Act becomes law, in part because of the efforts of organized labor. *See p. 109.*

SOURCES FOR FURTHER STUDY

Baxandall, Rosalyn, and Linda Gordon. *America's Working Women: A Documentary History, 1600 to the Present*. Revised edition. New York: W.W. Norton, 1995. This remarkable anthology contains first-hand accounts of women telling about their workplace experiences over three centuries of American history. It includes numerous powerful selections that illustrate how women strengthened the American labor movement—oftentimes despite ugly resistance from male labor organizers and management executives alike.

The Dramas of Haymarket. Chicago Historical Society and Northwestern University. Available online at http://www.chicagohistory.org/dramas/overview/over.htm. An ambitious and fascinating web resource that provides detailed coverage of the infamous 1886 Haymarket Riot. The heart of the website is a selection of materials from the Chicago Historical Society's digital archive of holdings on the tragedy. This electronic project interprets these materials and places them in historical context, drawing on many other items from the Historical Society's extensive resources.

Eugene V. Debs Foundation Website. Available online at http://www.eugenevdebs.com /index.html. The foundation that operates this website maintains Debs's historic home in Terre Haute, Indiana, as a museum. Features of the website include overviews of Debs's life work as a labor organizer and political activist, as well as an extensive online photo gallery.

Skurzynski, Gloria. *Sweat and Blood: A History of U.S. Labor Unions*. Minneapolis, MN: Twenty-First Century Books, 2008. Targeted at younger readers, this work provides a good summary of the origins and historical development of the labor movement in the United States. The text is also supplemented with many period photographs of leading labor leaders and important events.

Yates, Michael D. *Why Unions Matter*. New York: Monthly Review Press, 2009. Written by a labor and economics professor, provides an easily understandable overview of how labor unions function, as well as background on the role that unions have played in addressing racism, sexism, and economic inequality in America over the last two centuries.

BIBLIOGRAPHY

Books and Periodicals

Badger, Anthony J. *The New Deal: The Depression Years, 1933-1940*. Chicago: Ivan R. Dee, 1989.

Barnard, John. *American Vanguard: The United Auto Workers during the Reuther Years, 1935-1970*. Detroit: Wayne State University Press, 2004.

Bernstein, Irving. *The Lean Years: A History of the American Worker, 1920-1933*. Baltimore: Penguin Books, 1960.

Bernstein, Irving. *Turbulent Years: A History of the American Worker, 1933-1941*. Boston: Houghton-Mifflin, 1971.

Bodnar, John. *The Transplanted: A History of Immigrants in Urban America*. Bloomington, IN: Indiana University Press, 1987.

Bodnar, John. *Workers' World: Kinship, Community, and Protest in an Industrial Society, 1900-1940*. Baltimore: Johns Hopkins University Press, 1982.

Boorstin, Daniel J. *The Americans: The Colonial Experience*. New York: Random House, 1958.

Boris, Eileen, and Nelson Lichtenstein, eds. *Major Problems in the History of American Workers: Documents and Essays*. Lexington, MA: Heath, 1991.

Boyle, Kevin. *The UAW and the Heyday of American Liberalism, 1945-1968*. Ithaca, NY: Cornell University Press, 1995.

Chinoy, Ely. *Automobile Workers and the American Dream*. Urbana: University of Illinois Press, 1992.

Dollinger, Genora (Johnson). *Striking Flint: Remembering the Flint Sit-Down Strike, 1936-37*. As told to Susan Rosenthal. 2008. Available online at http: susanrosenthal .com/wp-content/uploads/2008/08/coldtype-edition-strikingflint.pdf.

Dulles, Foster Rhea, and Melvyn Dubofsky. *Labor in America: A History*. 5th ed. Wheeling, IL: Harlan Davidson, 1993.

Fantasia, Rick, and Kim Voss. *Hard Work: Remaking the American Labor Movement*. Berkeley: University of California Press, 2004.

Foner, Philip S. *The Industrial Workers of the World, 1905-1917*. Volume Four of *History of the Labor Movement in the United States*. New York: International Publishers, 1965.

Genovese, Eugene. *Roll, Jordan, Roll: The World the Slaves Made.* New York: Pantheon, 1974.

Gutman, Herbert. *Work, Culture, and Society in Industrializing America: Essays in American Working Class and Social History.* New York: Knopf, 1976.

Hindle, Brooke, and Steven Lubar. *Engines of Change: The American Industrial Revolution, 1790-1860.* Washington, DC: Smithsonian Institution, 1986.

Johnson, Marilynn S. *Violence in the West: The Johnson County Range War and the Ludlow Massacre.* Boston: Bedford/St. Martin's, 2009.

Leuchtenburg, William E. *Franklin D. Roosevelt and the New Deal.* New York: Harper & Row, 1963.

Lichtenstein, Nelson. *The Most Dangerous Man in Detroit: Walter Reuther and the Fate of American Labor.* New York: Basic Books, 1995.

Lichtenstein, Nelson. *State of the Union: A Century of American Labor.* Brunswick, NJ: Princeton University Press, 2003.

Lingenfelter, Richard E. *The Hardrock Miners: A History of the Mining Labor Movement in the West, 1863-1893.* Berkeley: University of California Press, 1974.

McGerr, Michael. *A Fierce Discontent: The Rise and Fall of the Progressive Movement in America.* New York: Oxford University Press, 2005.

Meltzer, Milton. *Bread-And Roses: The Struggle of American Labor, 1865-1915.* New York: Knopf, 1967.

Patterson, James T. *Grand Expectations: The United States, 1945-1974.* New York: Oxford University Press, 1996.

Roediger, David R., and Philip S. Foner. *Our Own Time: A History of American Labor and the Working Day.* New York: Greenwood Press, 1989.

Rorabaugh, W.J. *The Craft Apprentice: From Franklin to the Machine Age in America.* New York: Oxford University Press, 1986.

Stephenson, Charles, and Robert Asher. *Life and Labor: Dimensions of American Working Class History.* New York: State University of New York Press, 1986.

Tomlins, Christopher. *The State and the Unions: Labor Relations, Law, and the Organized Labor Movement in America, 1880-1960.* New York: Cambridge University Press, 1985.

Zieger, Robert. *American Workers, American Unions: The Twentieth Century.* 3rd rev. ed. Baltimore: Johns Hopkins University Press, 2002.

Internet

"The Flint Sit-Down Strike." *Historical Voices.* Available online at http://www.historical voices.org/flint/strike.php#.

"History of the National Labor Relations Board: The First 60 Years." *U.S. National Labor Relations Board.* Available online at http://www.nlrb.gov/publications/History/thhe _first_60_years.aspx.

"Labor History and Culture." *AFL-CIO: America's Union Movement.* Available online at http://www.aflcio.org/aboutus/history/.

Samuel Gompers Papers. University of Maryland Department of History. Available online at http://www.history.umd.edu/Gompers/bio.htm.

DVDs

A. Philip Randolph: For Jobs and Freedom. DVD and VHS. California Newsreel, 1986.

At the River I Stand: Memphis, the 1968 Strike, and Martin Luther King. DVD. California Newsreel, 1993.

Eugene Debs and the American Movement. DVD. Cambridge Documentary Films, 1977.

Lewis, John L. "I Solemnly Warn the Leaders of Industry," Speech delivered on the Red Network, National Broadcasting Company, Washington, DC, December 31, 1936.

PHOTO AND ILLUSTRATION CREDITS

Cover and Title Page: George Grantham Bain Collection, Prints & Photographs Division, Library of Congress, LC-DIG-ggbain-10357.

Chapter One: The Granger Collection, New York (p. 10); The Granger Collection, New York (p. 13); Print Collection, Miriam and Ira D. Wallach Division of Art, Prints and Photographs, The New York Public Library, Astor, Lenox and Tilden Foundations (p. 15); Prints & Photographs Division, Library of Congress, LC-DIG-pga-02822 (p. 17); Prints & Photographs Division, Library of Congress, LC-USZ62-117120 (p. 19).

Chapter Two: Illustrated by Bernhard Gillam in *Puck* (1883 Feb. 7), Prints & Photographs Division, Library of Congress, LC-USZC4-3108 (p. 25); Southern Labor Archives, Special Collections and Archives, Georgia State University Library (p. 29); Illustrated in *Harper's Weekly* (1886 May 15) by T. de Thulstrup, Prints & Photographs Division, Library of Congress, LC-USZ62-796 (p. 31); Illustrated in *Harper's Weekly* (1886 Dec. 25), Wood engraving after photograph by J.H. Ryde, Prints & Photographs Division, Library of Congress, LC-USZ62-82969 (p. 33); Illustrated in *Harper's Weekly* (1892 July 23), Wood engraving by T. de Thulstrup after sketch by F. Cresson Schell, Prints & Photographs Division, Library of Congress, LC-USZ62-55544 (p. 37); The Granger Collection, New York (p. 39).

Chapter Three: Prints & Photographs Division, Library of Congress, LC-USZ62-45662 (p. 44); Prints & Photographs Division, Library of Congress, LC-USZ62-23702 (p. 48); Prints & Photographs Division, Library of Congress, LC-USZ62-105054 (p. 50); Harris & Ewing Collection, Prints & Photographs Division, Library of Congress, LC-DIG-hec-01359 (p. 54); Prints & Photographs Division, Library of Congress, LC-USZ62-88632 (p. 55); Prints & Photographs Division, Library of Congress, LC-USZ62-118677 (p. 56); Denver Public Library, Western History Collection, Z-199 (p. 59).

Chapter Four: George Grantham Bain Collection, Prints & Photographs Division, Library of Congress, LC-DIG-ggbain-12728 (p. 64); National Photo Company Collection, Prints & Photographs Division, Library of Congress, LC-USZ62-77539 (p. 66); Walter P. Reuther Library, Wayne State University (p. 69); Harris & Ewing Collection, Prints & Photographs Division, Library of Congress, LC-DIG-hec-25045 (p. 72); AP Photo (p. 74); Harris & Ewing Collection, Prints & Photographs Division, Library of Congress, LC-DIG-hec-22560 (p. 76); Walter P. Reuther Library, Wayne State University (p. 78).

INDEX

North American Free Trade Agreement
(NAFTA), 104, 211
NRA. *See* National Recovery Administration
(NRA)

O

Obama, Barack, 107, 109, 211
Occupational Safety and Health Act, 100, 144
Occupational Safety and Health
Administration (OSHA), 100
Olson, Floyd, 72
open shop, 55, 56
Orchard, Harry, 126, 127, 170
organized labor. *See* labor movement; labor
unions
OSHA. *See* Occupational Safety and Health
Administration (OSHA)
outsourcing, 100, 101, 209
overtime pay, 75

P-Q

PATCO. *See* Professional Air Traffic
Controllers Organization (PATCO)
Pattinson, Robert E., 38
Peabody, James H., 46
Pearl Harbor attack, 81
Perkins, Fannie Coralie "Frances," 72-73, 72
(ill.), 74 (ill.)
recollections of Wagner Act, 180-83
Peyser, Theodore A., 74 (ill.)
Philadelphia and Reading Railroad, 48
Pinkerton Detective Agency, 37-38
Powderly, Terence, 28, 29 (ill.), 158
Prinz, Joachim, 93 (ill.)
Professional Air Traffic Controllers
Organization (PATCO), 102, 197-98
Progressive Era, 43, 51-53, 55-58, 116
Provenzano, Anthony, 132
Public Contracts Act of 1936, 75
Public Works Administration (PWA), 71
Pullman, George, 40

Pullman Palace Car Company, 38-40, 116
Pullman Strike, 38-40, 116, 124, 160
PWA. *See* Public Works Administration (PWA)

R

racketeering, 94
Randolph, A. Philip, 92, 93 (ill.)
Reagan, Ronald, 101-02, 103 (ill.), 197-98
Reason Foundation, 199
Reconstruction, 24
redemption, 11
Republican Party, 211
Reuther, Walter P., 87, 88, 89 (ill.), 93 (ill.),
95-96, 145 (ill.)
and AFL-CIO merger, 89-91, 143, 193
biography, 145-49
support for civil rights movement, 92-
94, 188-92
Revolutionary War, 12
right-to-work laws, 86, 103-04, 205
robber barons, 26
Robinson, Helen Ring, 177
Rockefeller, John D., 26, 60, 136, 173, 176
Rockefeller, John D., Jr., 136, 176
Roosevelt, Eleanor, 186
Roosevelt, Franklin D., 70, 74 (ill.), 82, 83
(ill.), 140
New Deal policies of, 3, 63, 72-73, 139,
180, 182
Roosevelt, Theodore, 47-49, 48 (ill.), 51, 117
Rose, Alex, 194, 195-96
Russian Revolution, 64

S

Sage, Russell, 26
scabs. *See* strikebreakers, 35
School Milk Program, 92
Screen Actors Guild, 102
Sedition Act, 65, 118
SEIU. *See* Service Employees International
Union (SEIU)

V

Vanderbilt, Cornelius, 26
Vietnam War, 97, 144
Voting Rights Act of 1965, 94

W

Wagner, Robert, 73-75, 74 (ill.), 180, 182
Wagner Act, 75, 85, 139, 180-83
Wal-Mart Corporation, 106
Walsh-Healey Act, 75
welfare capitalism, 67-68
West, George P., 173-79
Western Federation of Miners (WFM), 46, 54, 125-27
WFM. *See* Western Federation of Miners (WFM)
"What Can We Do for Working People?" (Debs), 160-63

"What Does Labor Want?" (Gompers), 164-69
wildcat strikes, 143, 201
Wilkins, Roy, 93 (ill.)
Willkie, Wendell, 140
Wilson, Woodrow, 60, 65, 117-18, 123, 127
Wobblies. *See* Industrial Workers of the World (IWW)
Woll, Matthew, 183
Workingmen's Benevolent Association. *See* Molly Maguires
workplace safety regulations, 58, 100, 106, 144
World War I, 63-65, 117, 123, 127
World War II, 81-82, 140, 142, 147

X-Y-Z

yellow dog employment contracts, 55, 56